THE VIRTUES OF
THE TABLE

THE VIRTUES OF THE TABLE

How to Eat and Think

Julian Baggini

GRANTA

Granta Publications, 12 Addison Avenue, London W11 4QR
First published in Great Britain by Granta Books 2014

A CIP catalogue record for this book is available
from the British Library.

1 3 5 7 9 10 8 6 4 2

ISBN 978 1 84708 714 0

Printed and bound by CPI Group (UK) Ltd, Croydon, CR0 4YY

To know how to eat is to know how to live.

Auguste Escoffier[1]

Contents

Contents

Contents

Contents

Introduction

We are supposed to be living in a golden age of food. Cooking, for so long associated with domestic drudgery, has been rediscovered as a creative pleasure. The quality of high-street restaurants has gone up, and the number of truly good ones has increased. Nutritional science, although incomplete, gives us a very good idea of what a healthy diet looks like. Ingredients that were until recently thought exotic and hard to obtain are available in every supermarket. Humanely reared animals and environmentally friendly produce have never been more widely available.

Yet there is the niggling doubt that all this might be as devoid of substance as the asparagus foams that are served up in Michelin-starred temples of gastronomy. Sceptics are increasingly challenging the zeal and excesses of the new foodism. Steven Poole captures this contrarian mood in the title of his wonderfully acerbic *You Aren't What You Eat*. Even serious food writers like Adam Gopnik have voiced the concern that 'Having made food a more fashionable object, we have ended by making eating a smaller subject.'[2] The drive to keep up with the latest ingredient, restaurant, dietary fad, piece of nutritional advice, cookery book or kitchen gadget takes on its own momentum and we forget – if we ever knew – why we should be so concerned with eating in the first place.

What has been missing from the food renaissance is a rigorous thinking-through of why food matters and what our relationship to it should be. Without such a philosophy of food, our practices just become a contradictory mishmash of fashion, common sense, received opinion, prejudice and rationalised desire, and, indeed, the new food culture is patchy and incoherent: takeaway on Friday night, farmers' market on Saturday morning; local chard for dinner, premium imported orange juice and coffee for breakfast next day; low-GI spelt bread with high-fat artisan cheese.

This book is an attempt to bring some clarity to this confusion, by articulating a thorough and wide-ranging philosophy of food, one to eat, drink and live by. This is not primarily a philosophy of rules and principles but one of virtues, by which I broadly mean dispositions, habits, traits, skills or values that help us to live better lives. Not all of these are familiar from traditional lists of virtues, in part because of our limited vocabulary. For example, to be able to appreciate art properly is a virtue, but there is no one word that names this capacity.

I advocate the virtues of the table because rules are too rigid an instrument to deal with most of the complex issues around food, and the good life in general. And if you base behaviour on rules that you know from the outset will have to be bent or broken, too often the result is hypocrisy or confusion. Virtues, however, are inherently more flexible and adaptable to different situations and changing times. They are also more enabling, since they foster individuals' abilities to choose well for themselves, rather than simply follow guidelines set by others.

Each of the chapters in this book focuses on an aspect of food and eating, and also on a virtue associated with it. The virtues, however, are connected, and the overarching theme of this book is the challenge of figuring out how we can live in a way that does justice to our complete selves: we are creatures of mind, body, heart and – in one sense – soul. Food is not the only key to understanding how they form one whole, but it is a particularly well-cut one because it involves every essential aspect of human nature: the animal, the sensuous, the social, the cultural, the creative, the emotional and – as I hope this book demonstrates – the intellectual. Thinking seriously about food requires us to consider our relationships to nature, to our fellow animals and to each other, as well as the unity of our minds and bodies. Furthermore, whereas philosophising can easily lead us up into the clouds, food grounds us. There is nothing more basic than the need to eat and drink, and so even when we marry food and philosophy, there is no danger of forgetting David Hume's advice: 'Amidst all your philosophy; be still a man.'[3]

The first part of this book ('Gathering') covers many of the big issues familiar from recent debates about food ethics, such as organics, sustainability and animal rights. The focus here is on the question of how to live in relation to others. Although the subjects are familiar, there is a need to interrogate them more thoughtfully than the usual, tired for-and-against debates conducted between converts and critics. Part II ('Preparing') centres on how we ground our judgements of what is right and wrong, better or worse. Parts III and IV ('Not Eating' and 'Eating') mark a turn inwards, with an emphasis on developing the character and habits that enable us to make good choices, live well and flourish as individuals.

The overall progression of the book is away from the big issues of interpersonal morality towards less familiar, often more personal and everyday aspects of food and how our ways of eating shape our selves. These two sides of the ethical life are of course connected: the good life concerns how we help the flourishing of both ourselves and others.

To keep sight of the practical, I have included at the end of each chapter some thoughts on particular foods, many of which take the form of recipes of a sort. If thinking better, living better and eating better all come as part of the same package, as I contend they do, this book should be one for the kitchen as well as the study, bedside or living room.

Overall, the book could be said to address the age-old question

'Should you eat to live or live to eat?' by rejecting the false choice it implies. Food is neither a mere means to the end of living nor the ultimate end of life itself. It is rather an integral part of life, and living well means putting food in its rightful place. If you can do that, you know how to eat, and you know how to live.

PART I

Gathering

If you don't know where it comes from, you don't know what it is.

1

Check it out

When I first had the idea of talking about the connection between cheese and the philosophy of Immanuel Kant, I thought the conjunction of the two would be unprecedented. This, after all, was the writer of *The Critique of Pure Reason*, not pure Boursin, and the *Groundwork of the Metaphysics of Morals*, not mozzarella. What I didn't know is that cheese and Kant are already linked, and not in a good way.

According to Kant's friend and biographer E. A. C. Wasianski, Kant's deteriorating health towards the end of his life was exacerbated by a poor diet containing too many English Cheddar sandwiches. On 7 October 1803 he indulged his craving more than usual. The next morning, out for a walk, he lost consciousness and fell. Another biographer, Manfred Kuehn, suggests, 'The excitement over the forbidden food might have raised his blood pressure and brought on the stroke.'[4] Kant was never the same again and he died on 11 February 1804, his last words being, '*Es ist gut.*' (It is good.) This was a judgement not on his life or work but on the bread and wine he had just been given by Wasianski.

There is something wonderful about the most basic trio of cheese, bread and wine playing a leading role in the last days of one of the greatest thinkers in history. Food can bring even Kant right down to earth. It is perhaps then a fitting tribute to Kant that one of his most important ideas can be exemplified not by a timeless metaphysical dilemma or a thorny moral problem but by simple, humble cheese.

Kant opens his famous essay 'What Is Enlightenment?' with the words:

> Enlightenment is man's emergence from his self-incurred immaturity. Immaturity is the inability to use one's own understanding without another's guidance. This immaturity is self-incurred if its cause lies not in lack of understanding but in indecision and lack of courage to use one's own mind without another's guidance. Dare to know! (*Sapere aude*.) 'Have the courage to use your own understanding' is therefore the motto of the enlightenment.[5]

If you thought this exhortation applied only to weighty, intellectual matters, you'd be wrong. Enlightenment requires 'freedom to make public use of one's reason in all matters'. Kant offers 'a physician who prescribes my diet' as an example of a lazy reliance on authority. Deferring to him means 'I have no need to exert myself. I have no need to think, if only I can pay; others will take care of that disagreeable business for me.'

Food is a quotidian example of how we fail to apply the principle of '*Sapere aude*'. Mostly we buy it without knowing where it is from, whether its production is sustainable or whether those who produce it are able to feed themselves as well as it feeds us. You might protest that you do in fact ask all these questions. But how far do you really go to find the answers for yourself? Even when we try to shop with discrimination, we mostly rely on a combination of reputation, hearsay and the reassurance of appellations like organic, free-range, PDO (Protected Designation of Origin), Vegetarian Society Approved and so on.

Cheese is a good example of a food where knowing more can really open our eyes. If you care about animal welfare, what do you do? Buy a vegetarian cheese? But all that means is that it contains no animal rennet, an ingredient necessary for the setting of hard cheese that is obtained from the stomachs of beasts and comprises a tiny proportion of the total mass. It tells you nothing at all about the welfare of the dairy animals from whose milk the cheese was made. You might buy organic, but as we will see later, although that may be a decent rule of thumb for animal and environmental welfare, it's an imperfect one.

Perhaps the most interesting example of how reliance on labels can mislead is the European Union's PDO scheme. Many assume that this system exists to ensure that certified products are made locally in the traditional way, from ingredients that are also produced locally in traditional ways. But it does no such thing. 'The PDO legislation that came into effect in 1992 does a lot more to support the interests of large businesses, especially in northern Europe, than it does to actually preserve any kind of tradition,' cheese buyer Bronwen Percival told me when I visited Neal's Yard Dairy in London.

Take Pecorino Romano, for example, which was made by the Ancient Romans and is described in the PDO specification as 'a hard, cooked cheese produced exclusively from fresh full-fat sheep's milk'. Area of origin is the key issue here, so 'The milk production, production and maturing of "Pecorino Romano" cheese and the marking operations must be carried out on the territory of the area stated in paragraph 4(3)', namely Sardinia, Lazio and the province of Grosseto. Other than that, the rules simply specify the size, shape and weight of the cheeses, the minimum fat content, the temperature of souring and cooking, and the length of maturation. Nothing in this requires the use of traditional methods. The rules actually make it quite simple – in some ways better – to produce on a large industrial scale, since strict control of factors such as temperature is easier in a sterile, mechanised environment. 'It's very important not to conflate big with bad,' says Percival, warning that '"industrial" is such a loaded word.' But clearly buying a PDO Pecorino Romano does not guarantee you're getting what you would think of as a traditional cheese.

What about Parmigiano Reggiano, which, like Roquefort and Brie, has been known by its current name since the Middle Ages?[6] Made with milk from the happiest cows grazing freely? Well, no, the rules actually insist that they are reared on feed, mainly hay. This may indeed be traditional and necessary to produce the high-fat milk required, but then force-feeding geese is also traditional and necessary to engorge their livers to make foie gras: it doesn't automatically mean it's acceptable. As it happens, feeding can depart from the traditional way quite significantly, as 'Cows may be fed using the unifeed technique, which consists in the preparation of a homogeneous mix of all the daily feed ingredients before giving them to the animals.'

Since Dr Becky Whay, senior lecturer in animal welfare and behaviour at the University of Bristol, visited the Parmesan-making area, the cheese has been blacklisted in her house. She found quite large, 'zero-graze' herds, where the focus was on dietary manipulation to produce really high-fat milk. Whay saw 'shocking lameness problems', and with the kind of feed the cows were being given (short-chop, low-fibre lucerne, aka alfalfa), they weren't ruminating properly or 'behaving like normal cows, who would regurgitate their food, chew it and swallow it'.

In short, if you want to know the quality and origins of the cheese you buy, you cannot simply allow others to do the thinking for you and pass on their judgement in the form of a logo. Unless you know exactly what the standards of certification schemes are, there is always the danger that they will provide false reassurance. To give another example, the magazine *Ethical Consumer* regularly rates different products, so you might think something that scores highly is more ethical than the alternatives. But of course there is no algorithm for ethics, and *Ethical Consumer*'s priorities might differ from, or even conflict with, yours. For instance, points are deducted for companies implicated in nuclear power, even though the magazine acknowledges that the green movement is 'split' on the issue. It also counts any kind of animal farming apart from organic as unethical.[7]

Sapere aude. It doesn't even need that much daring really. It just means taking a little time to look for yourself. What's more, it seems knowledge really does increase people's appreciation of what they're eating. In Todmorden, a small market town in West Yorkshire, people were buying meat at the local market with no idea that most of it came from the hills around them. When the group Incredible Edible Todmorden gave the butchers blackboards to write down everything that came from within 30 miles, more people started asking for it.

Henry Dimbleby of the quality fast-food group Leon tells the even more striking story of what happened when the prices of some imported ingredients in their 'superfood salad' soared. Unable to absorb the cost, they 'put a sign up saying there had been a big frost in Spain and for a few weeks veg was going to be quite expensive until the British crop started to come through. So we put a pound on the salad and not only did sales of that salad increase, people were so amazed to be connected. That sharing of the knowledge, they loved it.'

Of course, you can't know everything about the provenance of everything you eat, but the more you know, the more informed and truly free your choices are. Nor should we confuse finding out for ourselves with not relying on others at all. The acquisition of knowledge is a social and collaborative enterprise as well as a personal one. There is no virtue in reaching our own conclusions if that means ignoring the arguments and evidence provided by others. We haven't got time to find out all the facts and go back to first principles about everything, so we rightly look for books, documentaries, articles, talks and podcasts that can do some of the work for us, by identifying, articulating and critiquing the most important information and arguments. All we need to avoid is simply absorbing what we find

11

uncritically, or adopting lazy rules of thumb, the crude moral heuristics that fool us into assuming we are doing the right thing when we haven't stopped to check the facts.

To live by the principle of '*Sapere aude*' therefore means neither doing all our thinking in a private bubble nor simply accepting what we are told. The opinions to which we are most entitled are neither purely the product of our own minds nor wholly adopted from others. The need to rely on at least some expert knowledge provides the clearest example of this. If I'm interested in animal welfare, for example, veterinary scientists know much more than I do. Indeed, it might be because Kant became too unwilling to listen to expert medical advice that he persisted in eating more cheese than was good for him.

Daring to know requires daring to admit what we don't. It also means daring to accept that some of what we have most firmly believed to be true may not be so after all. As we're about to see, certainly when we check out what lies behind the new food orthodoxies – such as the value of sustainable, organic, seasonal and local produce – we discover that pretty much everything is far more complicated than it seems.

THE CHEESEBOARD

The great early-nineteenth-century French food writer Brillat-Savarin was guilty of overstatement when he said, 'A dinner that ends without cheese is like a beautiful woman with only one eye,'[8] but the underlying sentiment is sound. So here's a mainly British cheeseboard I implore you to know for yourself.

Rachel. Made by White Lake Cheeses in Somerset, Rachel is a delicate, semi-soft goat's cheese, but not as goaty in flavour as you might expect. I've seen the farm, the cheese-maker and the goats, and although the animals aren't gallivanting around the hills as you might imagine, I am satisfied that they are as well kept as Rachel is well made.

Manchego. Because this is a sheep's-milk cheese from the Manchega breed, you can be sure that animal welfare is not a major issue, because these sheep are not intensively reared. What you can't be sure of is that just because it's PDO Manchego it's as good as it can be: much of the supermarket stuff is disappointingly bland and rubbery. A good one, however, provides an intense and distinctive, sharp, salty, nutty hit.

Laverstoke Park mozzarella. Authentic mozzarella has to be made from buffalo milk and come from Campania in southern Italy, but mozzarella is a very young cheese and the best is always the freshest. So if you live in the UK, try this wonderfully creamy variety, made from the milk of an organic buffalo herd grazing outdoors in Overton, Hampshire.

Cornish Yarg. When I first tried this delicious grassy, hard cow's-milk cheese, wrapped and matured in nettle leaves, I assumed with a name like that – you can imagine a West Country farmer saying it – it was a traditional variety. In fact, it was invented in the 1980s by Alan and Jenny Gray, and Yarg is just their surname spelled backwards. It's proof that a new cheese made well in a traditional way is better than a traditional cheese made badly in a mechanised way.

Stichelton. Every cheeseboard needs a blue, even though in the UK it makes up only 2 per cent of cheese sales, much of that taken up by Christmas purchases of Stilton.[9] Stichelton is pretty much what Stilton used to be, when it was still made from raw milk. It's one of a number of excellent artisan British blues, including Dorset Blue Vinny, Bath Blue and Shropshire Blue. Each of these is like several cheeses in one: different parts contribute sweetness, saltiness, creaminess and the distinctive metallic sharpness of the mould itself.

Lincolnshire Poacher. Cheddar has become a generic word for traditional hard British cheese, and although the only one still to be made in the village of Cheddar is pretty good, the best varieties don't carry the name. You can almost taste the pasture in this raw-milk variety, which combines notes of Continental mountain cheeses like Comté with those of a traditional Cheddar. If you can't find it, Mrs Kirkham's Lancashire is a delicious alternative: strong, a little sharp, but not overpowering.

2

Be self-insufficient

INTERDEPENDENCE

'How's your scorched earth policy going?' The allotment manager's question was asked in good humour, but the policy itself was born of despair. The summer of 2012 was a terrible year to start growing food in England, the wettest since records began. Farmers saw wheat yields drop by nearly 15 per cent, and the apple crop was down over a quarter.[10] With full-time professionals struggling, even the most seasoned veterans of the small plot complained that little had grown.

It was the fourth season for fruit and vegetables in our compact back garden, but the first for our new allotment. There is a centuries-long tradition in Britain of making land available for people to grow their own food on, but the modern allotment took its current form with the passing of the Small Holdings and Allotments Act 1908, which obliged local authorities to 'provide small holdings for persons who desire to buy or lease and will themselves cultivate the holdings'. The purpose was the 'Welfare and Happiness of the Poor', as the Allotments Act of 1832 put it, when such land was primarily a source of turf and wood, cut for fuel. Allotments remained largely the preserve of the working class until fairly recently, when the middle class discovered them, with the result that waiting lists in some areas can be longer than those for top public schools. We got ours in a little over four years, which is around average.

The wet weather, however, was a minor problem compared to

the menace of ubiquitous bindweed. Our first battles had merely forced it into retreat, from which it resurged with aggressive vigour. So we had resorted to covering all the ground with black plastic, starving the weed of the sunlight it needed to grow, hoping that next year it would be weak enough to control, even if it was not defeated.

No one should be under any illusion that growing food is easy. If it were, hunger would have been abolished millennia ago. It's a constant struggle against uncooperative weather, bugs, diseases and weeds. Nonetheless, there are numerous good reasons to cultivate a small strip of land. Many people find it a welcome contrast from the rest of life: quiet rather than noisy; outside rather than within four walls; in contact with the earth and elements rather than protected from them. The word many people reach for is 'therapeutic', and sometimes this is meant quite literally. There are formal schemes to provide 'horticultural therapy' for people with learning disabilities, the isolated elderly or the depressed, and for many it seems to work.

However, there is one value associated with allotments that, I think, gets things exactly the wrong way round. Self-sufficiency has always had an attraction, especially in an uncertain world. The supposed ideal is to feed yourself from the fruits of your own land, perhaps exchanging some of your surplus with that of others nearby. Second best is being able to survive on food grown not just by you but by others in your local area. The minimal aspiration is for national self-sufficiency – for a country to be able to feed itself without recourse to imports. It seems obvious that self-sufficiency makes us more secure, less dependent on others and therefore more resilient. But this is wrong. What makes us stronger is not independence but interdependence.

The allotment is a good place to see this in action. Its very existence depends on a formal system to divide common-owned land into plots for individuals to cultivate, provided by local authorities and mandated by central government. They are run by committees made up of allotment holders, and an individual's ability to cultivate a plot depends very much on how efficient this management is. It is by collective rather than individual action that water tanks are provided, bulk deliveries of wood chip dumped for everyone to use for their paths, compost toilets provided and so on. Far from being independent, the allotment holder depends heavily on her peers.

Aside from the formal aspects of coordination, the allotment is a fertile breeding ground for informal mutual aid. People will watch over and water each other's plots when they go away; they will share surplus crops and seeds, knowing that they too will get shares of others' in due course; and they will also readily share experience, expertise and tools. This is not just a utilitarian informal economy. Allotments are extraordinarily sociable places. Within weeks we had got to know by name more of our fellow plot holders than we had neighbours on our street in five years. These social interactions are also admirably egalitarian. The first question here is not 'What do you do?', and many of the clues to social class are hidden under mud-coated old clothes. Along with hospitals, allotments are one of the few public spaces where people mingle irrespective of social background.

Then there is the question of what you actually need to grow your food: manure bought from a national chain or delivered by a local farmer; tools and sheds more likely to have been made in China than Chew Magna; how-to books printed in Poland and shipped by Amazon. The dirty secret of home growing is that far from being an exercise in thrift, the annual expense very often outweighs the value of the crop, and what is being bought in literally outweighs what is carried out.

Finally, there are the crops themselves. The modern allotment would look very different without the potatoes and tomatoes brought over from the Americas, orange carrots from Holland, spinach from Persia, parsnips from the Romans and all the other alimentary immigrants.

Overall, then, it is clear that the allotment is the example par excellence of how all that we do depends on a complex web of social and historical links with others, who are often far away. It is a reminder that we can only eat because of our interdependence, that human sociability and exchange lie at the root of our success and productivity as a species. We should be glad that our growing is made possible by these links, not kid ourselves that it is all our own doing.

The need to counter the insular cult of self-sufficiency is even more urgent in the public sphere. Of the now holy trinity of seasonal, organic and local – 'SOL food', as I call it – local has become the first among equals. A recent American survey, for example, found that more than half of consumers believe it's more important to buy local produce than organic.[11]

There are many good reasons to buy local, one of which top chefs know better than anyone. Stockholm's two-Michelin-starred restaurant Frantzén/Lindeberg boasted in 2011 that 95 per cent of its ingredients came from within Sweden. When I met head chef Björn Frantzén, he explained that biodynamic, organic, locally produced ingredients are generally better because they are fresher and have not been chilled, stored and transported. However, this is not true of all ingredients, which is why in 2012 Frantzén tweeted, 'It has gotten a little bit too far regarding ingredients. It is NOT where they coming from that matters, it's how they TASTE.'

Take Swedish truffles. 'They're nothing compared to the Alba truffles; they're nothing compared to the excellent Australian truffles that come here in a couple of weeks; nothing compared to the Périgord winter truffles in France,' he told me. Likewise, the British kitchen is enriched by olive oil from the Mediterranean, dates from the Middle East, cocoa from Central America, coffee from Brazil and tea from India. Restaurant supplier Charlie Hicks concurs: 'Chefs will tell you, if they're being honest, "Quality first, local second." I had it beautifully put to me at a lovely country-house hotel where they have their own walled garden and they grow a lot of fantastic stuff.' There, Hicks was told, 'Local is not an excuse for shit.'

So, yes, local often does mean fresher and tastier, but not always. Nor does local invariably mean more sustainable. The concept of 'food miles' has taken off in recent years, with many small shops boasting of how short a distance the food has travelled from farm to shop. But this is not always an indicator of less environmental impact. Take two examples. London has to bring in the vast bulk of its food from outside. The nearest place that grows potatoes is Essex, but yields there are much lower than in Lincolnshire, which is prime potato country. So when you look at the total carbon footprint of a bag of potatoes, taking into account amount of land, manures and fertilisers needed to grow it, alongside the energy used harvesting and transporting, the more distant Lincolnshire spuds usually tread more lightly on the Earth than the more local Essex ones.

An even more extreme example is New Zealand butter. Being thousands of miles from pretty much everywhere, New Zealand's international trade is threatened by the new cult of the local. So it was reassuring when a team from Lincoln University found that 'The UK emits 2,921 kilograms of carbon dioxide per tonne of milk solids compared to just 1,423 in NZ (including transport to the UK).'[12] Conditions for all-year outdoor grazing are perfect in New Zealand, which means that butter and lamb can be produced with comparatively few carbon-producing inputs. Furthermore, container ships are the most efficient form of transport in the world. One study found that an 'entire container voyage from China to Europe is equalled in CO_2 emissions by about 200 kilometres of long-haul trucking in Europe'. Hence a bottle of French wine shipped from Marseilles to New York could have a lower carbon footprint than a bottle of Californian wine trucked to the same restaurant,[13] and your pat of New Zealand butter probably has a smaller carbon footprint than one churned in Britain.

So local doesn't necessarily mean tastier or more sustainable. Does it make an area more self-sufficient, though? In Bristol, where I live, the cult of local is at its height, and self-sufficiency is a major part of its rhetoric. The local authority has joined the Bristol Food Policy Council and has published a Food Charter, one of whose ten ambitions is to 'make the city more secure in terms of being able to meet its own food demands from as close to the city as possible'.[14] But we are not more resilient when we source as locally as possible. On the contrary, we are more vulnerable. Throughout history places all over the world have suffered famines because crops failed locally and they did not have the capacity to bring in food from outside. A warning of what happens if you rely too much on local agriculture came in 2012, when the UK's poor wheat crop forced Premier Foods, maker of Hovis bread, to drop its pledge to bake only with British flour. A food economy that has numerous supply lines, some short, some long, makes it possible for us to eat well all year round, irrespective of what kind of spring or summer we've had.

We are all better off being able to trade and exchange, sometimes across large distances. Trade is what enables people to concentrate on what they are good at, achieving economies of scale that are unattainable when we do everything for ourselves. Having one person bake bread for everyone in the village liberates others to produce more of the other things that the village needs. In Castell de Ferro, Granada, fishermen catch only fish, while up in the hills farmers grow only almonds. It makes no sense for the farmer to invest in a boat or for the fisherman to grow some almond trees, when they can just swap their surpluses and have plenty of both. No other animal has such an elaborate division of labour and system of exchange, which is why what really marks us out as a species is that we are *Homo cambiens*: exchanging humans.

The cult of localism leads to all sorts of perverse attempts to defy this evident logic. For a price, you can now buy tea grown in

Cornwall, which is no small achievement. It probably has a distinctive taste and is worth a try, but it would be mad to attempt to grow lots of our tea in Britain when the conditions for its cultivation are so much better elsewhere. Similarly, with enough artificial light and heat, maybe you could grow coffee or cocoa here too, but that would be a ridiculously poor use of resources. In general we should use British land for what grows or grazes well here.

At its best, trade brings people together. It is no coincidence that the great centres of Western civilisation have always been trading hubs, where people of different nations have come and gone: Athens in the fifth century BCE, Venice in the fourteenth and fifteenth centuries, Amsterdam in the seventeenth century, London, New York and Tokyo today. When people exchange goods, they also exchange ideas and experiences. Trade is arguably at the root of human civilisation. The honouring of contracts requires reciprocal trust and a strong civil state.

So why is the idea that we are less vulnerable if we import less so appealing? In part, it's because we have reached the lamentable stage where we seem to trust nature more than we do human beings. We are more afraid of capricious foreigners cutting off supplies than we are of too much or too little rain shrinking our yields. The educated urbanites who often lead these calls to localism have simply lost all sense of just how fickle nature is. Their allotments should teach them better, but like gamblers, hobby gardeners tend to remember only their wins. The one crop of ours to grow really well in 2012, for example, was raspberries. How satisfying it was to walk into a shop and see small punnets selling for £3 that contained less, worse-quality fruit than that we had picked from the bush fresh that morning, and every morning before for weeks. Isn't nature bountiful? we think, ignoring the scrawny beans and piddling green tomatoes destined never to ripen. Anyone who trusts nature to provide does not know nature. On the other hand, we don't need to trust human nature in order to be confident that others will honour their side of the bargain: if a trader loses his reputation, he is finished.

The fear of being dependent on strangers points to the political and ideological failings of the new localism. Not so very long ago, people who saw themselves as socially progressive championed internationalism. For example, even if it was an economic mistake, many of us liked the idea of a European single currency because it symbolised the coming together of nations. Now, progressives are more likely to champion the exact opposite: local currencies such as the Bristol pound that you can't even spend in the next village. Its slogan – 'Our City, Our Money' – echoes the catchphrase of the grotesque shopkeepers in the comedy series *The League of Gentlemen*: 'This is a local shop for local people.' What was once satirised as narrow-minded and parochial is now asserted proudly, without irony. 'To adhere to a principle of "buy locally" irrespective of the consequences for others,' write the philosopher Peter Singer and his co-author, Jim Mason, 'is a kind of community-based selfishness.'[15]

The idealising of the local risks creating a parochial mindset that confines people to the cultures they were raised in. There is a hint of this in the food sovereignty movement, which taints its otherwise laudable definition with an unnecessary two words: 'Food sovereignty is the right of peoples to healthy and *culturally appropriate* food produced through ecologically sound and sustainable methods, and their right to define their own food and agriculture systems.'[16] (My emphasis.) Of course people have a right to access foods from the cultures they belong to, but that is not because they are somehow more 'appropriate'. That is far too close to the frankly racist idea that bananas are for Africans and apples for Englishmen. We should remember that, in the past, the most passionate advocates of national food self-sufficiency have been the ugliest of nationalists, demanding that people stay or go back to where they came from. Mussolini, for instance, imposed import tariffs on wheat and encouraged Italians to eat only home-grown produce.[17] That is not to equate localism with fascism, of course, but simply to warn that there is a fine line between healthy local pride and pernicious, divisive nationalism.

What is needed, I think, is a way to combine the positive aspects of the new localism with the old virtues of internationalism. Something like this has been proposed by Carlo Petrini, founder of Slow Food (on which more later), who talks of a 'virtuous globalisation', by which local traditions are strengthened and made sustainable by their connections to the wider world through trade and exchange.[18]

The real problem of globalisation has nothing to do with the proximity or otherwise of those we trade with. The contemporary malaise is the depersonalisation of trade and the reduction of all goods and producers to commodities. The worst symptom of this was the financial crisis of 2008. Financial markets had become so abstracted from real relations between real people selling real goods that in some cases computer programs analysing nothing more than statistics were trading things that did not yet even exist. This was almost certainly one of the reasons why stock market and property bubbles had grown: traded values and real values had become divorced.[19] It was made possible in part because *Homo cambiens* had transmogrified into *Homo economicus*, a single-minded maximiser of financial gain.

That is not to say all trade is always and automatically better at a more human scale, of course. Car or computer production, for instance, cannot be carried out economically in artisanal workshops. But when impersonal corporations come to dominate all areas of commerce, we lose some of our humanity and come to feel and act more and more like cogs in an economic machine.

I think the cult of localism is in part a desire to recapture the human dimension in economic life. But it misunderstands the problem. What matters is not whether food is *local* but whether it is *located*: whether it comes from a particular place and a producer we can, however indirectly, treat with respect and fairness. So all other things being equal, it is more ethical, for example, to buy coffee we know comes from a well-managed estate in Kenya than it is to buy milk from a British herd kept in industrial conditions by a faceless conglomerate. What we should want is for human-scale, ethical businesses to be supported, in our locality and with other localities.

We promote localities anytime we buy something and are confident about where it comes from, however far away. The ideal is described by one importer of Spanish food to Britain, which says, 'Our products come from small companies with history, experience and local producers to establish an excellent and unique connection "from local to local".'[20] For example, Londoners who eat Mrs Kirkham's Lancashire cheese paired with Eccles cake at the high-class restaurant St John are in their way celebrating the local as much as Lancastrians who buy it at Bury Market. After all, it is a strange kind of local pride that turns inwards and does not want to share what it is proud of.

This points to how the pro-local and globalisation tendencies can be reconciled. The clearest example of how this can be done comes from the Fairtrade movement, which tries to ensure a better deal for producers in the developing world. (I use 'Fairtrade' throughout this book to refer to formally certified schemes, to distinguish these from 'fair trade' more generally.) Harriet Lamb, the CEO of Fairtrade International, described the situation to me in terms of the 'hourglass economy'. With coffee, for example, around 25 million smallholders worldwide produce 80 per cent of the world's coffee, which ends up being drunk by millions, if not billions of consumers. But between producer and consumer are just a handful of middlemen. Forty per cent of the global coffee trade is in the hands of 4 companies, and 60 per cent of the retail trade is captured by 5 global brands.[21] The problem with globalisation is not that people at each end of this hourglass exchange with each other; it is that they do so via a faceless, placeless, multinational intermediary. On the whole, these global giants have sucked up commodities from around the world and melted them down to create one, homogenised, uniform product, erasing all trace of the specific locality from where they came. If, however, we could restore more direct links between producer and consumer, then much of the unease people feel about globalisation would vanish, to be replaced by a positive delight.

So whereas local is usually contrasted with global, local-to-local implies a trading relationship that extends wider than the immediate community. That is why I did not find it contradictory when Catherine Gazzoli, the CEO of Slow Food UK – a vigorous supporter of local food traditions – prepared a lunch for me made entirely from Italian foods: prosciutto crudo di San Daniele and Livio Felluga white wine from Friuli; Parmigiano Reggiano; ravioli bought at Slow Food International's Salone del Gusto in Turin, served in a sauce made with Neapolitan tomatoes brought over by visiting friends. Only the cake her colleague had made was British, but the meal fitted the vision of virtuous globalisation, which is all about exchanges between people and places who have their own strong, local traditions.

A shift in our understanding of where the true value of the local lies could be helped by a linguistic switch. Italians do not speak so much of *località* as *tipicalità*. Food is *tipico* if it is distinctive of a particular place, and such is the value placed on this characteristic that if a dish is described as *tipico*, it hardly needs saying that it is also *buono*. The advantage of using this word is that you can eat a *tipico* Tuscan bean stew in Birmingham, but not a local one. *Tipicalità* is a form of locality that can travel. Indeed, a risotto Milanese made from good ingredients in Manchester is more *tipico* than a ready-made one reheated in a microwave in Milan.

There is plenty to be commended in growing our own food and

supporting local producers, but we should not slip into the error of seeing it as a declaration of independence. Rather, we should understand that without other people, places and cultures, we are nothing. Our interdependence makes it imperative to widen our horizons and open our doors, not so that we are swamped by a homogeneous force called 'global capitalism', but to exchange with millions of others who love their own land and people as much as we do.

RISOTTO

One of the best ways of turning the spring harvest into a tasty meal is to combine it with ingredients imported from across the sea. I take finely chopped shallots and garlic from our garden, sweat them in olive oil from Greece and then add Arborio rice from Italy. Once the grains are coated, I might add a generous splash of white wine, possibly from France. I'll throw in peas and tender, unpeeled broad beans from the garden and then, ladle by ladle, add hot stock from a pot, stirring at a low simmer continuously until the grain has absorbed all the liquid and is cooked almost through, but retains a little bite. Then I stir in some chopped mint and a squeeze of lemon, possibly from Spain, turn off the heat and leave the risotto to sit for a few minutes before serving.

All risottos follow the same principle. What varies with the meat or vegetables is when you add them and what kind of fat and stock you use. So for pea and prawn, for example, the (preferably raw) prawns are added near the end and a chicken or fish stock is best. Some, such as mushroom and/or leek, benefit from plenty of butter and some grated Grana Padano stirred in before serving, and sprinkled on after as well for that matter. If you use dried porcini mushrooms, the water you soak them in can be the base of a vegetable stock.

You can make an entirely local version of the same dish. Just use British pearled spelt instead of rice, something like rapeseed oil or butter – which is what most Italians would use in risotto anyway – and stick to British herbs and vegetables. With leafy greens such as kale, its earthier, nuttier taste makes it arguably better than risotto, but not because it's local. I would hate to think of people depriving themselves of the reassuring pleasure of an authentic risotto out of a misguided desire to keep it local. After all, 'speltotto' is itself inspired by a foreign dish, and how many of those home-grown vegetables are assimilated immigrants anyway? Peas were a Roman import, and broad beans originated in North Africa. 'All-British' speltotto is yet another declaration of our interdependence.

3

Watch the time

Here are three meals that you could prepare over the course of a year in the United Kingdom. As a conscientious eater, would you be happy to cook all three?

January

Free-range chicken and mushroom pie,
julienne carrots, garlic mash
Apple tarte tatin with organic clotted cream
All ingredients sourced within the UK, most within 25 miles

March

Sustainable certified MSC (Marine Stewardship Council)
wild salmon, organic Fairtrade peas and organic
Fairtrade saffron basmati rice
Organic Fairtrade fig and almond cake with mascarpone

September

Swordfish, roasted butternut squash, creamed leeks
Berry crumble
All ingredients sourced within the UK and its waters

It's not a trick question, but it is a tricky one. It highlights the difficulty of paying homage to all three parts of the holy trinity of seasonal, organic and local. March's menu, for example, is entirely organic, but it is also completely unseasonal and therefore not local, since everything has to be imported, with the peas airfreighted. Adding to the ethical confusion is that all ingredients that could be Fairtrade are Fairtrade.

September's menu is entirely seasonal and local, containing only ingredients that are available in the UK at that point in the year. At the time of writing, however, swordfish is considered an at-risk fish and most campaigners would urge you not to eat it, under normal circumstances at least. And what if these seasonal foods have been grown on conventional farms of the most soil-depleting, fossil-fuel-hungry kind permissible under existing legislation?

January's meal is as close to seasonless as you can get. All the ingredients can be sourced from UK farms almost all year round, sometimes because they store well. It is in some ways a better menu than the seasonal one since food has travelled shorter distances and comes from better-managed farms, some of them organic. The animal flesh is sustainable, and the chicken itself slaughtered instantly, not left to suffocate on a boat like the wild salmon.

Overall, then, seasonal, local and organic are not in themselves trump cards, and sometimes these desiderata conflict with each other. However, the difficulties of elevating the seasonal-organic-local mantra to the level of a golden rule run deeper than the specifics of SOL food. The root of the problem is an inescapable feature of ethics: its plurality.

Whatever we base our morality on, we often find that our values conflict. We want to avoid airfreighted food, for example, but we want to support Fairtrade blueberry growers in South America. So what do we do? The sceptical response is that all moral values are relative, little more than preferences really, so there is no right answer.

Whatever works for you. But hardly anyone who pays lip service to this kind of laissez-faire relativism acts as though they really believe it. They tend to condemn the lying politician or the cheating spouse as strongly as the next person.

Another option is to maintain that moral values form a kind of hierarchy, so if they conflict, one trumps the other. So, for example, most people think the imperative not to kill trumps the right to defend your property: you do not shoot a pickpocket running off with your wallet. The ways in which this hierarchy is determined can be very complicated, so it is not just a matter of ascertaining which rules apply, but gauging the specific nature of the situations to which they apply. For instance, there may be no simple rule that says supporting Fairtrade trumps keeping CO_2 emissions to a minimum or vice versa. Rather, it might be true that supporting Fairtrade is usually more important, but there is a limit to how heavy a commodity can be for airfreighting to be justifiable.

Pluralism is a third position, one which agrees that we often have to balance competing moral values and that sometimes one will weigh most heavily. But it goes further and insists that the scales do not always tip one way or the other. There are many legitimate moral values and sometimes there is no way of determining which should prevail when they clash. Whichever you choose entails some kind of loss, and there is no formula or master principle that enables you to determine which option you should take.

I believe that pluralism is probably true. I accept that ultimately it might not be: perhaps all moral dilemmas are in principle resolvable, if only we could see all the facts and values in play clearly enough. But in practical terms, this is beside the point. Pluralism describes the situation we find ourselves in, whether that is because of the limits of our moral knowledge or because of the limits of morality itself.

That's why my menu dilemma is so tricky. There just isn't a

formula for deciding which is superior on ethical grounds. Each has its merits and drawbacks. That is not to say we cannot think more clearly about the grounds on which we choose one or another. What helps most of all is clarity about the nature of the values we are balancing. We have already thought about the merits of locality, and later I'll look at organics and fairtrade. What, though, is so virtuous about seasonality?

Answering the question is not helped by the fact that the very concept is muddled. In broad terms, the definition seems clear: food is in season when it is fresh and ready to eat. But of course, by that definition alone, all fresh food is seasonal. What you need to add to the definition is some notion of locality. In Britain, asparagus is in season when it is available fresh from British farms in May and June, not in January when it is being airfreighted from Peru. But what defines local? If I'm eating my meal in, say, Folkestone, where I grew up, I'm closer to the farms of France, Holland and Belgium than I am to those of Yorkshire and Lancashire, while parts of Spain and Italy are closer to me than many in Scotland. Why is rhubarb picked 200 miles away in Lincolnshire seasonal, while tomatoes picked 200 miles away in France are unseasonal?

Another complication is that growing seasons have been greatly extended by the use of polytunnels, hydroponics, artificial heating and so on. Are British strawberries in October in season?

You could try narrowing the definition of seasonal to foods that under more or less traditional growing methods are only available at certain times of the year within a fairly small radius, say a few hundred miles. This isn't an exact definition, but some concepts and rules work better with fuzzy edges than sharp ones. So, for example, it would be silly to rule a strawberry that is 200 miles and 1 inch away unseasonal and one a foot closer seasonal. Nor can there be a clear definition of what counts as 'more or less traditional' farming.

The trouble with going down this route is not its unavoidable imprecision, but that it requires us to make ad hoc revisions to the rules to fit our intuitions about what we think we mean by 'seasonal', without being clear on what those intuitions are based, and whether they are sound. So before we try to set rules, we need to be clear about what good reasons we have to attach value to seasonality, and only then see what rules preserve those values most completely.

The first value is environmental. There are foods that grow well, on our doorsteps, at certain times of the year, and it is better to eat them only, or mostly, then. That is more efficient than transporting produce from afar or using energy-rich inputs like heating and fertilisers to make crops grow at otherwise unsuitable times or in unsuitable places. The principles behind this argument may be sound, but they do not always lead us to seasonal food. Bananas, for example, can be shipped at very low environmental cost from countries where they are grown abundantly, and so are as environmentally friendly as local, seasonal fruits.

The second value is aesthetic. Some foods simply taste better during their natural season. The strawberry season has been extended considerably, but you get the best flavour from those in 'peak season' around June. When fruits and vegetables have to be transported long distances, many lose their freshness, in part because they have to be picked before they are ripe so they can last long enough to survive the trip. That's why Italian tomatoes in Britain rarely taste like Italian tomatoes in Italy. But there are some seasonal foods that travel well. Take cheese, for example. The milk that makes a young pecorino Toscano is at its best from spring through summer, when the pastures the sheep graze are at their most lush. Given it is only aged for around a month, that means it is best eaten from late spring to early autumn, whether you enjoy it in Florence or Felixstowe. Truffles are another example: an autumn Alba truffle is as delicious and as seasonal in Manchester as it is in Milan.

Another aesthetic consideration is that pleasure is heightened when you know you only have a short window in which to experience it. Flavours that have disappeared for nine months taste all the richer when they return and can become dull when indulged in too much. I remember one year, for example, being delighted by the early arrival of strawberries in the shops. That warm summer I kept buying them, making the most of them on the assumption the season would soon end. But in these days of polytunnels, it dragged on well into September, and so the following year I was still too sated to buy the new season's.

A final aesthetic reason to honour the seasons is that modern life is an increasingly homogeneous experience. Our homes and workplaces are a constant 18 degrees Celsius all year round, there is little vegetation in city streets to distinguish summer from winter, and few jobs have any kind of strong seasonal rhythm. The more we attend to the ways in which the natural world changes with the months, the more differentiated the days become. And the more a day differs from others, the more there is to appreciate in it, while the more the days resemble each other, the less precious each one becomes.

This links with the third reason to value seasonality, which is more than just aesthetic: it makes us more aware of the flow of time. This for me is one of the main benefits I get from our allotment and vegetable garden. When you grow food, the transitions between the seasons become much more apparent, to the extent that you become aware of the next one before it has even begun. In August, for example, you already start noticing that growth is slowing down. Some crops have been harvested and the brown wilt of autumn has already begun. Similarly, there are signs of spring, in terms of shoots, in February or even January.

This is not about the romantic idea of being 'in touch with the rhythm of nature'; it's about the rhythm of human life. Between beasts and angels, we live neither entirely in the present nor in a timeless eternity. If you want to hear the clock that ticks in sync with our lives, you'll find it in gardens. To grow, you have to think beyond the moment, but your timeframe will remain on a human scale. The quickest crop, such as rocket, goes from seed to table in a few weeks. Fruit trees can take several years to establish themselves, a vine even longer. If you rotate your beds, you'll be working on a three- or four-year cycle. Gardens make you think in terms of weeks, months and years, not seconds, minutes, centuries or millennia.

Within this frame, things never stand still. In spring you can see some crops grow on a daily basis. Last year we were given particular pleasure by our fruit bushes. Each morning would reveal some more berries that had ripened and were ready to pick, yet each bush produced this bounty for only three or four weeks. If you attend to it, this can give a poignant, bitter-sweet sense of the transience of all things, the inevitability of the cycle of life and death, and the extreme privilege of being able to savour what life presents to us while we can. At the same time, the ever-changing nature of the garden encourages an attitude of letting go, accepting that good things pass and simply hoping that you'll still be around next year to enjoy the ride once again.

This kind of sensitivity to the seasons is more prominent in some other cultures than it is in the West. It is perhaps most developed in Japan, which has the aesthetic concept of *mono no aware*, the 'pathos of things', which involves an awareness of their impermanence and a wistful sadness at their passing. The idea that developing sensitivity to the seasons is a kind of virtue would therefore seem very natural in Japan, and it's one that we should embrace too. That, rather than any environmental consideration, is the most convincing reason to live and eat more, but not completely, seasonally.

APPLE AND BLACKBERRY CRUMBLE

I've got to know some of the best places for picking blackberries near my home in autumn and I'm always on the lookout for more. Around the same time, not far away in Somerset, in a good year for apples you'll find people leaving boxes of the fruit at the ends of their drives for people to take, rather than see them go to waste. From these gathered foods, one of my favourite seasonal dishes takes shape.

Crumble is absurdly easy. First, just peel and chop apples into smallish pieces, not necessarily of a uniform size. Mix in as many blackberries as you like. If you use eating apples rather than cookers, no sugar needs to be added. If the berries are tart, though, or you're using lots of them, then you might want to add some sugar or mix in some honey to counter the sharpness.

The crumble topping is simply a combination of plain flour – white or wholemeal, as you prefer – sugar, butter and a pinch of salt. The proportion of sugar to flour is to your taste. You'll know you've got the right proportion of dry ingredients to butter when it mixes between your fingers into a crumbly texture, but will bind if you take a little and squeeze it together. I like to put oats and crushed nuts in with the dry mix too. How much of this you make depends on how thick a layer of crumble you like.

The crumble then just goes on top of the fruit and the ensemble is put in the oven at around 180 degrees Celsius (360 degrees Fahrenheit, gas mark 4). It's ready when brown, after about forty-five to sixty minutes. It somehow seems even nicer cold from the fridge the next morning with some Greek yoghurt. Sweetest of all are the first and last crumbles of the season, as you greet and say goodbye to a much-loved annual visitor, knowing that you will never get bored by too much of its company.

4

Look beyond organic

Lunch with the Helen Browning, chief executive of the Soil
Association, is in many ways a vindication of the organic movement she leads in the UK. We met at Canteen on Bristol's Gloucester
Road, a very socially mixed café-bar in a neighbourhood where
people didn't just sign petitions against the opening of a national chain
supermarket, some planned to firebomb it, a plot that led to riots
when police raided the squat where they believed it was being
hatched. It is a sign that organic ideals are not a middle-class preserve
that the food here is not only delicious but seasonal, from small local
farms with high animal welfare and environmental standards. What's
more, Browning's pea risotto and my sustainable mackerel cost less
than many takeaways. But one word is conspicuous by its absence on
Canteen's daily-changing chalkboard menu: organic.

A similar story could be told about Tom Bowles's farm near Bath
in Somerset. Farming has been in his family for nearly two centuries,
and his father has lived through all the major changes in modern agriculture. A few decades ago this farm was almost a monoculture,
supplying as much wheat for the supermarkets as the land could produce. Now it has returned to mixed use and sells almost all its
produce directly through its farm shop and café. The cows' pasture
is enriched by clover, not fertiliser, and chemicals are all but banished.
But although many people who drive through the farm gate assume
it must be organic, it isn't.

Over the last few decades organic has emerged from the fringes to become the cornerstone of the new food gospel's holy trinity, with seasonal sat to its left, local to its right. For many, it seemed organic was the future. But in several markets that march has been halted, and in some it has reversed. Sales of organic products have been falling in the UK year on year since the credit crunch first bit in late 2008. Thrift alone does not seem to be enough to explain what is now a medium-term trend, though, since Fairtrade, another ethical certification that often carries a price premium, has not suffered the same reverse, with its sales continuing to rise strongly, up an estimated 19 per cent in 2012 alone.

What seems to be happening is that uncommitted customers who bought organic vaguely believing it was better in some way have prioritised economising, while many of those who once used the organic label as a kind of proxy for good, sustainable produce now look to the specific virtues that most concern them: sustainability, seasonality, locality, fair trade or animal welfare. Ironically, this greater discernment is in part a sign of the organic movement's success. As many of the broad principles that organic farming advocates have become more mainstream, the prestige of actually being certified organic has diminished.

The question of how we should farm is an urgent one. The world's population is not due to peak until around the middle of the century and there are serious question marks over whether we will be able to feed the roughly 9 billion people who will be on the planet by then. Yet there are also doubts that modern industrial agriculture – by which is meant large-scale farming that uses a lot of synthetic inputs – is sustainable. It depends on resources such as oil, nitrogen and phosphates, which are finite and many think are running out, at least in their practically accessible forms.

The dilemma we face is exemplified by the Spanish village of Polopos, a few miles from the coast in the mountains of Andalusia.

Walk the narrow stone streets and you'll come across mules in stables below the houses of farmers who still use the beasts to work their fields, producing grapes and almonds. You can knock on the door of the local shepherd and buy one of his goat-milk cheeses. It sounds idyllic, but five minutes here is enough to show you that it isn't. Polopos is dying. The population is elderly, most of the young people have left, the school closed years ago, and you hardly see any children or young people in its streets. This way of farming might have been fine when people were happy to be poor and barely subsisting, but it just isn't efficient enough to provide a decent living for those who want basic twenty-first-century comforts.

Those who remain can't live on almonds and the local *costa* wine alone, however, so they have to buy their fruit and vegetables in supermarkets in nearby towns, from a truck that comes to the village every Saturday or at one of the nearby markets. And here's the shock: these last upholders of the bucolic rural life eat fruit and vegetables that range from the bland to the flavourless. In the market of nearby Cádiar, for instance, you are lucky to find a tomato that smells of anything. Look out towards the coast from the hills surrounding Polopos and the reason is clear. As far as the eye can see, the white sheen of polytunnels in the sun fills the valleys and spreads onto the hillsides, which have been violently razed to create new land for growing produce, not in the earth but hydroponically: plants are rooted directly into a base of feed, which is then kept watered. These modern techniques are generally fine-tuned to maximise volume, not flavour. Much of the crop goes to export, to British supermarkets where customers have a very different image of the Spain they come from.

The past is past. There is no point pretending that we can go back to the time of the mule, but the present doesn't look too attractive either. So how did we get from one to the other, and is there an alternative?

The history of Tom Bowles's farm provides a neat encapsulation of the issues. Before the Second World War it was what we might call a traditional mixed farm which sold its produce in small local markets. The war, however, gave Europe a shock: it was barely able to feed itself. So understandably, post-war, the Continent was determined to go for agricultural growth and make sure it had the capacity to provide more than enough food for its citizens. These were boom years for farmers, who were given huge subsidies to modernise their methods and boost production, replacing the gentle methods of old with machinery and sprays.

The next, slower revolution was the emerging dominance of supermarkets. They were very clever, says Tom's father, Richard. They went round the farms finding out exactly what it cost to produce what they needed. They then effectively set their prices by paying everyone on the basis of the costs of the most productive farms. Tied in by contracts, the farms had to do whatever was necessary to meet the targets.

Bowles, like many, decided in the end that enough was enough. 'I can't see any farm in this location of this size ever being profitable in today's commercial farming world,' he told me. It was then that his son decided to take the farm in a new direction. They gave up on supplying supermarkets and tried something else, something that was in a sense a return to the original farm: mixed production, selling locally and directly. The farm shop is not on a main road, catching passing trade, so most of its custom is not from day-tripping middle-class city dwellers but from the local villages. Yet so far the plan seems to be working.

The changes being made by farmers like these, as well as changing consumer behaviour, mean that supermarkets are changing their game too. Although they still drive hard bargains at times, they are being forced to accept that squeezing farms only works for so long. All are now trying hard to improve relations with farmers, both to secure good-quality supplies and to show increasingly savvy customers that they are not corporate bullies.

Where does organics fit into this? In Bowles's case, not at all. But you can see how organics came to prominence by offering an attractive alternative to each of the lamentable developments in this tale.

First and foremost, organics addressed the health concerns of people worried by the huge increases in the quantities of synthetic sprays and fertilisers being used on crops. This first came to the wider public's attention with the publication of Rachel Carson's *Silent Spring* in 1962, which alerted people to the dangers of agricultural chemicals for human health, seeing the detrimental effects of pesticides on bird populations in particular as a warning sign. Ever since, people have been wary of conventionally grown crops, convinced they are loaded with toxic residues. Organics offered an attractive alternative. Although it is not true that organic crops are grown with no sprays or chemicals at all, their use is extremely limited. Research by the Soil Association and Sustain suggests that the belief that organic food is 'healthier for me and my family' is one of the main reasons why people buy organics, with 52 per cent of customers citing it as a motivation, more than high animal welfare standards (34 per cent) or its being more ethical (33 per cent).[22]

However, the story of conventional farming is not one of ever-increasing chemical usage. Since and in part thanks to *Silent Spring*, legislation on the use of pesticides and fertilisers has become much stricter. 'Conventional growers' standards are so much higher than they were twenty, thirty years ago,' says fruit and veg supplier Charlie Hicks. 'I know a lot of growers and they've got very high standards. People don't cheat when it comes to sprays. If you speak to farmers, what they keep saying is, "Do you know how expensive this stuff is?"'

In a recent academic book surveying the evidence from the last few decades, Professor Robert Blair, former principal scientific officer of the UK Agricultural Research Council, concludes that

'Organic and conventional foods are fairly similar in terms of their nutritional quality and freedom from harmful chemical residues,' and that this 'is in agreement with conclusions reached by many other scientists and government food agencies worldwide'. Indeed, having formerly not worried enough about pesticides and chemicals, we now almost certainly worry too much. Farmers are the people most exposed to pesticides, yet Blair reports their cancer rates are 'very substantially lower than that of the general public', probably because they have a healthier, more active lifestyle than the typical contemporary Briton. Another study showed no difference between the sperm counts of organic and conventional farmers.[23]

We also tend to assume more spraying is worse than less, but what actually matters is how 'residual' the chemicals are: how long they remain in the soil or on the plants. The reason farmers spray the herbicide Roundup so often, for example, is because it breaks down quickly and so needs regular reapplication. In that sense, the safer the spray, the more often it has to be used.

Many people, however, do not trust scientific definitions of 'safe levels' and believe that any trace is bad. But this is just a superstition based on a deep-rooted psychological aversion to contamination: it is only human to feel repulsed by the thought of any contaminant, significant or not, for good evolutionary reasons. But rationality has to be a better guide here. We know, for example, that there are all sorts of naturally occurring carcinogens, such as the tannic acids found in tea, coffee and cocoa, and the heterocyclic amines in cooked meats. Most of us rightly do not avoid these foods, and nor should we fear vegetables that have even lower levels of substances that are only dangerous in excess.

Even if conventionally grown food is free from harmful levels of synthetic toxins, some worry that the pumped-up, fast-grown produce it creates is less nutritious. But again the evidence suggests otherwise. A review by Professor Alan Dangour of the London

School of Hygiene and Tropical Medicine found no significant differences in the nutrient content or health benefits of organic food. Blair concluded in his book that 'There is broad agreement ... [that] ... there is no proof that organic food is more nutritious or safer.'[24] All this simply reinforces the most comprehensive study to date, an independent 2009 report commissioned by the Food Standards Agency, which surveyed over fifty years of evidence and concluded, 'Organically and conventionally produced crops and livestock products are broadly comparable in their nutrient content.'

It is true that some farming practices can result in lower nutritional content and potential health risks, but this is not down to whether they are organic or not. For example, grass-fed cattle have been shown to produce more nutritionally rich milk, but while many more organic herds than conventional ones are grass-fed, many grass-fed herds are not organic. So although it is claimed that organic milk contains higher levels of omega-3 fatty acid, that is only true when the milk is compared to that produced by conventional feed-reared dairy herds, not that from non-organic grass-fed ones.

Bit by bit the claims for the health benefits of organic food have been refuted. In 2012 another review of the evidence published in the journal *Annals of Internal Medicine* concluded that 'There isn't much difference between organic and conventional foods, if you are an adult and making a decision solely on your health.' The case for the health benefits of organics is now so flimsy that the Soil Association has effectively been banned from making any claims for them. 'Anything we say we ASA-proof it now, absolutely,' says Browning, referring to the need to avoid sanction by the Advertising Standards Authority.

Another reason why people might choose organic is that it claims higher animal welfare standards. This is generally true, if you compare a random organic farm with a random conventional one. Compassion in World Farming, for example, believes that of the certification schemes, organics guarantees the highest welfare standards.

But that does not mean organic is always or automatically better for animals. As animal welfare researcher Becky Whay told me, the research that has been done on whether organic standards are all really better for animals 'is not very clear cut'. The only way to know how well the animals are cared for is to go to the farm, not look at the label. Good animal husbandry is about more than following rules.

Indeed, there may be some cases where organic animals are worse off. 'I would never raise livestock organically,' wrote Susan, a Maryland sheep and goat producer and college-educated scientist who writes the blog, the Baalands. She believes American 'organic standards do not allow you to treat a sick animal with anything that is scientifically proven to be effective. You can't use antibiotics, anthelmintics, anti-inflammatories, coccidiostats, steroids, hormones, feed additives, or many other conventional therapies.'

'There are certainly areas we know they're struggling to deal with in the organic sector,' says Whay, 'such as digital dermatitis, an infectious disease of cattle where we know that mass antibiotic treatment is very, very effective.'

The rules do state that the animal's welfare must come first, even if that means it loses its organic status by being treated, but this does create potentially bad incentives. As Whay put it, 'From a farmer's point of view, if you've got a cow who loses her organic status, she becomes quite a problem for you.'

Roger Longman of the non-organic White Lake Cheeses spells out what this can mean: 'A lot of farmers go, "Well, she's not really, really sick. I won't treat her. I'll just hope she gets better," and that's wrong, to my mind. If I get sick, I'll go to the bloody doctor and get antibiotics, and I'd expect to be able to do the same thing with my animals.'

There is even one area of animal welfare where McDonald's appears to be ahead of the organic movement. Recent research has suggested that an enriched environment, with shrubs and shade, is more important for poultry welfare than minimising flock size and maximising ranging area. At the time of writing McDonald's had already moved ahead in rolling out its Range Enrichment Programme for its egg suppliers, whereas the Soil Association was still consulting on a change to its standards to accommodate the evidence.

The final selling point of organics has been that conventional farming is environmentally damaging and unsustainable. It's certainly not difficult to find examples of very bad practice, past and present. Perhaps most notoriously, nitrogen run-off from fertiliser applied to agricultural land along the banks of the Mississippi has spewed out into the ocean, creating a 'dead zone' in the Gulf of Mexico, unable to support most marine life. A 2008 study found more than 400 such dead zones around the world.[25] But it would be wrong to judge all non-organic farming by its worst examples. If you do take evidence seriously, unless you cherry-pick – which both defenders and detractors often do – it appears to be very mixed, and complicated. For example, one study into what we would call high-intensity maize production in Nebraska suggested that highly irrigated and nitrogen-fertilised crops had higher yields, used less energy and had less environmental impact than alternative systems.[26] Even Helen Browning doesn't deny that the evidence doesn't all stack up on the side of organics. 'On biodiversity, organic clearly has a lot to offer. On climate change, on the greenhouse gas side of things, it does in some areas and not others.'

Advocates for organics are hostages to fortune if they continue to use sustainability as their trump card. What recent history has shown is that conventional farming adapts and it has very strong incentives to reduce its dependency on finite resources such as oil and synthesised nitrogen. Some would claim that the hydroponic farms that blot the landscape of southern Spain are already fully sustainable, in the sense that they are extremely efficient, do not pollute surrounding soil and do not require the excessive use of chemicals, water or fossil fuels.

Even if you don't buy the case for hydroponics, if sustainability is the key, then it is probably only a matter of time before we see truly sustainable and safe agriculture that is also industrial and ugly. And if it is, we have one very good reason to prefer it over organics. Washington State University professor John P. Reganold is no apologist for big farming, having led the US's first and still only undergraduate major in organic agricultural systems. But writing in *Nature*, he noted that the most recent meta-analysis showed 'Organic farming systems in developed countries produce yields that are 20 per cent lower than their conventional counterparts.'[27] Few outside the organic movement, and not even everyone within it, believe we would be able to feed the world if the entire planet's agricultural production went over to organic overnight.

That is not to say we need the most rapacious mega-farms either: 70 per cent of all food in the world today is grown by smallholders with 2 hectares or less, so we are hardly reliant on large industrial farming.[28] Both sides of the debate often present the issue as though it required going to one or other extreme when the truth seems to be that the most problematic routes either would be to make the world entirely organic (which not even a Friends of the Earth report advised)[29] or industrialise to the maximum. It is not an either-or choice. Even the Soil Association's own president, Monty Don, acknowledged as much when he took on the role in 2008: 'I would much rather someone bought food that was local and sustainable but not organic than bought organic food that had to be shipped across the world,' he said.[30]

As Tom Bowles shows, farming is not neatly divided between small and organic, and large and industrial. Although broadly supportive of organics, Dominic Coyte of Neal's Yard Dairy said, 'You can get massive organic farms, and is the husbandry any better there than a farmer who's not because he can't afford a Soil Association certificate or he just thinks it's all a bit barmy? For me, scale is more important – some of the organic herds are too big.' Indeed, some organic operations are now so large that the writer Michael Pollan uses the phrase 'industrial organic' to describe them.[31] It is not at all clear that these operations meet the ideals associated with organics. The founder of Slow Food, Carlo Petrini, has complained about the exploitation of migrant workers on large American farms, saying that 'No *civilised* country advances organic agriculture, as California is doing, by enslaving so many Mexican growers.'[32] Is a huge herd fed with organic pellets bought in from hundreds of miles away better than a small herd grazing on grass that has been lightly fertilised? Should we prefer acres of an organic maize monoculture to a small mixed farm that sprays pesticides sparingly?

One reason why this is so complicated is that 'organic' has no clear, single meaning. Standards vary between and sometimes within countries. Farmed salmon can be certified organic in Scotland, for example, but there is no EU standard for farmed fish. In the UK, the EU sets the minimum criteria, but produce can be certified by one of ten different bodies, all of which have their own sets of rules. Most of the differences are quite small, but some are not: in America, antibiotics are completely banned; in the UK, their limited use is allowed.

This means that although organics is based around four principles – the health of every part of the food cycle, working with and emulating living ecological systems, fairness to all and following the precautionary principle – it is run on the basis of a complex list of rules. So there are box-tickers who don't respect the principles but are just looking to add a premium to their produce, and farmers who affirm these principles of health, ecology, fairness and care without also ticking the boxes, such as the farmer at the market at Cádiar, Andalusia, whose sign read, '*Productos ecológicos*' ('Organic produce') in large print, with a smaller '*sin certificar*' ('without certification') below. But in an important sense he was wrong: organics is defined by its system of certification.

Having discussed and written about these issues over recent years, I find people often strangely reluctant to let go of the idea that there is something special and good about organic food. My charitable explanation for this is that they see there is something good in it, but it's not quite what they think. Yes, food production needs to be compassionate to animals, environmentally sustainable, safe and healthy, but not only are there non-organic systems that met these desiderata, so do some extremely industrial ones.

My suggestion is that organics is good in so far as it embodies a virtue that is not explicitly there in the four principles of health, ecology, fairness and care, but is lurking in the background nonetheless: stewardship. The importance of stewardship is arguably the most important ideal that conservative political thought has consistently defended. It is the idea that the land is not ours to do what we want with, but something we have inherited from previous generations and that we must safeguard so that we pass it on in as good, or better, condition for generations to come. As the most eloquent conservative philosopher of his generation, Roger Scruton, put it, 'We come to see that this present moment is also past, but the past of someone else, who has yet to be.'[33] How we deal with this is the challenge we confront in places like Polopos, where the old inheritance has run out and cannot be replenished, yet what is replacing it seems so abhorrent.

If we think in terms of stewardship, we are led neither to organics nor to the maximal efficiency of technological agriculture, nor to the preservation of as many traditional ways of producing food as possible. Good stewardship does demand that our agriculture is sustainable into the future, but that is only part of what it means.

Stewardship requires that we ought to protect our land and our landscape. If you are only concerned with sustainability, there may be nothing to object to in the swathes of polytunnels blighting Andalusia and Almeria. What is problematic about them is that a once-beautiful part of the country has been rendered ugly, mountainsides dug away and land flattened. In the 1950s and 1960s the Spanish *costas* were ruined by tasteless developments built to attract mainly British holidaymakers in search of a cheap break. Now, behind the beaches, the foothills are being ruined to provide tasteless food to, often British, consumers in search of cheap meals. The Spanish have blown their inheritance in search of quick rewards. Of course there are always going to be trade-offs between protecting natural beauty and the needs of development, but stewardship does not mean knee-jerk preservationism. The good steward has the courage to protect the things that should not be changed, the sensitivity to manage the changes that must be made and the wisdom to know the difference between the two.

Stewardship also requires that we protect the culture of the table whereby humans do not just feed; they eat, and eat well. That means a respect for the quality and flavour of food, not just its quantity and price. Admittedly there is a danger here of a kind of elitism that denies the importance of those on limited incomes to feed themselves cheaply. I do not buy the argument that everyone could eat the kind of tasty organic food beloved of the chattering classes, if only they learned to cook properly and were frugal. But I do believe that the vast majority could eat better within their budgets. It is in part a matter of priorities. Michael Marriage of Doves Farm, for instance, defends the higher prices of his organic flours and biscuits by asking rhetorically, 'Why do we have to buy the cheapest food all the time?' As he rightly points out, there's virtually nothing else we choose on the basis of price alone, including drink. We spend a lower proportion of our household budgets on food than at any point in history, but at the same time we spend plenty on eating out and takeaways. In Britain in 2011 for every £1 spent on household food, 43p was spent eating out.[34] We don't need to spend more overall to contribute to the stewardship of good food; we just need to spend differently.

Stewardship is thus a virtue that encapsulates all that is truly good about organics, but it also captures much more, and it is not limited to organics. It is the virtue of being good custodians of our inheritance, neither throwing it away nor preserving it in aspic. This is what we need to be thinking about when we decide what food to buy, not whether it carries an organic logo. The Gospel According to Organics thus turns out to be an Old Testament that merely paved the way for a New Testament, based on more robust virtues, of which stewardship is an important one.

EINKORN BREAD

It's certainly not difficult to work out why einkorn, one of the most ancient wheats, vanished from British tables long ago. Even Michael Marriage of Doves Farm, who recently started growing the crop with his wife Clare, told me that 'You get a pretty pathetic yield, the heads are tiny, and you get pretty small grain.' Plus, whereas most modern domestic wheat is 'naked', meaning the husk around the seed falls off during threshing, each tiny einkorn seed is encased in a hard shell and needs de-hulling.

But any suspicion that the grain is more effort than it is worth vanishes when you taste it. My bread-making skills are strictly elementary, but even the quick, simple recipe on the side of the flour packet resulted in a loaf far tastier than anything from an in-store supermarket bakery. It had an almost cake-like, soft, close-crumb texture and a flavour with hints of corn and nuts.

To make a loaf, you simply mix 500 grammes of einkorn flour, a teaspoon (5 grammes) each of quick yeast, salt and sugar, and 325 millilitres of lukewarm water. I tend to add a dash of olive or nut oil too, and sometimes use a bit of honey instead of sugar. Knead this into a dough for five to ten minutes, shape it into a loaf and leave it covered with a tea towel in a warm place to prove for thirty-five to forty minutes. Then bake at 200 degrees Celsius (180 degrees Celsius fan/400 degrees Fahrenheit/gas mark 6) for 40 to 45 minutes.

If einkorn is hard to find, you can make a similar loaf with the now widely available spelt, another heritage variety first revived by Doves Farm. Use a little more water (360 millilitres), and for optimal results, give it a second knead and a second proving. Spelt rises quite quickly, and you know it's ready for the next stage when it has more or less doubled in size.

By supporting the production of these grains, you will be contributing to the stewardship of both a valuable part of our agricultural heritage and a delicious part of our culinary one.

5

Kill with care

COMPASSION

For the first time in over twenty years I decided I was going to have a bacon sandwich. There were plenty being sold at Breakfast at Timothy's, a popular mobile roadside café on the A38 near Langford in Somerset. I had just visited an abattoir less than a mile away, where pigs had started their transformation into butty fillings. The experience had made me a rare example of someone who had become more, not less, likely to eat meat after seeing for himself how the animals were killed. I had also seen how the pigs were reared, in a spacious pen in the grounds of a friend's country home: they were well fed, well looked after, safe and as happy as pigs in muck prover-bially are. I was satisfied that I could eat their flesh with a clear conscience. The same could not be said with any confidence of the pigs who were now between slices of white bread or stuffed in a baguette at Timothy's, so for now a steaming cup of strong tea in a polystyrene cup would have to do.

This was the latest staging post in a long journey for me. It had started when I gave up eating mammals and poultry as a teenager. My father had been a pescatarian – someone who does not eat most ani-mals but will eat dairy products, eggs and fish – for many years. When my sister followed suit, I decided to give it a go, not because I was convinced meat was murder, but because I was not sufficiently con-vinced it wasn't. I could easily stop eating animals, and when it came to life-and-death matters, it seemed best to err on the side of caution.

I never called myself a vegetarian, partly because I would still eat most sea animals and couldn't see the point in refusing the odd bit of beast, particularly chicken, if it was already dead and placed before me unrequested. Nonetheless, for over a decade, I chose not to cook or buy any meat or poultry and bought only vegetarian versions of foods such as cheese that contained animal-derived ingredients. After around a decade of this, I sat down and thought through my reasons and concluded that I needed to apply my principles more consistently and rigorously.

The one thing I was always sure of was that the case for not killing any animal life at all didn't add up. There is no 'sanctity of life' principle that applies to every living creature, otherwise we would not kill vermin, disease-spreading insects, bacteria or viruses. To be even close to consistent in your respect for the sanctity of life, you would need to be like the Jains, who cover their mouths to avoid swallowing flies. You would also have to choose your vegetables carefully, since mechanical harvesters and insecticides kill millions of field animals like rabbits, mice and pheasants.[35] You certainly shouldn't keep a cat that is free to run around outside, since they do not stop killing just because you feed them. In the US, researchers estimate that 'Free-ranging domestic cats kill 1.4–3.7 billion birds and 6.9–20.7 billion mammals annually.'[36]

This is why it makes no sense to object to killing animals on the basis that it requires human beings to play God, deciding where to draw the line between what kinds of lives are sacrosanct and which can be taken away for our convenience. Everyone, even a vegan, draws such a line. Only the mad would draw it at killing bacteria and viruses. Almost all are prepared to kill the lice that infect human bodies. Most would kill vermin, although many would prefer to trap them – and then what? Release them into a rat sanctuary? The argument is about where, not if, the lines are drawn, and the only sensible criterion for drawing it is a degree of consciousness. The only kinds of life that have interests that need respecting are those that sustain some kind of ongoing experience worth having. That is why vegans treat plant life differently from animal life. No sensible person can argue that a carrot suffers if it is uprooted, except in some very loose metaphorical sense.

However, although most vegetarians and omnivores both accept this basic principle, they differ as to what follows from it. For many vegetarians, the critical point is that, however limited the conscious capacities of animals, they still feel pain. As Jeremy Bentham memorably put it, 'The question is not "Can they reason?" nor "Can they talk?", but "Can they suffer?"'[37] Causing unnecessary pain is bad, and so if we can avoid it, of course that is good.

But this argument is far from decisive when applied to eating meat. For just how serious a matter is the pain animals suffer in the first place? Here I think it is important to make a distinction between pain and suffering. Pain is simply that unpleasant sensation we have that has evolved as an alarm system for bodily damage (although some alarms are false). There is no reason to doubt that any animal with a basic central nervous system feels pain, and even some crustaceans may feel some. To suffer, however, is not just to have a moment of pain, or even a series of pains. It is for pain to compound itself by accumulation, and that requires a certain amount of memory.

To illustrate this difference, imagine a person who retained no memory, conscious or otherwise, of any experience she had. Everything that happens is forgotten immediately. Imagine that this person is painfully pricked every ten seconds. These pricks, if unnecessary, are of course bad, but each individual prick is hardly terrible, and each successive prick is no worse than the one before it. It is as though on each occasion the person is being pricked for the first time. Now imagine if I were to prick you every ten seconds. It would not take long for you to be driven half mad. 'Stop it,' you'd say, because you were aware of this as an ongoing torment and would dread its indefinite continuation. The total amount of pain you felt would be the same as that of the amnesiac, but your suffering would be immeasurably greater. And this reflects a general truth: pain is bad, but suffering is much worse.

There is actually a good deal of experimental evidence to show that suffering and pain differ, as suffering is memory-dependent and we care more about it than mere pain. In the most striking experiment, patients who were given an endoscopy were asked to report their level of pain and discomfort while the procedure was being undertaken. Then, once it was all over, they were asked to rate how unpleasant the entire experience had been and how willing they would be to undergo it again. There were therefore two sets of results: a series of judgements made at the time and a final, retrospective assessment. It turned out that this final judgement depended more on when *the most intense moment of pain* was experienced than it did on the *total amount of pain* felt. As it happens, the most painful part comes right at the end of the procedure, and if it is stopped at this natural point, the patient judges the whole experience to have been very painful. But if you keep the endoscope in place, creating continued mild pain and allowing the discomfort to calm down a little, the patient's final assessment is that overall the procedure was less painful than it otherwise would have been. This is deeply counter-intuitive, because, of course, the second case, although judged to be less distressing, is exactly the same as the first, apart from the *addition* of some extra, mild discomfort at the end. There is more total pain, but less total suffering.[38]

The reason for this is simple: pain itself is an unpleasant sensation, but it is experienced in present moments of awareness, which pass. What makes our self-consciousness more developed is not that we can experience moments – all animals can do that – but that we can create a narrative of our lives based on these experiences. This higher form of self-awareness is not simply an aggregate of lived moments; it is something different, built from them. In these terms, then, suffering is a kind of construct based on pain, but not in a straightforward additive way.

That's why suffering and pain differ, and why suffering matters much more. It does not mean that causing one instance of excruciating pain is never worse than causing ongoing but mild suffering, of course. There can be no neat algorithm for even comparing such things. But I think it does show that merely causing pain need not be a great wrong, if it is not contributing to significant suffering. Apply this to animals and the moral is clear: the fact that an animal may feel momentary pain at some points in the farming or hunting process is not necessarily a great wrong. We should only be seriously worried if we are causing real ongoing suffering or repeated severe pain.

I heard a fascinating story that illustrates the difference between animal pain and human torment perfectly. A woman was travelling with a group in Kenya and a goat was brought along, which many found delightful and were petting. She could see it was going to end up in a pot, though, and this was confirmed when it was strung up to a tree to have its throat cut. It was clearly in some distress, but the knife was too blunt and the first attempt at slaughter didn't work. So while the knife was sharpened, the goat was let down. As soon as it was let loose, it just continued munching grass as though nothing had happened. At that point the traveller saw the chasm between herself and the goat. Had she been through the same experience, she'd have been traumatised. The goat, however, had no existential anxiety. It was terrified, the terror passed, and that was it.

Although this is just one impressionistic anecdote, the scientific evidence supports this interpretation, with some caveats. First of all, animals vary, and a dog, for example, seems to be bothered by a trauma for a bit longer than a goat. Also, repeated maltreatment does cause animals to suffer, as their stress hormones become permanently activated. Even so, that does not contradict the basic insight that animals clearly are much more in the moment than we are and that, as a result, temporary pain or discomfort need not have any significant ongoing effects.

That is why I have yet to hear any convincing animal-welfare-based argument as to why I should not eat shrimps, whose nervous systems are far too minimal for them to suffer in my sense at all. Pigs, in contrast, are probably capable of suffering, but what that means is that we should rear them so as not to suffer, not that we should refrain from killing them, even if that requires some momentary pain (which it should not).

What about animals of intermediate sophistication, say fish? Is a fish truly suffering as it suffocates on a ship's deck, or is it only ever conscious of the present, experiencing a sequence of painful moments in much the same way as our amnesiac human? The question is perhaps badly put, since it implies an either/or when we have every reason to think that all life is on a continuum, and that there are no sharp lines between the capacities of species, only gradations of difference. The chances are that the suffering of a fish is more than that of a prawn but less than that of, say, a dolphin in the same situation. If suffering requires a certain amount of self-consciousness, one that combines memory with a sense of oneself as a continuing subject of experience, then it seems clear that certain species have greater capacity for suffering than others.

When considering how much importance we should place on pain, we must not forget that a certain amount of it is an inevitable part of any animal's life. For those wild animals we hunt as game, death at our hands is no worse than most alternatives and often better. Wild animals do not just live joyous lives, then curl up peacefully to die. If they are prey, the chances are they will perish in the jaws of a predator not bound by conscience or welfare legislation to provide for as quick and easy a death as possible. Before being slowly ripped apart, they will often be dragged around between sharp teeth, sometimes for hours. If they catch a disease or go lame, they will die slowly. So it is not clear that shooting them results in more pain than leaving them alone would.

To insist that any pain caused by farming is intolerable ignores the fact that an animal that has a pleasant life on a good farm almost certainly feels less pain over a lifetime than one in the wild, with no vets to cure disease and a low probability of meeting a quick, clean end. Watch any wildlife documentary and you'll see animals fighting to fend off starvation, and most infants dying in the first few weeks of life, the weaker ones weeded out, picked off by prey or denied food by a healthier sibling. In that sense the animal born on a good farm is a winner in life's lottery, while its wild cousin loses out.

But what, then, is a good farm? Is such a thing possible, from an animal's point of view? One problem with thinking about this is that we all have an idea of what's good for animals and it always looks something like this: small groups in open pens or fields, living 'free-range'. As soon as we see animals in less natural-looking environments, we tend to think they are being deprived in some way.

Take a farm I visited in Shepton Mallet, Somerset, which provides the milk Roger Longman uses for many of his excellent White Lake cheeses. The day I went, the cows were out grazing in the fields. However, I saw the large shed that was to be their winter home. They would spend several months in what looked like small stalls, on beds of straw. But Longman insisted they actually preferred it that way. In the winter, fields become muddy, cold quagmires. Just as we'd rather be sat inside than wandering about in such conditions, so cattle will happily sit around all day chewing the cud if hay or grass is put right in front of them. Nothing could make them happier. To imagine that Ermintrude is wistfully dreaming of roaming free from field to field is infantile.

Longman acknowledged that towards the end of winter, cattle do start to show signs of frustration when they are kept in sheds. 'You put cows out in the spring and they'll charge around the field and they're jumping up and down. It's lovely to see. Next day, you put them out and it's like' – Longman pulls a long face – "'I've got to walk all the way up there for the food!'" Another cattle farmer confirmed the pattern, suggesting that their spring bounce lasts about half an hour. The cows are no more deeply damaged by their winter indoors than children who come jumping out of classrooms are damaged by their schooling. 'You go and watch a bunch of cows in a field: they don't move,' says Longman. 'It's humans who go running for fun.' It is true that some animals are distressed by confinement, needing, for instance, to establish a territory of their own. Such animals should not be penned up; but distressing confinement is not the inevitable fate of any farmed animal.

This isn't just a farmer's self-serving justification. 'Come winter, the cows are quite ready to come in. Come spring, they're quite ready to go out again,' says animal welfare expert Becky Whay. 'They really wouldn't want to be standing up to their udders in mud in the fields in winter, and they particularly dislike strong wind and rain – that's when they're at their most miserable.' Indeed, this is one area where organic standards, which try to maximise the amount of time cows spend outside in their 'natural' environment, can be 'pushed too far', as Whay puts it. This is especially true for 'young stock when they're outside in really unpleasant conditions, almost to the point where they're compromising legislation because they shouldn't be standing up to their hocks in mud'.

Another romantic image is of the milkmaid at her stool, gently coaxing the milk from the cow's udder. The sight of a modern milking machine is not so inspiring: a metal box with pipes protruding with rubber liners at their ends, squeezed by the action of a pulsating vacuum pump. It looks like the kind of modern hospital kit no one would be pleased to be attached to, but, says Longman, 'It's not dragging the milk out; it's just gently squeezing. If you hand-milk, you end up doing more damage to the cow's teat than using a machine.'

Around the corner were the goats, from whose milk the best of the award-winning White Lake cheeses, such as Rachel, Little Wallop and White Nancy, are made. Again, you might expect them to be outside, grazing, but they were in fact in large communal pens. The reason is that if they freely roamed over the soil in this particular area, they would end up riddled with parasites against which they have little or no natural immunity. It's healthier for them to be inside eating feed than wandering around chewing anything that comes into sight.

The pen also challenges romanticism in another way. The goats had recently been kidding and a few corpses of the weak and stillborn were lying around the enclosure, yet to be taken away. It was a little gruesome, but nothing in the behaviour of the goats suggested they found it distressing.

For those who take the trouble to look, it does seem possible to farm animals in ways that give them a decent life. That is not to say that the kind of good farming I have praised is as common as it should be. Despite improvements in welfare standards in the UK and EU, for instance, Becky Whay told me that 22 per cent of the national dairy herd is lame, unable to walk without difficulty, almost all down to poor husbandry. And the worst excesses of industrial live-stock farming – thousands of animals cramped in sheds or pens day and night, unable to move – remain horrendous and very common in the US, as Peter Singer and Jim Mason document in their book *Eating*.

Another problem is that many modern farm animals have been bred so far to their limits that they are in effect incapable of having a decent life. The confinement and limitations placed upon them are then justified on the basis that they can't survive without them. The best-known example is of broiler chickens, who grow so quickly that their legs cannot support them. They simply could not survive in an open range. Less known is the modern Holstein, the most common dairy cow in the UK. Whay told me it has been bred to eat a lot and to produce gallons of milk. It has even lost its ancestors' instinctive response to reduced feed, which is to lactate less. Such is the extent of its requirement for nutrients that it may be better for the cow to have its food brought to it rather than to have to go out and graze. As Philip Lymbery of Compassion in World Farming put it to me, 'Cows have been pushed genetically so hard that the higher-producing breeds cannot survive on grass.'

Longman described such modern dairy breeds as 'prime athletes', super efficient at producing food from the 'rocket fuel' they are fed. Michael Marriage of Doves Farm used the same analogy to point out what has gone wrong with modern arable crops as well as animal breeds: 'Modern varieties are like highly trained athletes or a Ferrari. They go very well, but they're very highly tuned, and therefore if something goes wrong, they fail very quickly. Whereas these old varieties are more like donkeys or carthorses, which are much more resilient but may not go quite as fast.' The moral issue here is not how we treat the animals we have, but how we breed them to lead such difficult lives in the first place.

At the same time, it would be a mistake to think that an animal has an inherent right to live the kind of life it is fashioned by nature to enjoy, that it would not be enough for a rabbit to have a happy life in captivity, but that it should also have a bunny-like life in warrens in open fields. This is surely romantic nonsense. All farm animals have been bred for a purpose and so we should not think that farming robs them of the free life they would otherwise have had, pursuing their independent interests. Their nature is actually deeply tied up with the farm. The natural life of a Dorset Down sheep, so far as it has one, is on a farm, producing early lambs. Nor does a domestic cat crave life permanently outdoors. If it did, it would just go away and live it.

That is not quite the same as the bogus argument I heard surprisingly often from people who raised animals: that it is acceptable to kill them because that is what they were reared for. If we bred human beings to be slaves, that would not make it right to enslave them. The fact that an animal is reared for meat is not a justification for slaughter, but is exactly what needs to be justified.

Nor is it the same as the equally specious argument that without farming there would be no farm animals at all and so it is in the interests of the animals that we keep rearing them. A species does not have any interest over and above that of its members. If we had to choose between letting a species go extinct or conserving it by keeping its members living in awful pain, then we would not be doing the animals a favour by saving them. The point about the domesticated nature of farm animals is that it means it is not against each individual animal's interests or nature to be farmed, not that we ought to farm in order to maintain a species' population.

If you consider what makes for a good life for an animal, there is no good reason to believe farming cannot provide one, even if too many farms do not. But what about a good death? The omnivore cannot ignore the fact that every happily rooting pig or grazing sheep ends up hanging skinned on a hook. That is why I took my friend's pigs to an abattoir, to see the process for myself. Although the kinds of arguments I have presented here had led me to eat other kinds of meat from well-reared animals, I had not yet eaten pork. With my worries and uncertainties, I thought it would be a good idea to refrain from eating at least some animals as a kind of reminder of the continuity between us and them, to keep vivid the idea that animals are living creatures who deserve some kind of respect. By reputation pigs are very intelligent and I had heard that unlike sheep, who literally go like lambs to slaughter, they sense what is happening and resist all the way. I needed more convincing that a pig could have a good life and death before I would eat pork.

I was not alone in being more concerned by pigs than other farm animals. In Todmorden, I even met a former pig farmer, Estelle Brown, who turned vegan because she 'could not justify killing something that intelligent just to eat it because I liked the taste, when I don't need to'. One pig in particular had a big impact on her, a saddleback who could unlock every gate on the farm unless you took away the key. They even tried putting in special supposedly pig-proof locks that do up with a screw, but 'She would put her lips round and wind and wind and wind and she knew how to pull it apart and open the door, and she would not only let herself out, but everybody out.'

The young pigs I was to take to slaughter certainly stirred my sentimental side when I saw them in their pen. They are oddly cute creatures, the natural shape of their mouths beguiling us with its resemblance to a human smile. As they were being herded into the pick-up truck, though, the limits of their intelligence became obvious. In order to stop a pig heading in a given direction, all you need is a 'pig-board', a rigid sheet of some kind. When pigs see one, they assume it's a solid wall that they can't go through. Hold that between the pig and where you don't want it to go and it won't try, even if it is powerful enough to push through it. They may be smart, but they're not that smart.

Once at the abattoir, the pigs trotted from the truck to the 'kill pens', where they are held before slaughter, with no signs of any distress. This was a model facility, part of the University of Bristol's veterinary school, the kill pens were far from crowded, and the animals were kept there for as little time as possible. Nonetheless, the head slaughter man, Colin, has also worked at larger facilities and he told me he did not think these are necessarily worse for the pigs. It's people who stress them, not other animals, and so the mechanised, dehumanised nature of the commercial abattoir can make it easier for them.

The process itself is efficient and, for me, remarkably undistressing.

Four animals are moved to the stunning area, then brought forward two at a time to be stunned. The stunning equipment – bearing a plaque indicating that it is sponsored by the Humane Slaughter Association – is a kind of giant pair of pliers with ragged metal teeth, which the slaughter man tests and brushes before using. Once his colleague has gently got the pig into position, he pinches its neck between the pliers. Most of the pigs fall instantly to the ground in silence, while a few let out only the smallest of yelps. The colleague wraps chains round the pig's hind legs and it is carried off on a hanging conveyor, twitching through automatic reflexes as it goes.

Contrary to what I had believed, the waiting pigs seem unaware of their fate and that of those around them, even when the pig just stunned is only inches away, sometimes even touching. One was so oblivious to what was happening to the pair before him, he was actually trying to mount his companion. It would be far too fanciful to suggest that he had realised his number was up and was trying to make the most of his last minutes on Earth.

The pig is carried by the belt through a high opening in the wall to the main processing area, where another man pierces its throat, creating an impressive gush of blood, which he effortlessly dodges. The beast is left hanging a while above oval Rubbermaid black buckets that collect the blood, to be thrown away rather than made into blood sausages. There are fresh red splashes up the white wall where he works, a sight reminiscent of gangster movies.

The pig is then unhooked from its chains and dunked, stirred and prodded in a large tub of scalding water to remove the hair from its skin. Once the hair and the nails of the trotter come off when pulled, it is ready for the next stage and the animal is scooped up by rotating metal bars and deposited onto an adjacent platform, which violently shakes like a mechanical potato peeler to scrape off the fur. The noise and violence of this action makes it the most disturbing part of the process, even though the pig is by now long dead. Still fully intact and viewed through hanging semi-transparent plastic flaps speckled with blood and fur, it looks like a living creature being brutally treated.

The shaking stops and the pig slides down onto a metal platform on the other side of the tub. Two men take one end of the pig each and shave the remaining fur off using an open knife and scraper. Then it's hooked up, hung once more and hosed down to reveal a smooth carcass. A long vertical slit is cut along its stomach and the guts and viscera are removed and thrown out. In times past this would have been used to pad out cheap shaped human food or animal feed, but this has just been banned by the European Union to counter the spread of transmissible spongiform encephalopathies, of which mad-cow disease is the most well-known form. However, this means more of the animal goes to waste, so it produces less money and the meat is more expensive.

And there it is: a finished carcass, awaiting butchery. The whole process is a kind of alchemy, transforming live animal to meat without any one stage seeming to mark the point of change. Perhaps it is fitting that the line between pig and pork is not so clear cut: after all, it is only a convention of language that we do not normally talk about sitting down to a plate of pig.

Taking my overalls off in the changing room on the way out, I briefly chat with one of the scientists from the veterinary school. He thinks that anyone who eats meat should visit an abattoir and that having done so should be a requirement for a licence to buy meat. Some go further and say that you should not eat an animal that you are not prepared to kill yourself, but squeamishness is no test of ethical consistency. If it were, then anyone who was unable to take part in open-heart surgery without fainting or feeling ill should not be allowed to benefit from the procedure. Like many things that our culture depends on, animal slaughter is unpleasant and there is no reason why we shouldn't pay some people to get used to it for us. Similarly,

I don't think someone able to watch an animal be killed is more enti-tled to eat it than someone who isn't. That might merely reveal a harder heart, a lesser apathy or a greater familiarity.

What I do think is that for townies like me, listening to people who work at the front line of rearing and killing animals is essential to overcome the sentimentality and ignorance that stands between us and a truly compassionate attitude towards animals. 'We're all too divorced from the food chain,' said Tobias Jones, whose pigs I was taking to kill. There is an illustration of this in the film *Fast Food Nation*, which dramatises many of the horrors of intensive cattle farm-ing and meat processing. The hardest punch, however, is saved until last: a scene on the kill floor of the abattoir. Yet of all the practices exposed in the film, this is the only one that all meat production requires, however humane. I find it telling that the most natural part of the process is also the one viewers find most disturbing.

It is true that familiarity can simply lead to a kind of numbing, as people become habituated to what ordinary people would find obscene. As more vociferous animal liberationists will tell you, that is precisely the psychological mechanism that allowed otherwise decent, normal Germans to work at the death camps. But certainly none of the people I've spoken to seemed insensitive to the animals' welfare.

Take, for example, one of my Italian uncles, who, in a process that takes a whole day, will kill, butcher and make salami from a pig. For him, '*Il maiale è un animale nobile, intelligente.*' ('The pig is a noble, intelligent animal.') Respect for a creature is deepened by a close, vis-ceral relationship with it. Modern urban life makes this almost impossible. People often say that if you knew what went into a salami or a sausage, you'd never eat it, but that's not true of those who know most intimately.

At the slaughterhouse, people are matter-of-fact, but they do not seem oblivious to the living, breathing nature of the animals they process. Herding the pigs in, they refer to them with such terms of endearment as 'piggies', 'Dusty', 'darlings', 'sausages', 'boys', 'porkins', words that combine affection with a lucid sense of what they are to become. The veterinary scientist I spoke to in the changing room takes the killing of animals so seriously that he thinks the waste of uneaten parts is immoral. The man who actually slits their throats calls the sight of the animals hanging upside down, bleeding from the neck, 'gory' and says he couldn't eat a rabbit that he had killed and skinned himself. Those are not the words or feelings of someone who has come to kill automatically, with his emotional circuits switched off.

Many people who rear animals express some kind of sadness for the need for it to end in slaughter. Longman says he can't kill the unwanted male kids that are the inevitable by-product of goat farming: 'They're just too cute.' Most bizarrely, the woman who took my friend's animals to the abattoir, Kate, is a rare-pig breeder but also a vegetarian. She became one before she was a breeder because she 'couldn't bear going to Tesco or wherever and buying meat that I knew wasn't raised ethically, in a good manner'. Now the habit is so ingrained that she can't even eat the meat from the animals she has raised and had killed herself.

It seems to me that many who work with animals have the most acute sense of the virtue that ethical meat-eating requires: compassion. In this case the word's etymology really is illuminating: feeling ('*passion*') with ('*com-*'). It is rooted in the most basic moral emotion of all, arguably the foundation stone of all morality: empathy. Empathy is what enables us to adopt the perspectives of others, to understand that they too have interests, feel joys, suffer, hope and die. Empathy needs both intellect and emotion. As a wise character in the film *Barton Fink* puts it, 'Empathy requires understanding.' Without understanding, we can easily believe ourselves to be feeling others' pain, when it's really only a projection of our own imaginations. At the same time, without some feeling for that other person or creature, a purely intellectual understanding of their viewpoint is woefully incomplete. The need for the interplay between reason and emotion explains why abstract arguments about animal rights based on minimising suffering or respecting life are not enough. It is not just that they don't stand up logically, but they are too often premised on assumptions about what it means to live and suffer that have not been tested by both scientific evidence and first-hand experience of how farm animals actually live and die.

Of course, no one can really know what it is like to be a pig or a cow. Science can help us to some degree, since the most sensible conclusion to draw from a combination of animal behaviour and the observations of the similarities and differences in the central nervous system between us and them is that they do feel the same kinds of sensations that we do. Anyone who thinks that we can disregard the welfare of animals because they are mere insensible brutes is in some ways an even more insensible brute himself.

But our scientific knowledge only takes us so far. An experienced farmer who practises good husbandry is probably a better judge of how an animal is faring than a novice zoology graduate. I think the kind of compassion good farmers have for their animals should be the model for those of us who do not live cheek by jowl with them. What they teach us is that treating animals with respect is not incompatible with eating them.

Indeed, I would go so far as to say that in one way some vegetarians respect animals *less* than many meat eaters. True respect means acknowledging what you respect for what it really is, not how you imagine it to be. To respect someone with a different religion from yours, for example, you must accept that the differences are real, not pretend that they are worshipping the same God as you in their own way. Similarly, to respect a lamb, you need to accept that it is not like a baby in sheep's clothing, but has a way of being specific to its own species. And what almost all non-human animals have in common in this regard is that they simply abide, without plans for future, regrets about the past or thoughts about any of existence other than their own, at that time. They seek to avoid death simply out of instinct, not from any desire to realise an imagined tomorrow. To kill an animal swiftly is therefore not to rob it of a future it values.

Accepting this fact about the natural world can be profoundly discomforting. We know that the thought that life is without ultimate purpose can induce a sense of existential anxiety, threatening to overcome us with meaninglessness. It's a thought that's even harder to avoid if you see that the world is populated by billions of sentient creatures and yet it makes no difference whether any of them lives or dies. The sheer abundance of pointless life, suffering and death can be too much to comprehend, let alone accept. Vegetarianism can be one way of taming this anxiety, allowing us to treat the animal kingdom as though it matters much more than it does. It makes the world, and the life that is in it, seem more meaningful. The carnivorous alternative can seem too harsh by comparison.

Compassionate meat-eating – animal welfarism, as I call it – is therefore a manifestation of an ethics that resolutely resists the temptation to see the world as containing abstract, transcendent values, such as the sanctity of life, but doesn't retreat into mere materialist striving. It does not deny that animal life has value, but it does not overstate what that is. By being willing to kill and eat, we show that we are willing to accept that death is a fact of life, and that what matters is how we live while we are alive, not that we continue to live indefinitely. Eating meat is therefore life-affirming, in that it asserts the true value of mortal life and does not add to it any transcendent extras.

So for me, all lines of enquiry lead to the same conclusion. The death of a wild animal at the hands of a human hunter is no worse than the death of such an animal in the jaws of a different animal or of natural, often painful, causes. And if an animal can be reared in a way that does not cause it any more pain or suffering than its wild cousins, that animal has had as good a life as it could have wished for. Most farming and killing of animals does not meet these standards, and we have good reasons to try to end the cruel practices that condemn a lot of livestock to misery, but much meat, game, poultry and fish does indeed pass this test.

When I told a friend that adopting a more rigorous stance on animal welfare meant I was going to eat more animals than I did before, he laughed, very much at me, not with me. It sounds paradoxical, but the ethics of eating animals is complex, and for all that it is admirable in the intent, I now think that vegetarianism (and pescatarianism) based on welfare concerns is actually less ethically coherent than the most popular alternatives. On welfare grounds, an egg from a battery chicken or the milk from an intensively reared cow is worse than the veal from a calf that was treated well and put to death in an instant.

The most indefensible inconsistency of being a lacto-vegetarian on welfare grounds is that the dairy industry produces calves that then have to be slaughtered. So when you drink milk, you are supporting the killing of calves as surely as if you were eating their flesh yourself. This is an uncomfortable but undeniable truth that many vegetarians hide from. They hold on to 'common sense', which insists there must be a moral difference between eating meat and eating cheese. But common sense is often no more than received ignorance and in this case is little more than superstition: a sense that somehow killing an animal is worse if you ingest it than if you don't. If anything, it should be the other way round: to kill an animal and then discard its meat is less respectful of the beast's life than making good use of it.

Vegetarianism rooted in concern about animal welfare is incoherent – especially if it is not scrupulous about the sourcing of eggs and dairy – and bodies that promote it are sometimes compelled by their own lack of logic to gloss over awkward truths. Take, for instance, the 'Vegetarian Society Approved' mark that appears on many products in the UK. Apart from a requirement that all eggs are free-range, this ensures no animal welfare standards above the statutory minimum. (It does, however, guarantee that the food does not come from any genetically modified source, which has nothing to do with animal welfare at all.) From a moral point of view, I find this ridiculous. A cheese that contains no animal rennet can be Vegetarian Society Approved, for example. One made with calf rennet cannot, even though the cows producing the milk for the vegetarian cheese might have had a much less pleasant life in a factory farm than the calf from whom the rennet is taken in the non-vegetarian cheese. In this case, if you care about animal welfare, it seems perverse to prefer the vegetarian cheese to the non-vegetarian one. For the Vegetarian Society, however, this absurdity is unavoidable. For if it were to consider animal welfare per se rather than the simple question of whether or not a food contains animal flesh, then it would cease to become vegetarian. So the best it can do is make weak gestures towards these kind of concerns. Hence, in a statement issued to me, it said, 'The Vegetarian Society recognises that many vegetarians are concerned about welfare standards in the dairy industry; in particular they may want to avoid products sourced from cows who are permanently housed indoors (known as zero grazing). So we offer advice on our website.'

There are, of course, other ethical bases for vegetarianism. One is environmental: meat production is in general less efficient at turning land into calories than arable crops and it produces more greenhouse gases. However, if you take a scientific look at the evidence, the most environmentally friendly scenario is one where we eat less meat, not none at all. The simple reason is that there are resources that we cannot eat but animals can. Some grazing land is unsuitable for arable crops but ideal for sheep, cows or goats. Scraps, waste and by-products inedible to humans can also be fed to pigs and chickens. Rearing no animals at all would leave a significant amount of land and plant matter wasted, and if we did not fish, we would need more land to feed us too.[39]

There may be other motivations for ethical vegetarianism, but if welfare is the issue, consistency and evidence pushes vegetarians to become either vegans or careful, compassionate carnivores. Since, as I have already argued, I see no reason to become vegan, the only ethical option is to try to live as a conscientious omnivore.

Although I have said that welfare-based vegetarianism is the most incoherent ethical stance on animal welfare you could take, that does not mean that vegetarians are the ethically worst people when it comes to eating animals. Far from it. At the bottom of the moral heap are those who simply don't care about animal welfare at all and eat whatever they can find. They deserve no praise for being consistent in their indifference. Vegetarians at least take animal pain seriously and are trying to do something about it. By adopting a crude 'eat no flesh' rule, they are almost certainly contributing much less to animal suffering than most others. They are at least trying to live by the virtue of compassion, even if that has led them to adopt an imperfect rule. To exercise compassion at its best, however, we must always remember that it is not just a feeling and it must be directed by reason and evidence.

Morality is a minefield, and even when we have thought long and hard about an issue, we might still be very wrong indeed. But we cannot escape the fact that we have a choice: not to change our behaviour at all or to do our best. I think doing our best will have to be good enough. I'd rather be a somewhat mixed-up, inconsistent, ethically conscious person following imperfect and sometimes simplistic rules than someone who was morally indifferent. The moral life is lived in a state of bewildered enquiry between conviction and apathy. What matters first and foremost is to be morally serious, and sceptical about the certainty of our moral positions.

And the world is certainly a morally confused place. In the café of the veterinary school, for instance, I seriously considered having that first bacon sandwich, so I asked if the meat served came from the onsite butchery. It didn't. The server thought it came from Brakes, one of the largest catering suppliers in the country. Ironically, to my mind, the same café advertised the fact that it sold Fairtrade, sustainable coffee and Fairtrade biscuits and cakes. It was morally scrupulous about its suppliers from the other side of the world, yet it didn't source the ethical meat on its doorstep. Like most of us, it displayed compassion, but incompletely, imperfectly and without subjecting it to sufficient scrutiny.

LAMB BURGERS

I remember reading many years ago that Jonathon Porritt, then head of Friends of the Earth, was almost vegetarian except that he ate lamb. The reason was that lamb is a fairly safe choice for those interested in animal welfare. Outdoor grazing remains the most efficient way of rearing sheep, so less than 1 per cent of the world's flocks are intensively farmed.[40] The main welfare issue is the long distances the animals are sometimes taken from field to slaughterhouse, with the practice of live animal exports still all too common. So buy local.

Lamb mince is a particularly good ingredient because it will probably come from cuts that would otherwise be hard to sell and so helps make the most of the animal. Making burgers from it is remarkably easy. Nothing needs to be added other than some finely chopped onions or garlic, if you wish, some salt and plenty of herbs and spices to taste. Lots of chopped mint is an obvious choice, but I had great success adding cumin, coriander, oregano and pimentón (or smoked paprika). Mix it all up, divide into balls and squash into patties (perhaps using cookie cutters as moulds). Using cling film to keep each one separate, let them rest in the fridge for a few hours, which helps them hold their shape when you cook them. You can grill or barbecue them, or cook them in a non-stick frying pan without oil, as they will soon start releasing their own fat.

The same mixture can also be used to make meatballs, ideally stuck on a skewer and cooked over a barbecue, and since fresh lamb can be eaten rare, you don't need to be paranoid about cooking through.

6

Pay the price

JUSTICE

It feels a bit weird to be in the buffet car of a train between Copenhagen and Stockholm and to find a smoothie made by a company based in my adopted home town of Bristol. Small world. But the pulped fruit in front of me actually tells the story of a world much smaller even than that. It starts with mangos in Peru, bananas in Ecuador, oranges in Argentina, South African apples and Brazilian guavas. All would have been squeezed or pulped in their countries of origin, reduced to concentrate if necessary, frozen and then shipped to Rotterdam. There, they were mixed and blended, before being transported in vats to Britain and bottled in Bridgwater, Somerset. More trucks and ships took them to Scandinavia, and finally to the buffet car of the Swedish intercity train. The company that ostensibly makes them is just three people in an office in Bristol, through which the fruit never passes.

It's a vivid example of the global nature of contemporary capitalism, and the strange way in which people can in one sense make things without making anything at all. But far from representing all that is wrong in global trade, the Natural Beverage Company (NB) exemplifies how there is nothing wrong with the capitalist system itself; it's all in how you use it, for NB's fruit smoothies are 100 per cent Fairtrade certified. Rather than exploiting farmers in the developing world to produce cheap drinks for relatively rich Westerners, NB pays a fair price, including a social premium that provides for a decent living for growers and helps fund things like local schools and sanitation projects.

It sounds wonderful, but Fairtrade's critics argue that at best it doesn't work and at worst it is positively harmful. Others accept its efficacy but see it as a kind of optional charity purchase. I think it is not only perfectly viable but that we have a moral obligation to buy goods that are fairly traded, a range that includes but is not exhausted by those certified by schemes like Fairtrade and the Rainforest Alliance.

The moral case is, I believe, straightforward and can be made by a simple thought experiment. A vulnerable person you know knocks on your door and says that unless he gets £10 to repay a notoriously exploitative loan shark within twenty-four hours, he will be severely beaten. It just so happens that you want to clear a large, weed-infested area of your garden to plant vegetables. Would it be morally accept-able to say, 'I'll give you the money, just as long as you spend the next twenty-four hours digging'? Assuming that you are able to pay him more or demand less from him without any significant self-sacrifice, and that no other bad consequences follow from paying more than the minimum, the answer is obviously no.

The reason this is so manifestly wrong can be expressed in a gen-eral principle, which all but the most rabid of free-marketeers must surely accept: it is morally wrong to exploit a fellow human being by using their need as leverage to make them work for as little as you can possibly get away with paying them. Yet when it comes to workers at the end of supply chains in poorer parts of the world, and even in some low-wage jobs in the developed West, we break this principle all the time, whenever we buy food, clothes or electrical goods that are made by people receiving less than a living wage, often in filthy, sometimes dangerous conditions.

Consider now not twenty-four-hour digging but coffee-growing. Over recent decades the market price for coffee beans has at times fallen below the cost of production, meaning that farmers actually worked at a loss to satisfy the caffeine cravings of Western consumers. Because the vast majority of coffee is traded on open markets, manufacturers just paid the market price, irrespective of what that meant for growers. As a result, the commodity buyers – and through them the consumers – used the desperate need of farmers as leverage to make them accept as little as we could possibly pay them. Even when coffee prices are higher, we often pay over £2 for a latte while the growers can't afford to send their children to school.

As various fair trade schemes have shown, to rectify this does not require consumers to pay significantly higher prices. The difference paying workers and farmers properly makes to the retail price is so marginal that there are several mainstream grocery lines that have been converted to 100 per cent Fairtrade with no additional cost to the consumer at all, such as some supermarkets' bananas, KitKat chocolate bars, Maltesers and Co-operative teabags. This shows that fair trade is not a middle-class indulgence. Even if it did require some prices to be higher, it is hardly an expression of solidarity with the poor to justify cheap prices for the least well off in the West at the price of worse poverty elsewhere. As the academic Geoff Andrews says, any debate about wealth and class is incomplete if it ignores the fact that 'The cheap produce provided by mass supermarkets is guaranteed by exploitative labour in developing countries.'[41]

It should be pointed out that Fairtrade – the formal certification – is not necessary for fair trade. The Fairtrade label is granted as a licence by national bodies (such as the Fairtrade Foundation in the UK and Fairtrade Canada) that belong to Fairtrade International (FLO). This is a formal scheme that requires the producers and traders to be audited against social, environmental and trade standards. A minimum price is set and a social premium added.

Joining such a scheme costs money and does not suit every kind of business, but it is, of course, perfectly possible to develop good relations with suppliers outside the scheme to ensure they get paid a decent price. Many small speciality coffee roasters and tea merchants operate in this way. Without any external audit, it can be hard for consumers to know if the companies really live up to the ideals they claim to promote, which is one advantage of certification. But it is important to be fully aware that buying certified products is not the only way to avoid being in the position of the exploitative Westerner. There are other means of finding out a product's provenance.

As I have presented it, the virtues of fair trade and the vices of business as usual seem clear. Too clear, you might think. Surely it can't be the case that we are routinely in the business of exploiting people, every time we shop? There are plenty of arguments that can be lined up against the charge, but unfortunately, none works.

First, it is objected that the people we 'exploit' are not poor relative to those they live with. But the same line of reasoning would lead us to say that slavery is acceptable because slaves are no less free than their fellow slaves, or that we should not worry about inner-city deprivation because that is normal for inner cities. The point is that they are kept poorer than they need be, given our capacity to pay them more without significant cost.

The second objection is that although some businesses in the supply chain might be exploitative, none of that guilt transfers to us. We do not pay workers at the end of global supply chains directly, and they live thousands of miles away. Both of these differences are psychologically powerful but morally irrelevant. If I kill a man 1,000 miles away with a high-tech rifle, I am no less culpable than if I had shot him in the chest from 3 feet. The geographical distance between wrongdoer and victim is immaterial. The same is true of indirectness. If I contract a builder who uses slaves, I am as much in the wrong as if I own the slaves myself, just as I am equally guilty of murder if I take out a contract on someone as I am if I kill him personally.

Other spurious defences are a little more sophisticated. Johan Norberg, author of *In Defence of Global Capitalism*, argues that 'In a typical developing nation, if you're able to work for an American multinational, you make eight times the average wage. That's why people are lining up to get these jobs.'[42]

There are actually two arguments here that often get confused. One is that people freely choose to take the jobs they do, so that makes it all right. The second is, 'A lousy job is better than none at all', as the free-market National Center for Policy Analysis (NCPA) put it.[43]

Take the free-choice defence first. It would be comforting to believe that since people choose to work for peanuts, that makes everything all right. When it comes to the likes of sex workers, people who work in sweatshops, soldiers who get shot, the people who have to clean the toilets you use, you can always tell yourself, They didn't have to do it – it was their choice. But the idea that there is no problem as long as there is consent is flawed for several reasons. First, people sometimes have to choose terrible things because in practical terms they have no choice. Prostitution is a good example. There are some, maybe many, Belle du Jours for whom sex work is not a last resort but a deliberate career move, but in many cases women are driven to prostitution out of desperation. Any man who thinks prostitution is unproblematic just as long as the woman isn't being physically forced into the job is surely deluded.

Second, the fact that something unpleasant is the best choice available to someone doesn't make it all right, if we could be offering them a better one at little or no cost. It is not uncommon for managers in factories in the developing world to refuse their workers sufficient toilet breaks, deny them drinking water, fail to follow local laws or health and safety procedures – the list could go on. So what if working in one of these places is still the best option locally? If paying a little bit more could remove all these hardships, why not do it?

There are always more options than the free-market apologists set out. For instance, Lucy Martinez-Mont wrote in the *Wall Street Journal* that 'Banning imports of child-made goods would eliminate jobs, hike labour costs, drive plants from poor countries and increase debt. Rich countries would sabotage Third World countries and deny poor children any hope of a better future.'[44] True, but the choice is not between the status quo and banning such imports, nor is it between sweatshops or Western pay and conditions. It's between allowing someone the opportunity to earn a decent living in a decent job and making them work long hours in poor conditions for barely enough to survive on.

Most fair trade campaigners are sensitive to this. For example, the Maquila Solidarity Network advises, 'Don't promote a blanket boy-cott of all goods produced by child labour,' precisely on the grounds that simply withdrawing custom and leaving nothing in its place is harmful to those they want to help.[45] The UK-based Ethical Trade Initiative's Base Code prohibits '*new* recruitment of child labour' (my emphasis) and insists that member companies 'shall develop or par-ticipate in and contribute to policies and programmes which provide for the transition of any child found to be performing child labour to enable her or him to attend and remain in quality education until no longer a child'.[46]

The point is simple. Poor working conditions may be better than nothing, but that does not justify our supporting them. The alterna-tive should not be nothing, but making things better. Parents cannot justify feeding their children junk food because that is better than no food, if proper food is an option.

It is somewhat baffling that so many criticisms of the fair trade alternative to exploitation are rooted in free-market thinking. The Adam Smith Institute, for instance, insists Fairtrade means 'its favoured farmers do not have to respect market conditions which might tell others to cut back production in the event of a world surplus'.[47] *The*

Economist claims Fairtrade encourages overproduction by 'propping up the price' of commodities.[48]

What these criticisms often neglect is that Fairtrade only guarantees a minimum price, not a minimum quantity, so it is no incentive at all for overproduction, since if the farmer grows too much, she just can't sell it. In fact, farmers in the scheme typically only sell around 30 per cent of their crops through it.[49] The reality is that initiatives like the Fairtrade label are free-market mechanisms par excellence. Fair trade is not like government subsidy, which fixes prices of a whole nation's crops. It is a voluntary, consumer choice, no more contrary to free-market economics than the decision to volunteer an extra 25p to have a shot of syrup in your latte. The premium paid on Fairtrade coffee is not market-bucking but market-dependent. The price is higher solely because consumers want to pay the extra for the benefits they believe that produces. As Sushil Mohan put it in a report published by the pro-market Institute for Economic Affairs, 'All that is happening is that Fair Trade opens up an alternative specialist trading channel within the free market. The market fundamentals, the demand, supply and market competitiveness conditions for Fair Trade products, follow conventional trade practices.'[50]

The Fairtrade premium is in fact smaller and more justifiable than many others. For example, people are willing to pay a lot extra for a celebrity-endorsed product, or one with a logo, and yet I do not hear economists protesting that the prices of Adidas T-shirts are kept 'artificially high' by designer labelling schemes. What people are willing to pay can be motivated by a desire for fairness as well as value. We already have plenty of examples of where demand has led societies to decide on a fair price for labour that is not set wholly by the market. Even the US has a minimum wage, and London now has a living wage: the Greater London Authority and all its suppliers must pay their workers enough to live decently in the capital. So the laws of supply and demand are not being distorted by fair trade: we demand that our suppliers are able to make a living, and we pay accordingly.

Some see the promotion of fair trade as a distraction. What the developing world needs most of all, they claim, is a genuinely free global market. Coffee farmers would have no trouble making a good living if advanced Western nations eliminated import tariffs, farm subsidies and other distortions to the market.

The problem with this argument is that the question facing us is not how we should behave if global trade were truly free, but how we should behave as things are now. Maybe farmers in the developing world would be better off if borders were open, but they are not. So, in the real world, the question is, how should we act faced with the choice between buying goods in a distorted market that squeezes suppliers or buying goods that don't contribute to this squeezing? The only ethically acceptable answer is obvious. The free-marketeer, if genuinely concerned by morality, should both campaign for freer trade and in the interim avoid reinforcing the injustices of the current system.

The only reasonable conclusion to draw is that the way we treat suppliers in the developing world is a moral disgrace, and we are all complicit in it. Our position is comparable to that of slave-owning societies, in that we have a moral outrage at the core of our economy that most people fail to see as such. Like slavery in the nineteenth century, this is something that for a long time a minority, often seen as do-good cranks, have made a noise about but that the vast majority accept fatalistically as part and parcel of ordinary life. Along with other great injustices that we have taken steps to reduce – such as racism and the subjugation of women – it will come to be seen as wrong because there is simply no justification for treating workers in the developing world differently from the rest of humanity. And also like slavery, racism and sexism, there are many 'common sense' justifications that crumble on examination.

Confronted with this charge of manifest injustice, we are likely to react as the slave owners did. Because the victims are far away and harmed only indirectly by our indifference, it just seems incredible to think we're implicated in a massive injustice. Because the status quo seems so natural and nothing feels wrong about drinking coffee, we convince ourselves that it just can't be true that good, decent people such as ourselves are systematically behaving so badly. Therefore, we conclude, we can't be either. But this logic proceeds in the wrong order. It starts with the presumption of our innocence and works backwards, whereas what we need to do is tackle the case for our guilt directly.

While the sins of our forebears are all too evident, the wickedness of our own age is much harder to discern. Familiarity takes the edge off wrongdoing. There is no behaviour so morally repugnant that some people at some time have not got used to it and come to see it as normal. Slave owners were not generally moral monsters. They were people considered, by themselves and others, to be decent, virtuous people, like George Washington, the first president of the United States. In Britain, slavery was only finally abolished in 1833, women only received the same voting rights as men in 1928, and racism only started to become widely unacceptable in the late 1960s. It would take a great deal of moral certitude, a kind of hubris, to suppose that we are the first generation in human history not to be blind to some kind of systemic wrongdoing.

Of course, even the greatest philosophers have been as blind as everyone else. In a notorious footnote, Hume wrote, 'I am apt to suspect the negroes, and in general all the other species of men (for there are four or five different kinds) to be naturally inferior to the whites.'[51] Aristotle believed 'The male is by nature superior, and the female inferior; and the one rules, and the other is ruled; this principle, of necessity, extends to all mankind.'[52]

When we ask ourselves about moral horrors, we tend to look back in history, and overseas, but as Descartes said, 'When one spends too much time traveling, one finally becomes a stranger in one's own country, and when one is too curious about things which went on in past ages, one usually lives in considerable ignorance about what goes on in this one.'[53] He was right. The injustices of global food supply persist because of psychological weakness, not moral rightness. And I don't claim to be immune from this. I argue this case passionately and adjust my behaviour to a certain extent, but I don't check the provenance of every item of clothing or foodstuff I buy. This weakness is natural, but that only explains; it doesn't excuse. We need to be aware that what looks like the delectable platter of the new food renaissance is too often a heavy plate being carried on the breaking shoulders of oppressed producers. If we believe that justice is a virtue, then we should not turn a blind eye to the ways in which our own choices can work against it.

MONKINS

By adapting a few other recipes (thank you mainly to Hugh Fearnley-Whittingstall), I've come up with this base list of ingredients for a muffin-like bun that is so wholesome as to be virtually monastic, hence I've dubbed them 'monkins'.

240g plain flour of some kind (e.g. wholemeal, white, spelt)
5 level tsp (25g) baking powder
½ tsp bicarbonate of soda
a good pinch of salt
2 large eggs (3 if small)
250g whole-milk yoghurt
4 tbsp oil

If you use wholemeal flour and don't have them very sweet, a monkin is practically a health food. You can add to this a wide range of fairly traded ingredients to make them even more virtuous, such as cocoa, chunks of chocolate, sugar, nuts, small pieces of chopped banana, dried fruit and runny honey. If you don't use those that are fairly traded, these ingredients will most probably have been produced by squeezed farmers.

For sweet monkins, you'd swap some of the flour for sugar or use honeyed yoghurt and, depending on the variety, cocoa powder, ground almonds or both. A nut oil will also complement the other flavours better than a vegetable one. Try dried fruit and nuts with cinnamon, or chocolate and hazelnut chunks.

For savoury, you'd probably use wholemeal flour, swapping 40 grammes of it for oats, and you'd use a vegetable oil, probably olive. You'd then add savoury ingredients like courgettes, sun-dried tomatoes, porcini mushrooms (rehydrated), cheese (grated or in small pieces) or spinach (cooked, chopped and squeezed). You can also adjust quantities of the raising agents, since bicarbonate of soda does a similar job as two to three times the amount of baking powder. Sun-dried tomato, olives and feta is a good combination, as is spinach and cheese.

The generic instructions for whatever version you make are to heat the oven to 200 degrees Celsius (400 degrees Fahrenheit, gas mark 6), then mix together the dry ingredients, excluding any large pieces of filling, in a large bowl. In another bowl or plastic jug, whisk together the eggs, yoghurt, oil and honey, if using. Pour this over the dry ingredients and gently fold together with a large, flattish spoon or spatula until they are combined. The secret, apparently, is not to over-mix, and certainly not to beat. Add the remaining ingredients and stir just enough to mix them evenly. Spoon into muffin cases and bake for about eighteen minutes. They're ready when a knife or toothpick stuck into the middle comes out dry – except if it encounters melted chocolate, of course. You'll probably find that on first try, they are too something or not enough of something else for your personal taste. Adjust next time accordingly.

7

Loosen your chains

'Foodies' – originally a mocking term for ardent food enthusiasts, coined by Paul Levy and Ann Barr in 1982 – are often comically religious in their zeal. Rituals of preparation take on the necessity and seriousness of the rites of priests; ingredients are treated with a holy reverence; amazing meals are described as though they were spiritual experiences; no opportunity to evangelise unbelievers is lost; their Bible is a collection of holy cookbooks written by people venerated as saints; and there is an orthodoxy to the creed which, like that of the Church, is as rigid at any given moment in time as it is malleable over time.

Much of this is merely laughable, such as the passionate conviction that there is only one right way to make hollandaise. But there is one respect in which the religiosity of many foodies is pernicious: they divide the world into the good and the bad, the righteous and the damned, the pure and the fallen. Any vaguely reflective person will readily agree that the world is not this black and white, and that ethics is difficult precisely because there are so many shades of grey. Nevertheless, what we know on reflection, we often forget in action, since it is much easier to live in a world divided into heroes and villains than it is to accept that everyone is a composite of both.

At the moment, the commonest and laziest moral heuristic around food is that small, local independent stores and restaurants are good, while chains are bad. Certain multinational brands have become so 'unclean' that for some, a sinner spotted munching on McDonald's fries or sipping a Starbucks coffee requires confession, repentance and purification. Although there are good reasons why, all other things being equal, we should prefer the independent over the multiple, this justifiable general preference should not become an unjustified absolute rule.

Some of the most demonised companies are actually among the better performers in terms of corporate social responsibility. McDonald's is a very interesting case in point. A favourite target of anti-capitalist rioters, the company has been blamed for all sorts of evils, from destroying the Amazon rainforest to making everyone fat. The nadir of this demonisation came with the entertaining but absurd documentary *Super Size Me*, in which the seductively affable Morgan Spurlock 'demonstrated' how unhealthy McDonald's was by eating nothing but its food for a month, gobbling supersize portions if offered, whether he was hungry or not. As an experiment it was deeply stupid. You may as well set out to eat nothing but cheese, always ask for more if the cheesemonger asks, 'Anything else?' and commit yourself to leaving nothing uneaten. If you did that, you'd be in much worse shape after a month than Spurlock was, but it would not prove that cheesemongers are forcing unhealthy slabs of salty saturated fat onto the gullible Manchego-munching public. Foods aren't bad for you, diets are, and any diet that restricts itself to foods that provide a limited range of nutrients, with fat high among them, is going to be bad for you.

In fact, on many counts, McDonald's UK doesn't perform too badly at all. It has a surprisingly good record on animal welfare, for example. It has received three RSPCA (Royal Society for the Prevention of Cruelty to Animals) Good Business Awards, and Compassion in World Farming's Good Egg Award, since all the eggs used in its products are free-range, and have been for many years. It funds as well as keeps up to date with research on animal welfare, which, as we have already seen, has resulted in its Range Enrichment Programme for egg-laying hens. McDonald's has 'very strong animal welfare credentials', Philip Lymbery, the head of Compassion in World Farming, told me, and, 'I would be more confident in recommending someone buy a McDonald's egg product, an egg McMuffin, for example, than a non-specific egg product on the high street.'

Compare that to your apparently noble greasy-spoon caff. Not many of those make an effort to source eggs, meat and dairy ingredients that surpass the statutory minimum welfare standards. Not many use only Rainforest Alliance-certified coffee or organic milk for tea and coffee, as McDonald's does. What's more, many of the people employed by such small businesses do not enjoy the pay and conditions of someone with what is disparagingly called a 'McJob'. My first job was as a fourteen-year-old working illegally in a McDonald's imitation, putting in six-hour shifts with a ten-minute break, meal not provided. At 99p an hour, I was at least better paid than some of my mates earning half that washing up for other local, independent caterers. In contrast, McDonald's was in the top ten of the *Sunday Times*'s list of 'Best Big Companies to Work For 2012'.

That does not mean we should all rush out and start eating Big Macs, of course. I would want better cattle welfare standards before I ate their beef, and even then, I'm not a great fan of undifferentiated masses of sweet or savoury carbohydrate, protein and fat, finely calibrated to ensure they are as inoffensively moreish as possible. What it does mean is that it would be silly to single the company out as a kind of pariah when its competitors are almost invariably much worse.

The company is so used to being criticised for every little flaw, real or imagined, that it has become somewhat paranoid. I spent months trying to arrange an interview with a member of its UK senior management team, and when it eventually happened, it was on the understanding that it was only to be used for this book and not for any journalistic features. 'There is a multiplication factor that McDonald's places on any conversation you have with anybody,' said Nick Hindle, senior vice-president of Corporate Affairs. 'Do not be surprised if you say something that for another brand or business would be relatively benign, it could end up on the front page of the paper,' he tells new members of his communications team. 'That drives a certain amount of control and discipline, as you would expect. The problem is, in the past that's led to us retreating and not doing anything, and battening down the hatches, and that was a disaster.'

Not that the hatches have now been completely opened. I went to their massive restaurant in the Olympic Park in London, which could easily have been mistaken for the HQ of an environmentally conscious Scandinavian design firm, were it not for the familiar waft of slightly salty yet also sweet hot vegetable oil, one of a number of smells and flavours that are now part of the collective folk consciousness. Serving up to 1,000 customers an hour, it was an impressive feat of logistics, and they had also managed to construct a building that would be completely recycled at the end of the competition, squaring the circle of sustainable yet disposable fast food as much as is possible. At the Games' end, however, they did not make any big public announcement about how many people they had managed to serve, because they knew that releasing the figures would lead to accusations of massive profiteering, as though everyone else who tendered for the Olympic Park franchise was doing it out of charity or patriotic duty.

Supermarkets are the other object of righteous foodie opprobrium, even though almost everyone uses them. The argument is always that the people don't want national chains squeezing out small independent local traders, turning every high street into a clone. I fully support the aspiration, but if local people really don't want supermarkets, in most cases they don't have to shop at them. Near me, for example, is the Better Food Company, just the kind of local food shop the Church of Food would bless. Many of the fruits and vegetables come from a nearby community farm; most of the rest is organic or grown to some other high environmental or welfare standard; many goods imported from the developing world are Fairtrade; bread is from local artisan bakers and so on. Petitions against two proposed chain openings nearby have graced the checkout counter, but many of the very same people who signed voted with their feet when the stores actually opened. Despite the supposedly supportive demographic profile of the area, as revealed by the large piles of the *Guardian* in the newsagents, the longest queues are not at Better Food but at the Sainsbury's Local and the Tesco Metro.

The reasons are obvious. First of all, it's expensive. That's largely because most of the items that end up in the typical British shopping basket are of a lower quality or ethical standard. So instead of a mass-produced Warburtons medium-sliced white loaf at £1.45, at Better Food you have to get one from Hobbs House bakery at £2.45. You might baulk at paying £3.29 for a jar of Kitchen Garden Three Fruits marmalade, which is smaller than the Robertson's Golden Shred that costs £1.35, but the latter contains only 20 grammes of fruit per 100 grammes, rather than 34 grammes. On the few occasions when exact like-for-like comparisons are possible, Better Food is often cheaper. Still, when the benchmarks for everyday foods are set by the mainstream brands, even those who could afford to upgrade feel it extravagant to do so. It is true that many small greengrocers and butchers are very competitive against the supermarkets, but people are generally time poor and most prefer the convenience of a one-stop shop.

Of course, there is an argument that what looks like cheapness and efficiency in the industrial food world is unsustainable. The real cost of food is being 'externalised', as economists term it: passed on to future generations, underpaid farmers and agricultural workers.

Shop prices are also being artificially reduced by inefficient, protectionist farm subsidies. Sustainably, fairly produced food only looks expensive because we've got used to prices that do not reflect the true cost of feeding ourselves.

There is some truth in this, but it is too easy to think it is the whole answer. Not all the efficiencies of mass production and distribution come at the expense of producers and the planet. Time and again supermarkets have shown that they are able to bring what were originally premium products to market at a cheaper price. Fairtrade is a very clear example. A Fairtrade banana at my local Sainsbury's costs 18p; at Better Food it costs around double that. Three of the five bestselling mainstream chocolates – KitKat, Dairy Milk and Maltesers – have gone Fairtrade without hiking their prices. The Co-operative has started sourcing all of its imported winter blueberries from Fairtrade producers, and their price is the same as that of rivals.

The *bien pensant* moan about supermarkets can become so natural that we forget the very clear advantages they have brought. Their sophisticated delivery and stock-control systems mean that what you want is more likely to be in store and in pristine condition. Their scale means that they have squeezed profit margins to around 2 to 6 per cent of turnover, lower than most other major UK retail sectors. Independent shops just couldn't cover their costs on such low returns.[54] Although criticised for over-packaging, often rightly, they have reduced some waste by keeping food fresher for longer and reducing transit damage. If you run a small grocery store, you take what the wholesalers offer, whereas if you are a large supermarket, under national public scrutiny, you can and often must work harder to find out where that food is coming from. Similarly, a large, even non-unionised workforce can insist its rights are honoured more easily than one or two employees of a small enterprise.

Still, many maintain that however much you tame and domesticate them, supermarkets are at their core rapacious beasts we would do better without. This is a particular worry for campaign groups who often have to decide whether they are going to work with the big multiples. For instance, Todmorden's Incredible Edible campaign has promoted local producers, retailers and caterers, as well as setting up small plots in the town that volunteers tend and anyone can take produce from. Morrisons supermarkets wanted to get involved with them, which presented Incredible Edible with a dilemma: would accepting help result in supporting just the kind of retailer that takes people away from independent shops? With principled pragmatism, it accepted some no-strings-attached money to fund a number of local projects, but it decided against having an Incredible Edible Todmorden aisle in the supermarket, showcasing local produce. Although that would have got those goods in front of more people, the danger was that it would have made people believe that they were supporting the local food economy just by going to a national chain. Anything that drove more people into supermarkets and away from the high street conflicted with their goals.

Facing a similar dilemma, Slow Food UK went the other way, introducing 'The Slow Lane' into the aisles of Booths, the northern supermarket. As a result, a number of traditional foods, many of which have been in danger of dying out – such as Lyth Valley damson jelly (a kind of English membrillo), Cumberland rum Nicky (a Cumbrian pastry), Manx kippers, Morecambe Bay potted shrimps and unpasteurised Wensleydale cheese – got to customers who otherwise would never have even seen them. 'The bottom line,' says Slow Food UK's CEO, Cat Gazzoli, 'is that these guys have a lot of power and you can't just pretend they don't.' In this case, the gains for small producers were believed to outweigh the losses to small retailers. It helped that Booths, still family run, is not a large chain and is committed to many of the same values as the better independents.

In some cases, moving multiples in the right direction appears to be a win-win. Take Fairtrade, for example. There are some who cannot accept that KitKat has Fairtrade certification, because it is made by Nestlé, a multinational that has been the subject of a consumer boycott for decades over alleged bad practice in how it markets its infant formula milk in the developing world. From what I can see, nothing Nestlé can do would persuade many hard-core boycotters that the company is not Evil. In any case, KitKat's going Fairtrade means that millions more chocolate bars are being sold that properly benefit the cocoa and sugar producers than would otherwise be the case. Most people who make a point of buying Fairtade buy other more virtuous brands anyway. Certifying KitKat therefore does not drive consumers away from even more ethical alternatives; it simply expands Fairtrade's share of the market.

Philip Lymbery of Compassion in World Farming is unapologetic of his organisation's willingness to work closely with businesses of all sizes. 'The truth is that incremental change is going to happen incrementally. What we want is for companies to start making profound policy changes on an incremental basis and to be rewarded for that, to feel good about that and to be reassured that making the next step is going to be just as good for them, and the next step after that.

'One of the most misunderstood stories is that of David and Goliath. Everybody wants to be David because it's romantic, but the reason why that story is so powerful is that in ninety-nine point nine per cent of cases, David loses. We can't afford to lose on behalf of animal welfare and better food. Rather than be halo-driven Davids that lose most times, we want to walk with Goliath.'

I'm in broad agreement and think that we underestimate the extent to which it is possible to change the way the market works so that it reflects our higher values about food. For the neo-liberals, the market is omniscient, omnipotent and omnibenevolent, always knowing what the price is, always able to destroy attempts to 'buck' it and ultimately settling on the fair price for everything. For critics, the market ruthlessly and single-mindedly pursues only the maximisation of profit, trampling down any other consideration on the way, with no thought to human welfare. The mistake both parties make is to talk of 'the market' as though it were an independent entity with a will of its own, when all markets do is react to supply and demand. Ultimately, it is down to us what we demand. Some of that demand comes in the form of regulation, passed in response to the popular will. Most of it simply comes from what people choose to buy. If consumers demand the cheapest eggs possible, the market will deliver them, and damn the hens' welfare. If consumers demand cage-free eggs, that is what it will supply. As Wal-Mart's chief dairy purchaser, Tony Airoso, put it in the documentary *Food Inc.*, 'Actually, it's a pretty easy decision to try to support things like organic or whatever it might be, based on what the customer wants. We see that and we react to it, and so if it's clear the customer wants it, it's really easy to get behind it, and to push forward and to try to make that happen.'

McDonald's is a good example of how consumer demand is really the key. Nick Hindle told me that 'The changes we make are predominantly driven by what our customers want or are becoming interested in and we deem they will want or want more of in the future.' Note how there is an element of anticipation here: a nimble corporation will look to travel where the wind is blowing rather than find itself being flattened by its gusts. And because reputation is so important, it is possible for campaigners and activists who would never eat at McDonald's whatever it did to drive some changes. Nevertheless, Hindle says reputation is 'not our sole driving force', because the company cannot make changes in response to criticisms unless they create sufficient sell-through.

In practice this means the changes that get made are the ones that people are prepared to pay for. That's why McDonald's has been happy to switch to using only Marine Stewardship Council certified fish, as well as organic milk for tea, coffee, Happy Meal bottles and porridge. But, Hindle told me, the company 'would not see the uplift in sales or preparedness to pay more by going free-range chicken: I know because we've done the research'. The reason is that British consumers want breast meat, and the only way to make free-range breasts affordable would be if you could sell the rest of the carcass at a premium price too, and there isn't the demand for it. Similarly, McDonald's sees no point in using organic milk in their shakes and ice creams, because the other ingredients would not always be organic (especially in temporary promotional lines that use branded chocolate bars), so they could not be sold as organic and would not receive any added value.

There are companies that choose to raise ethical standards even in the absence of consumer demand, but generally speaking, businesses respond to what customers want. So if we are given beef from no-graze cattle, for instance, it is because we are not prepared to pay the extra required for pasture-reared beef. If we were, business would follow.

Anyone who cares to look objectively can see that there are chains that behave much more ethically than the majority of independents. Pret A Manger, the sandwich shop, provides an apprentice scheme for the homeless, saying, 'We don't mind if apprentices sleep on the streets or have a criminal record – we put that to one side and let them start with a clean slate.' It also delivers over 12,000 fresh surplus meals to homeless shelters in London every week. Carluccio's, the restaurant and deli chain, has a one-star rating from the Sustainable Restaurant Association, which is by no means an automatic reward for membership. Waitrose is part of the employee-owned John Lewis Partnership, which shares its profits among its staff.

You might see these as exceptions to the rule and insist that, generally speaking, the more human scale an enterprise is, the better the human relationships between owners, managers, workers, suppliers and customers. As a general trend, this is probably true. One striking study published in the *Journal of Environmental Psychology*, for instance, compared farmers' markets and supermarkets and found 'a similar number of perfunctory conversations in the two settings but more social and informational encounters at the farmers' markets'.[55] Having said that, there are also plenty of people who regularly chat with checkout assistants at Morrisons, and surly owners of small sweet shops who won't give you the time of day.

The other problem with fetishising size is that the most powerful drivers of change are not individual, conscious-driven consumers, but the big multiples, which Lymbery describes as 'super-consumers', who 'by making commitments such as going cage-free on their eggs, guarantee a market for higher-welfare products. And so they enable a whole suite of smaller, family producers to make a decent living in a better way.'

Many people want to avoid having to deal with the ambiguities of the food supply chain, but it is also possible to embrace them too much and to see shades of grey as just one undifferentiated blur. Moral ambiguity is not the same as laissez-faire relativism, and complexity need not lead to the shrugging of the shoulders and shirking of hard choices. All other things being equal, we have very good reasons to want to support smaller businesses, for the variety they bring and because, at their best, they do indeed enable commercial transactions at their most human. But all other things rarely are equal, so it is not enough to 'shop local' and 'support independents'. You need to seek out the good ones and be prepared to use multiples where they are better. The chains we need to free ourselves from the most are the ones that keep us tied to a simplistic view of who is good and bad in the world of catering and retail.

An appreciation for the ambiguities and complexities of the morality of food is a fitting conclusion to a section that started with the injunction 'Dare to know.' The pursuit of truth is daring because it involves discovering how precarious our claims to knowledge are. Many of our most cherished beliefs about how we should eat and live are far from being the definitive last word and we should all be willing to review and revise them. Doing the right thing can feel like walking a tightrope, but if the alternatives are either not bothering to try at all or falling off, all we can do is strive to maintain our moral balance as best we can.

MASS-PRODUCED CLASSICS

My partner confesses to having preferred some jarred mayonnaise to the fresh one made by her aunt, even though she is sure the latter must have been objectively better. But the guilt is misplaced, because it is not always the case that homemade is best. We should be honest enough to admit that a few of the best foods are mass produced, sometimes by big multinational companies

When thinking about what the best of a certain kind of food is, it can be helpful to borrow Plato's generally unhelpful theory of forms. Plato believed that all actual objects are imperfect copies of the one true perfect form of that object. So there is a form of the horse, for example, and all actual, physical horses are imperfect copies. The search for the perfect pizza or chocolate brownie – to name but two of my long-term wild goose chases – assumes a similar kind of idea. We have some notion of the way a food should be and we try to track down the one that most closely approximates to it. Factory-made foods sometimes fit that bill, because it is of the nature of some food-stuffs that they are made on a consistent, regulated, industrial scale.

You could, for example, try to make Bovril, Marmite or Vegemite at home, but your chances of beating the mass-produced originals are virtually zero. All these are the best of their kind because, in a sense, they define the class that they top. A rival could come along and do even better, but it's hard: such foods have become store-cupboard classics because they hit the spot so well.

Although sweet carbonated drinks are often condemned as the single worst contributor to Western obesity, most people love at least one kind, and it's the big brands who have perfected the recipes. You may hate all that the Coca-Cola Company and PepsiCo stand for, but most people who like cola find that the more low-scale, supposedly more ethical alternatives just don't compare in flavour.

I remember once being amused in a Bristol café that prided itself on its locally sourced, ethical ingredients when one of the workers was sent by his colleagues to buy some Cokes, 7-Ups and Fantas, which they didn't keep in stock. Similarly, I've seen stallholders at farmers' markets with their takeout Costa coffees. When even the guardians of the small and independent sometimes choose to buy from the big boys, you know that small is beautiful is only an approximation of the much more ambiguous truth.

PART II

Preparing

A meal begins long before the first forkful.

8

Tear up the recipes

A minor landmark in the cultural history of modern Britain came in 1998 when celebrity chef Delia Smith included instructions on how to boil an egg in her television series and accompanying book. 'I really don't believe that the majority of people cannot boil an egg,' complained one of her peers, Gary Rhodes, starting a national debate. 'It is insulting to their intelligence.'[56]

There can be little doubt, however, that in developed nations fewer and fewer people know how to cook even the basics. Countries that we think of as having rich food cultures are no exception. My Italian aunts and uncles report that none of the women of my generation cooks much anymore, and that is not because their husbands and partners are sharing the burden. Ready meals and frozen food are on the rise in Italy just as they have been in Britain and America.

It seems obvious that the answer to this is to teach people how to cook again. The problem is that this is assumed to mean giving them recipes. This approach was exemplified by Jamie Oliver, who in 2008 set out to save the northern town of Rotherham from TV dinners and takeaways by establishing his 'Ministry of Food'. This was a kind of culinary pyramid scheme, in which a small group of pioneers would be taught simple recipes and then encouraged to pass them on to others, who in turn would pass them on to yet more people, until the cascade of wholesome food flooded the whole town. It didn't.

As I see it, the core of the problem is the very idea of the recipe. Talk to people like my aunts and uncles about how they learned to cook from their mothers and you'll find no mention of recipes. My Italian grandmother, like everyone else of her generation, didn't even have much use for scales. You learned, as one aunt put it, by watching and listening. Consider my aunt's 'recipe' for gnocchi. She takes mashed potato, adds a beaten egg or two and then mixes in flour until the dough reaches the right consistency, something she learned to judge by experience. A recipe is a poor substitute for this use of judgement, since different varieties of potatoes, or even the same variety harvested or cooked at different times, hold more or less liquid, so there just isn't a consistent quantity of flour to use. (That's also why recipes for Irish potato cakes often don't come out right.)

Recipes are thus the root of the problem, since codification is the death of judgement. As soon as you create fixed instructions, you reduce the need for the cook to make her own decisions and thus diminish her skills. When you rely on what is written rather than on what you see, smell and taste, you lose command over your kitchen. Reading and writing have therefore in a way been bad for cooking: the rise of verbal literacy has facilitated the decline of culinary literacy.

The reason why people can't cook well is therefore not that they don't have enough recipes but that they have too many. They have learned to become dependent on having instructions set out for them. If we want to revive the art of day-to-day home cooking, this is the problem we need to address. That is not to say there is no place for recipes at all and that they should be snobbishly dismissed as crutches for the benighted. Julian Barnes is right to loathe the 'air of superiority' of certain people who say, 'Oh, I don't follow recipes,' or, 'I read recipes, but only to get ideas.' This is often just a lazy excuse to be 'airy-fairily "creative" in the worst, self-applauding way'.[57]

What we need to do is to encourage people to develop a feel for food, whether they use recipes or not. How much garlic should you use in a dish? It depends on how much you like garlic. What are the best ingredients for a stir-fry, and in what proportions? It depends on how you like it, but also on what you have to hand. There is no Heaven-decreed answer as to which version of a dish is better.

This more improvisational attitude to cooking is often thought to be the preserve of the talented, those with flair. As with jazz music, it is believed that first you need to learn your scales and follow routines by rote, and only later can you indulge in free play. The comparison is both right and wrong. What it gets right is that you do need a good grounding in the basics to cook well. What it gets wrong is thinking that this basic grounding must be mechanical, like practising arpeggios. For my Italian family, for example, the equivalent of learning your scales was to learn how to make the classic core repertoire: risotto, minestrone, ragù and sugo for pasta. But that was never about following a scripted set of instructions. From the start it was a matter of learning to judge what was right, on the basis of observation – a way of acquiring the experience of others – and then of practice, so building their own experience.

One reason this is so hard to replicate is that we no longer have a national or regional core repertoire. Rather than cutting our teeth on a limited range of eternal classics, people want to cook the latest Nigella, the new Nigel, the Delia du jour. Novelty and experimentation have become the desiderata, and not enough value is placed on doing simple, timeless dishes well. So rather than allowing ourselves to develop our own good judgement, we defer to the judgement of others.

This is connected to a general problem of the decline of what Aristotle called practical wisdom (*phronsis*). In the modern world, often for laudable motives of transparency and consistency, we have increasingly replaced personal judgement with codified rules. Discretion is no longer allowed to determine who should be admitted to a club, who should be hired or how strictly rules should be applied. Rather, the rules are the rules and they are applied blindly to all. While this might seem fair, it removes the element of personal judgement that has always been a necessary component of good decision-making.

The psychologists Barry Schwartz and Kenneth Sharpe argue that this loss of practical wisdom has all sorts of negative consequences for society, as we rely more on 'rules and incentives' and 'sticks and carrots' to ensure things are done 'correctly'. In banking, medicine, education and even creative industries like publishing, we no longer rely on the experience of experts but on spreadsheets, checklists and formalised procedures. What we are discovering, however, is that 'Substituting rules for wisdom doesn't work.'[58]

This approach has effects all the way down the food chain. Modern Western societies understandably insist on certain standards in production. But when you codify the rules, judgement and discretion slowly die from neglect. Worse, instead of doing things in order to achieve desired outcomes, people start following the rules for their own sake, seeing them simply as duties to be fulfilled or as obstacles to be overcome. This means even the most well-intentioned rules can actually facilitate bad practice. So, for example, 'The problem with meat,' says restaurateur Henry Dimbleby, 'is that animal husbandry is incredibly complicated, so if you set rules, you'll always find some bastard who will do it cheapest within those rules and inevitably that will cause problems.'

Time and again the restaurateurs and farmers I spoke to based their relationships not on rules established by contract, but on trust. That makes perfect sense: rules can be bent and you can't spend all your time making sure they are being followed. Trust is the only sustainable basis for good, strong relationships, and it requires that you give up the illusion of control and leave those you trust to get on with it. In doing that, you are trusting not just their good intent but also their judgement. The decline of respect for judgement is also therefore connected with the decline of trust.

In the kitchen, the paradigm case of judgement is a category of dishes we might call the Simple but Infinitely Variable: 'SIVs'. Their defining feature is that to make a great one, you do not need more information or knowledge but some kind of knack. Every culture has them. In India, it seems to be dal. Do not offend an Indian by making the grave mistake of saying that the lentil is a plain, boring food. You may well be treated to a hymn to the wonders of dal, the innumerable ways in which people cook it differently. And like all SIVs, you will almost certainly be told that no one makes it as well as your interlocutor's mother.

Italians seem to have more SIVs than most. Certainly minestra and minestrone soups qualify, with regional as well as familial variations in which vegetables and herbs go in. Every cook also has her own ragù and sugo – the basic pasta sauces that are eaten with a regularity that never bores.

In England, the SIV is the roast dinner. Again, in theory there are only so many ways one can roast a joint of meat or boil a carrot, yet the ensemble can turn out very differently in different homes, and for most people, nothing beats their mum's.

One can get obsessed with a SIV because although in principle it is so simple that perfection always seems within reach, it is never quite achieved. That's why I became obsessive about hummus. It's not that it's my favourite food, or the one I eat most of. It's just that the perfect hummus is strangely elusive. The closest I got to finding 'the One' was actually a brand easily found in London, in particular in the small Cypriot shops of Green Lanes, where I used to live. Yefsis was delicious: smooth and flavourful. So what made it superior to the stuff I used to buy from supermarkets? I looked at the list of ingredients, which I'm pretty sure was just chickpeas, tahini, olive oil, lemon juice, garlic and salt, in that order. What I noticed was the large tahini content. When I went back and looked at the supermarket versions, I was surprised to see that the second-biggest ingredient was in fact vegetable oil. No wonder it didn't taste as good. Even more curiously, the 'reduced fat' version had tahini as its second-largest ingredient. This meant that the so-called low-fat option was the more authentic recipe and the standard supermarket hummus was actually an *increased*-fat bastardisation, padded out with cheap vegetable oil. From then on hummus has been the only product from a low-fat range I would buy.

Hummus is in essence just five ingredients – chickpeas, tahini, lemon juice, garlic and salt – but not only can the proportions vary, from this base different cultures and different cooks make their own alterations, with spices or olive oil, or even the odd additional ingredient. So having moved away from a regular supply of Yefsis, I set out to make my own. I have to say what I make is pretty good, although it can never be the ultimate hummus, partly because it is never the same on two occasions running. I could try to standardise my proportions by careful measuring, but this, I think, is counter to the spirit of true traditional, rustic cooking. So it is that lemons are more or less juicy or bitter, garlic more or less pungent, teaspoons of tahini more or less generous. Rather than fight the inconsistency, I go with it, always learning from the last batch I've made but knowing that there will never come a point when I turn out the same dish time and again. And this is what, I think, makes the difference between an adopted SIV and a native one. The mothers – and it was almost always the mothers – who made dal, minestra or porridge day in, day out did so with a remarkable consistency, one that could never be copied by anyone else, no matter how closely they observed the process.

A humble bowl of hummus thus stands as a constant reminder to me that what is simple is not always easy, what is complex is not always complicated, and that some of life's great pleasures are not exotic or unusual but regular, familiar, everyday delights. It also stands as testimony to the role of judgement in cooking.

What we need is a new kind of cookbook, one that replaces pre-scriptive recipes with looser suggestions for how to make things. It might help to remember that the word 'recipe' itself derives from the Latin verb *recipere*, meaning 'to take', which is not the same as simply copying or passively receiving. As you may have noticed, that is pre-cisely the approach I am trying to encourage with the 'recipes' in this book.

More crucial than such cookbooks would be a more general revival of and respect for the art of judgement. The great success of science has perhaps made us too willing to see its precise, quantified methods as the template for all good rational deliberation. But, as is increasingly accepted, not even science is free from judgement. Although results ultimately stand and fall on the basis of hard fact, research often proceeds on the basis of hunch and intuition.

Good judgement, or practical wisdom, differs from mere 'opin-ion' or even 'prejudice' because it is receptive to evidence and seeks justification. At the same time, it appreciates that in many domains facts and evidence together cannot settle an issue. Judgement there-fore is about filling the unavoidable gaps between knowledge and its grounds; it is not about creating such gaps for their own sake or not trying to close them.

Some people find this idea appealing and in some sense obvious – not everything can be established scientifically, logically or evidentially and so of course there is an ineliminable role for judgement – but many find it suspiciously vague. To allow a role for judgement would seem to open the door to all sorts of unjustified assertion and irra-tionality. The response to this understandable concern cannot be to close the door to judgement but to police the entrance as vigilantly as possible so that less desirable elements don't try to sneak in under its guise.

The chapters that follow attempt to apply practical wisdom, showing that judgement is a form of rationality that does not embrace vagueness and imprecision for its own sake, but which recognises that much of what is most important in human life cannot be precisely specified, quantified, measured or otherwise pinned down, both inside and outside the kitchen.

HUMMUS

All you need to do to make hummus is to mix chickpeas with up to around a third again in quantity of tahini and (optionally) olive oil, along with some lemon juice, crushed garlic and salt. Whizz with a blender and serve. Taste it. If you find it has too little of this or too much of that, adjust next time.

As for the ingredients themselves, the main reason I bought a pressure cooker was that I thought using dried chickpeas would improve my hummus. If it did, then it wasn't by much and these days I much more often use a tin. I've also found that the best tahini is the runnier kind sold in Middle Eastern grocers. The light variety you get in health food shops is fine but a bit thick: don't be afraid to add some water if your hummus comes out too firm.

You can build on the basic formula. I like to add pimentón (smoked paprika) and cumin to mine. The Fish Deli in Ashburton, Devon, does a fantastic version with orange and cumin. You can also mash up other kinds of beans with herbs, garlic and various seasonings to make different kinds of paste, such as butter beans with lemon and rosemary. New varieties await your invention.

9

Be inauthentic

Behind almost every tradition is a myth, and behind all traditions is the biggest myth of them all: that this is what our people have always done, if not from time immemorial, then at least since our people were a people. But, of course, cuisines are always evolving and with food 'for ever' simply means 'as long as we can remember', which is often not very long at all. The myth persists, however, because it is essential for the cult of authenticity, which worships dishes and recipes supposedly true to these timeless traditions.

The quickest and easiest way to destroy this illusion is simply to run through a list of 'traditional ingredients' and see just how many are relative latecomers to a national cuisine. Italy provides numerous examples of this.[59] Tomatoes are a central ingredient of what we now think of as *la cucina italiana*, but of course they did not even arrive in the country until after the discovery of the New World in 1492, and they only became common in the mid-nineteenth century. Pasta does have a very long history, predating Marco Polo, but it only became a national staple after the Second World War, and at one time it was eaten very soft, not al dente as is now considered de rigueur. Before the arrival of tomatoes, it was often eaten with a sprinkle of cheese or sugar and spice. As for balsamic vinegar, my family was typical in never once having had a bottle in their house.

What is true of ingredients is also true of whole dishes. 'When people say, "That's not traditional," that's really disputable almost all the time,' Giorgio Locatelli told me at his London restaurant, after I'd eaten a lunch so good I didn't care if it was traditional or not. 'With Italy it's even worse than any other place because by the time they codified the recipes, most of them were already spread all over Italy, so each one had its own interpretation.' The difference between the soup in one village and the next might simply be whether it has sage in it or not, but to the locals, that's vital.

More interesting than mere 'not as old as you think' debunking, however, is finding out how traditions have been constructed. Whisky is a rich case study. Take any distillery tour in Scotland and you'll be told how 70 to 80 per cent of the flavour of the spirit is determined by the used oak barrel it matures in, which these days is almost always a bourbon cask imported from America. Those aged in Spanish sherry barrels are sweeter and heavier. Taste two side by side and even if you are no connoisseur, the difference is clear. You would have thought, then, that the choice of barrel reflected centuries of accumulated wisdom, acquired through trial and error, as to which kind best suited the distinctive local characteristics of each Scotch.

The truth is far more mundane. Scotch whisky used to be matured almost exclusively in sherry barrels made from European oak. This had become the cask of choice for sherry-, port- and Madeira-makers after Napoleon increased oak cultivation to help build his warships and restricted the age at which they could be felled, which resulted in a plentiful supply of the wood. The fortified wines that filled the oak casks were popular in Britain, where distillers were only too happy to make use of the empty barrels left after their contents had been consumed.

In America, meanwhile, machine-made native-oak barrels were becoming cheaper to produce than handmade, European ones, and bourbon distillers favoured the flavour given by heavily charred new casks. Then in 1935 an edict turned this common practice into a necessity, when federal law made the use of new barrels compulsory, a protectionist measure to help foresters and coopers. So suddenly there was a glut of cheap used bourbon casks undercutting old sherry barrels. Scottish distillers took advantage of this and, in so doing, radically changed the flavour of their drinks. So what we now think of as the traditional mode of production and resultant flavour of Scotch was nothing more than an opportunistic response to changed market conditions, precipitated by a law passed by a foreign nation, which also ensured that bourbon too would settle to have a common, 'traditional' style and mode of preparation.[60]

Food history is full of such accidents of politics and economics ossifying into apparently timeless traditions. The 'authentic' British banger, for example, is distinguished from most other European sausages by its use of rusk, a kind of dried unleavened bread, but this was only introduced in response to wartime rationing, in order to make the meat go further. Thrifty butchers simply never saw the point in returning to more expensive all-meat formulations.

It also needs to be remembered that traditional is not always good anyway. Grocer and broadcaster Charlie Hicks cites Joy Larkham, who has done a great deal to revive lost 'heritage' varieties of fruit and vegetables, but who once pointed out that there's often a very good reason they stopped growing them in the first place: many aren't that nice.

However, it is easy to get carried away, or perhaps disillusioned, by these myriad tales of how traditions are not so good or deep rooted after all. Surely there is some sense and value in 'tradition'?

One key is to understand a tradition as something that is essentially alive and dynamic. As soon as anything stops living and becomes fixed as a kind of cultural museum piece, it ceases to be a tradition and instead becomes part of an historical heritage. So, for instance, while soda bread is still a traditional Irish loaf, a trencher – a piece of stale bread used as a kind of edible plate in the Middle Ages – is simply part of our culinary history. If revived, it would be a heritage foodstuff, not a traditional one, since it would no longer be tied to the past by continuous custom, but would be a self-conscious resurrection of a dead practice.

Tradition and heritage both have their value, but although they overlap, they are not the same thing. Tradition mirrors an aspect of language identified by Jacques Derrida.[61] Any word you can meaningfully utter, I or others could also use and be equally well understood. However, this fact has misled some into believing that there must be some kind of single meaning or 'essence' of a word that each iteration of it captures. Derrida's claim was that, in fact, the iterative nature of language means that each time a word is used its meaning can change very slightly. Each iteration is sufficiently alike that comprehension is unproblematic, but also sufficiently unique that the meaning of a word cannot be fixed for ever. That's why it was possible for 'dinner' in English to alter its meaning seamlessly over the centuries so that what once named a late-morning meal now refers to one taken in the evening (or to lunch, depending on the social class and region of the diner).

Traditions are the same. Each time someone makes a 'traditional' Christmas cake, for example, it will be sufficiently similar to those made by others that no one will have any doubt that it is indeed an example of the same dish, but of course no two cakes are ever identical, and over time, changing habits, ingredient availability and fashions may mean that the recipe changes. English Christmas cake, for example, evolved from a kind of plum pudding. Sometimes, as with words, a significant change is introduced self-consciously and the community either adopts or rejects it. More often, changes occur gradually and organically. As butter gained a bad reputation for causing heart disease, for example, many northern Italians who had previously used it generously gradually cut down or substituted olive oil. People throughout the world have also become more sparing in their use of sugar. 'There is always a kind of movement in the cooking,' says Locatelli, 'so tradition moves with society, with what you're doing around you.'

Because of this, there is no contradiction at all in a dish's being traditional and yet differing significantly from its historical predecessors. We should not be seduced by the idea that only the 'original' is truly 'authentic'. Of course, it can be very interesting to know in what ways contemporary iterations of traditional foods differ from their ancestors, but it is not straightforwardly the case that the older the version, the more traditional it is. How long the practice has been maintained matters more than how long ago it started.

If we accept that tradition is always about continuity through change and not simply preserving old ways, why should we value it? First and foremost, because our food traditions are part of our cultural inheritance and we have an obligation not to let that just die. This is another example of the virtue of stewardship, underpinned by the conservative insight that there is often wisdom in the evolved practices of the past and since it is easier to destroy than to create, we should take care to preserve what is good in what we inherit from our ancestors. That is not to say that just because something emerges out of a tradition it must be good, or that it exists for a reason that is still pertinent. But it is a cause for caution, to remember that even if we can't see exactly why something is how it is, we should presume there is a value to it until proven otherwise.

Some such values are purely aesthetic. Every culture has traditional dishes that contribute to the rich 'gastrodiversity' of the global food culture. A world in which many of these traditions died out, to be replaced by a homogeneous, globalised cuisine of American-style pizza, French fries and pan-Asian stir-fries would be an impoverished one. Just as the world becomes a duller place when every capital has high streets full of the same multinational chain stores, so it becomes less interesting when the pizza in Naples is the same as the pizza in

New York. This is another reason why rare breeds of pig, cattle and poultry; ancient varieties of apples and pears; the local and the seasonal, all matter: if we neglect them, then we end up with a narrower, more homogeneous range of one-size-fits-all foodstuffs and we lose depth in our food culture.

Ironically, however, over-zealous attempts to preserve traditions can just as effectively kill them. In living traditions, there are always differences between regions, and even kitchens in the same street. Witness the disagreement between Devon and Cornwall over what goes on a scone first in a cream tea: jam (Cornwall) or clotted cream (Devon). Once the preservationists get their hands on a dish or product, however, one formulation is frozen in time and becomes the uniform orthodoxy. This is one of the downsides of the European PDO and PGI (Protected Geographic Indication) schemes, designed to protect the special, distinctive status of regional foodstuffs. When it is formally specified exactly what it means for a cheese to be mozzarella di bufala campana, or camembert de Normandie, innovation is stopped. Codification is ossification. When you deny something the possibility of growth, you do not keep it alive; you kill and pickle it.

As with the old adage about business, what stops moving forward inevitably ends up sliding backwards. Academic and writer John Dickie told me of a very clear example of this. He lived for about a year in a small town called Genzano, near Rome. 'It's a town of fine food traditions, particularly its bread,' says Dickie. This is pane casareccio di Genzano, a kind of long, semi-brown bread baked in wood ovens and bought in quarters or halves. In 1997 it was awarded EU PGI status. 'This immediately led to a kind of levelling-down of the standards,' says Dickie. The incentives were put in place to meet the minimum criteria, but not to exceed them, since that did not allow the product to be clearly differentiated from others with the PGI certification. And so, 'The few bakers that made it in the proper way with the beech branches were carried along by the majority who wanted an easier and more marketable version. The result is that if you get this stuff which is called pane di Genzano elsewhere in Italy, "Italy's first bread", it's not remotely like the stuff I got.'

That's why the conservation of a product is not as important as the continuation of a living tradition. Indeed, arguably the torch of tradition is now glowing most brightly in the hands of people creating new products in traditional ways, rather than traditional products in new ways. Take, for example, the producers of Stichelton, an unpasteurised blue cow's-milk cheese in the old style of Stilton. The latter is now being produced according to strict PDO rules that require the milk to be pasteurised, which means Stilton has become 'a protection of an existing form of manufacture that in actual fact bears no relation to what the traditional Stilton is all about', according to Dominic Coyte of Neal's Yard Dairy. I would argue that the new Stichelton is the more properly traditional cheese.

We ought to be able to continue the best traditions of the past without denying them the right to change. Take, for example, the cheese-maker I visited in Valle d'Aosta who produces Fontina in a more or less traditional way. When I saw him, he was with his herds in the high alpine mountains, where they grazed on land that would be covered in snow a month or so later. By that time they would have moved down a little, and in the winter they would be feeding in the valleys.

When we entered his cheese-making workshop, he was stirring the milk and rennet in a huge copper bowl with a traditional curd cutter, but it was being heated by a gas burner and towards the end of the process he swapped the wooden cutter for an electric mixer. Similarly, the cheese drained on an old wooden table, but in modern plastic moulds, and he moved up and down the mountains in a four-by-four, not on a mule.

Although I think the best way to make the past matter today is by maintaining living traditions, that is not to say there is no value in what I contrast as heritage. Gastrodiversity is also served simply by keeping alive or bringing back lost or threatened foods. The Slow Food movement has been instrumental in promoting this through its Ark of Taste (known in the UK as the more prosaic Forgotten Foods). One such product is einkorn, for which I gave a bread recipe earlier. Apart from its cultural and culinary value, in a world in which there is a tendency for agriculture to put all its eggs into one or two baskets, in the form of the most productive cultivars for any given plant, it is good that some small-scale production of alternatives is kept going to maintain biodiversity. If some sort of virulent pest or disease attacks the dominant cultivars, we may need others to help develop new, resistant hybrids.

Tradition at its best is therefore not about looking backwards, but about looking both ways, taking the good that has come from the past into the future, while not being afraid to see it continue to change and grow. In that context, 'authenticity' begins to look like a misguided value. This is something I have been slow to realise. Growing up with an Italian family on one side, I got a little snooty about what I saw as inauthentic perversions of their culinary traditions. I was right to be horrified by the watery mince and carrot concoctions that passed for bolognese sauce in many English families, but only because they didn't taste good. In fact, what we had in our house was not a traditional bolognese either, and like most households in the 1970s and 1980s, the so-called Parmesan we sprinkled on top was the dried stuff in a cardboard drum that no one in Italy would touch. Similarly, I still think pineapple or chicken tikka on a pizza is an aberration, but on pure grounds of taste. If I were rigorous about 'authenticity', I would not allow anything more than the original toppings of tomato, basil and mozzarella to grace my dough, and I would leave my beloved capers and anchovies to one side.

Innovation is essential to keeping a tradition alive, but without an understanding of that tradition, innovation descends into destruction. Such understanding is hard to codify, and perhaps we should not try. It is another domain where our best understanding requires the imprecision of judgement and practical wisdom. It is no accident that we use words like 'sensitive' to describe someone who innovates well within a tradition, as their skill is more of a kind of perception than the result of rational deliberation.

A great contemporary Italian cook like Giorgio Locatelli, for example, understands that the cuisine of his country requires combining relatively few good, pure ingredients well. He also understands that there is a kind of core palette of flavours that provide the basis for anything that goes on top. Within these and other limitations, he can create genuinely new combinations that are nonetheless firmly located within the tradition, a kind of novelty that works precisely because it is never completely new. An Italian who sat down, as I did, to his roast partridge, Swiss chard, grape and chestnut, or the antipasto of cured neck of pork, girolles (mushrooms), balsamic vinegar and rocket, may never have eaten those dishes before, but he will instantly recognise them as belonging to the culinary tradition he knows and loves.

But because people have the wrong idea of tradition, it can be hard to take people on that journey. Tradition sells, says Locatelli, but selling requires sensitivity to 'supply and demand' and that means not challenging the expectations of customers too much, even if they are based on outdated ideas of what is authentically Italian. 'If I go to any Italian restaurant now in Italy which is a little bit nice, you'll have a raw fish carpaccio,' says Locatelli. 'It's something Italians eat all the time now. You can't do that here because people say, "I didn't come to a fucking Italian restaurant to eat raw fish!"'

To be aware of tradition in the best sense is to understand the culture that surrounds you and how it has shaped you, so you are better able to move forward without denying yourself either the promise of the new or the guarantee of the old. If 'authentic' means anything in this context, it is not 'original' or 'unchanging'. It is rather being true both to yourself and to what is good in the living tradition that you imbibe.

MARMITAKO

I have no idea how 'authentic' my version of this dish is, and I don't much care. It's a form of a traditional Basque fisherman's stew that I loved eating when I taught English in Bilbao. What's more, it's easy, one-pot cooking, with little to clear up afterwards.

For two people, you'll need one or two red peppers, a tin of chopped tomatoes, potatoes (quite floury varieties work better than waxy ones), garlic, hot pimentón (or smoked paprika) and a tin of tuna, preferably albacore, whose flavour works better in this dish and which is more sustainable to boot. For bigger quantities, just scale up.

Heat up some (preferably olive) oil in a saucepan and add the peppers, chopped, and garlic, sliced. How small? You decide. People like it differently. Cook over a moderate heat, stirring often, to soften the peppers without browning the garlic. When soft, add pimentón to taste. Again, you have to find the quantity that suits you. A whole rounded teaspoon will make this pretty hot; around half will just add a lovely smoky, spicy note. Mix in the pimentón well with the peppers and garlic. Add a tin of tomatoes and chopped potatoes. Once again, the exact quantities depend on your preference: this can be more or less potatoey.

To simmer, you need at least enough liquid to just cover all the ingredients, so you may need to top up the tomato juice from the can. If you've got red wine to hand, add some of that, otherwise a little water will do. If you want it as more of a soup than a thick stew, add even more.

How long it will take to cook once you bring it to a simmer will depend on two factors: first, how small you've cut the potatoes. You may well find that this takes much longer to cook than you'd have thought. I've often needed to give mine an hour or more. The second factor is how soft you like the potatoes. I think this dish is best when they are beginning to disintegrate, but maybe that's just me.

Right at the end, break up the tuna, stir it in, bring back to a simmer and heat the fish through. You can also make this with fresh tuna, although I don't think that version is much better. Serve as it is or with fresh bread.

10

Use the right kit

TECHNOPHRONESIS

A particular bugbear of high-end fruit and vegetable supplier Charlie Hicks is how romantic technophobia can easily get in the way of good sense. Or, as he more colourfully put it to me, 'The anti-science thing just gets right on my tits.'

Hicks describes a visit to a salami producer in Hungary. Each salami was put together in the traditional way. 'The ingredients were impeccable, there was nothing nasty at all, and we watched the process all the way through,' he says, but the curing was done in a high-tech facility where they could completely control temperature and moisture, which are ultimately what matter. 'We used to put it in caves,' said the man controlling it all via his laptop. 'We knew what the ideal temperature was and we'd try to get it right, but we'd lose about thirty per cent. Now we keep the whole lot. It's exactly the same; we just got better at it.' From Hicks's point of view, if you can use such technology to avoid losing a third of your production, it would be immoral not to.

It can be hard to accept that modern machinery really can beat traditional ways. I've been to a sherry distillery in Sanlúcar de Barrameda where they insist it's the warm, salty air off the Atlantic that makes the difference to the ageing. In Trevélez, Granada, it's the combination of warm air off the southern Mediterranean hitting the cool heights of the Alpujarra mountains that makes their hams some of the best in the world. If you think about it, though, the reason

120

these places became centres of excellence is because the air matters, and pre-technology, you couldn't change it; you just had to be where it was best. Once you can control the immediate atmosphere, its exact physical location no longer matters. There may be some natural environments that we can't better, but there are sure to be others we can.

Even people who are generally technophiles often have an inner technophobe who comes out when the science gets too unfamiliar, too scary. You see this often in reactions to genetically modified organisms (GMOs). To express support for them in polite company these days is tantamount to revealing an admiration of Stalin.

Part of the trouble is that, as is so often and tiresomely the case, it's a debate that has become polarised. Many opponents maintain a simple blanket 'No GMO' stance, turning a pros-and-cons issue into a simple for-and-against one. Although it seems to me that there are three very good reasons for wanting to avoid the vast majority of GMOs currently in production or development, none justifies completely ruling out their future use.

Harriet Lamb, the CEO of Fairtrade International, explains the first. 'If we believe in farmer empowerment and farmer organisation, the problem with GMOs is that the traditional way of farmers keeping back a portion of their harvest for the next year, they can't do anymore. They've lost control of the crop.' That's because commercial varieties are owned by large conglomerates who insert 'terminator genes' into the seeds so farmers need to buy new ones every year. Those same companies also supply the weedkillers that destroy everything else apart from the crop. As Helen Browning, the head of the Soil Association, puts it, 'The whole history of GM has been about corporate control.'

Second, there are reasons for doubting the sustainability of the way most commercial GM crops are grown. By leaving only one plant standing, GM turns farms into absolute monocultures, in which the soil dies without artificial fertilisers, and wildlife cannot flourish.

The only way to keep such farms productive in the long run is to throw more and more chemicals onto them, which may not be dangerous, but is expensive and requires lots of carbon-based energy input at a time when we need to reduce CO_2 emissions.

Third, natural selection means that this approach can only lead to a prolonged adaptive war with nature. Herbicide-resistant weeds are already evolving to fill the niche left by their vanquished predecessors. Nature abhors a vacuum and it could be that by hastening the demise of the weeds we currently have, we are speeding the arrival of ones that are even tougher to deal with.

There may be answers to these criticisms, although I haven't heard any good ones yet. Nonetheless, what these and other reasonable objections have in common is that they are not objections to GM per se. The problem is with the current system of ownership and the particular crops now around. The only objections against all forms of GMOs are extremely weak indeed. The 'playing God' charge is so pathetic as to hardly merit a reply: in short, we have been selectively breeding and making life-and-death choices for millennia.

The more serious objection is that we cannot say for certain what effect the introduction of new species will have on the wider ecosystem. That is true, but all it means is we need to be careful. Had we never introduced new species, then there would be no tomatoes in Italy, potatoes in Ireland or tea in India. Almost every species found in a country like Britain was at one time imported from elsewhere. Some introductions have gone badly wrong, such as rabbits to Australia, but even that hardly led to the collapse of civilisation.

Indeed, we have already introduced thousands of new species and varietals into agriculture over the last century. Since the 1930s, one of the most common techniques for creating these is to bombard plants with radiation to accelerate the natural process of random mutation, selecting the resulting crops that do well and repeating the process until the ideal variety emerges. If this technology were new and the resulting products given their technical label, 'mutagenic', they would probably be resisted as strongly as GMOs.

The balanced position is to be rightly cautious of GMOs, and perhaps even opposed to the spread of current commercial varieties, but not to oppose research, especially by non-profits, into new plants that could be of tremendous help. The Golden Rice Project, for example, is a Rockefeller Foundation-funded humanitarian attempt to develop rice that will provide the vitamin A lacking in the diet of many poor people for whom the crop is a staple. Drought-resistant crops could also play a major role in increasing food security, even if the current research leader, Monsanto, is not the organisation to deliver on its social benefits. In both cases, there may need be no fundamental change to the ways the crops are currently cultivated and so little if any risk of unintended side effects caused by aggressive insecticide use.

All this seems crystal clear to me, and yet people opposed to GMOs in their current form are often remarkably reluctant to concede they might one day be useful. Harriet Lamb, to be fair, does say Fairtrade standards, which currently ban GMOs, are 'live' and, 'You have to keep debating and be ready to change your view if the technology and ownership of it changed.' Helen Browning is, however, constrained by the need of the organic movement to have a simple message and 'maintain a clear tension between very strong forces that would take GM into our food supply and control it in a pretty wholesale way'. Even so, shouldn't the Soil Association acknowledge that the current ban is provisional? 'The *Daily Mail* then says on the front lead story, "Soil Association says GM is fine,"' replies Browning. 'That's the world we live in. That's why half the time you can't have sensible conversations.' Unfortunately, she is probably right. The organic movement has to play politics, because food is a political issue, and so sensible conversations become impossible.

For those of us less constrained by politics, however, more nuance is possible. Neither a technophile nor a technophobe be. What we need instead is what we might call 'technophronesis': practical wisdom about technology that enables us to judge on a case-by-case basis whether the innovation in question is unnecessary, extravagant, wasteful or useful.

Technophronesis would not only lead to much more sensible thinking about the big issues of food technology that confront society, it would also have its uses in the domestic sphere. Technology is all around our kitchens; it's just that most of it is so simple and familiar we don't think of it as such, like corkscrews, tin openers, vegetable peelers, electronic scales, kettles and blenders. But most kitchens contain more rarely or never used gadgets than ones that see regular service, their buyers too easily seduced by a new machine that will transform their lives into an endless parade of home-made ice cream, fruit smoothies, breads, yoghurt and fondues.

However, even the most notoriously underused gadget, like the juicer, can be a boon if it falls into the right hands. I have one prized bit of technology that I hear many others leave languishing in the back of a cupboard: a bread machine. It's so good that I'll happily tell you it's a Panasonic SD-255 with my full assurance that the company has not even been told about this voluntary product placement. I used it constantly for about five years. If I timed it right, I could have lunch with bread that was still warm. And then of course there was the smell that permeated the house when the loaf was baking, and the ease of making doughs for breads like focaccia. It passed the key tests of good domestic kit: it was simple to use, easy to clean and it worked. It was not a question of matching the produce of artisans, but bettering what you can usually get off the shelf. Mine certainly did, at least until a couple of brilliant bakeries recently opened nearby. Even if it doesn't find a new home, it will have had a long, productive life and has saved me much more than it cost, unlike the exact same model my neighbour has, which he has yet to work out how to use.

Could it be, however, that some machines can beat even artisans? In some spheres of human activity, perhaps, but not with food and drink, surely? That's what I assumed, until a revelatory moment just after I had finished interviewing Jonray and Peter Sanchez-Iglesias, the extremely likeable young chefs behind the Michelin-starred restaurant Casamia in Bristol. They had been talking, as most chefs do, about how they like to constantly challenge themselves, be creative, source the best local ingredients and so on. I mentioned in passing that I had enjoyed their contribution to a roundtable discussion on coffee in the industry magazine *Restaurant*. It was a bit of a joke, though, I said, that also sitting at the table was a representative of Nespresso, the capsule-based system, which just happened to be the sponsor of the feature. Not at all, replied Jonray. The coffee you had when you arrived, that was Nespresso. He ushered me over to the little machine that sat behind reception. All the top guys use it, he said, all the Michelin places. He slipped a capsule in, pressed a button and out came an espresso with a perfect crema – the thin, tan-coloured layer of foam on the top that for many connoisseurs is the hallmark of a well-made drink. It tasted good: smooth, a little nutty and not as bitter as many espressos.

I've done more important volte-faces in my time, but I don't think I've ever had my preconceptions and prejudices overturned so quickly. I checked it out, and although 'all' was of course a bit of an exaggeration, it is true that numerous high-end restaurants are now serving push-button coffee, including the two that at the time of writing were vying for top place on some of the most respected lists of the nation's best: the Ledbury and Heston Blumenthal's Fat Duck. In France, the legendary three-star L'Arpège in Paris, whose chef Alain Passard uses organic produce from his own biodynamic garden, is one of more than 100 Michelin-star restaurants supplied by Nespresso. Even Italy has embraced the capsule culture. When I stayed in a small, family-run hotel in the Valle d'Aosta, where the kitchen prided itself on its local food, the coffee came from a Lavazza capsule machine, discreetly designed to look like a more traditional one. Other companies like Illy, Segafredo and Kimbo also have their own versions. This goes completely against the food zeitgeist. We are supposed to be moving away from high-tech processes towards hand-made food made from good, 'natural' ingredients.

The capsule in the restaurant seems wrong in part because of the seeming dissonance between the creative, artisanal preparation of everything else on the menu and the any-idiot-can-do-it simplicity of the machine. But push that idea a little further and it collapses. Also on your table might be a bottle of wine, which the waiter simply had to open. Next to it could be a cheeseboard, which had merely been brought to room temperature and cut. Restaurants buy in what they cannot make better themselves, so why should coffee be any exception? Why not 'embrace innovation – new ingredients, techniques, appliances, information and ideas – whenever it can make a real contribution to our cooking', as four of the world's top chefs declared they did in their 'Statement on the "New Cookery"' in 2006. Ferran Adrià, Heston Blumenthal, Thomas Keller and Harold McGee insisted, 'A commitment to excellence requires openness to all resources that can help us give pleasure and meaning to people through the medium of food.'[62]

The best restaurants have good reasons for believing they cannot do better than a capsule machine. Making good espresso is extremely difficult and things can go wrong at every stage. Start with the beans. Even if you buy the best, once you have opened the bag, they start to oxidise and go stale. As soon as they are ground, that process accelerates rapidly. So unless you have a very high turnover, you are bound to end up serving coffee that is not as fresh as it should be.

Then you need to put the right amount into the portafiltro and compact it to the optimal pressure with the tamper, both processes that rely on human judgement and will not always be done exactly the same. Your machine also needs to be clean and calibrated to deliver water at the right pressure, which can be difficult, especially, apparently, in the mountains, where air pressure can vary a lot. Without a high turnover, the water in the machine will sit around hot for too long and lose oxygen, like water in a reboiled kettle.

Given all that, it can seem a miracle that cafés manage to make decent coffee at all. Indeed, it might explain why coffee nerds are so insistent that a decent drink is hard to find, and that it is only because most people are ignoramuses who prefer to drown out the flavour of the espresso with milk, sprinkles and syrups that most cafés get away with it. These geeks, who understand why making good coffee is so hard, should be the most able to see why automation is often a good compromise. Coffee-making lends itself to technical perfection, since all the key variables are strictly controllable.

There is nothing to stop a large company getting really good beans, then roasting and grinding them well. If it can do that and then immediately vacuum-seal them in capsules, where they will not degrade any further, it is already one step ahead of most baristas, since in effect it is using fresher coffee. If you then spend millions on R&D, drawing both on coffee-making expertise and technical know-how, you might well be able to design a machine that will force the right amount of water through the capsule at the right temperature and pressure, which is all that is needed to turn the coffee grounds into a great drink.

In theory, that might seem true, but it is hard to defeat an ideology with mere theory, and many of us hold as a tenet of faith that in spheres of human creativity, artisans always beat the machine. Well, that's what they used to say about chess. It is only since IBM's Deep Blue defeated Garry Kasparov in 1997 that people have started to say that it is obvious why computers are good at that sort of thing. Once you find a rigorous step-by-step procedure to achieve an end, automation becomes almost inevitable, so long as it is cost-effective. They did it for chess and now they've done it for coffee.

The proof of the pudding is in the eating, and top restaurants just wouldn't serve capsule coffee if they thought their own baristas could do better. These are places that don't cut corners, and that can have up to one chef in the kitchen for each diner. Nespresso itself has done innumerable blind tastings, and it was only because they knew they could hold their own against the best that they agreed to take part in one I organised.

It took place at the Latymer, the two-Michelin-star restaurant at Pennyhill Park in Surrey, because it had both a Nespresso and a traditional machine in situ. Counter-intuitively, the diners in the restaurant got the capsules, while guests ordering room service had their coffee handmade, because that was cheaper. Our samples were made by the highly experienced restaurant manager and fully trained barista Bruno Asselin. Bruno explained to me the care he had taken to make the test fair. He had serviced and cleaned the traditional machine the night before and was going to open a new bag of beans and grind them just before making. I handed him an unmarked bag of a third coffee to act as a kind of control. This was a high-quality single-estate coffee from Monte Sión in El Salvador, but it had not been roasted specifically for espresso and had been ground four days earlier. If our tasters rated this comparably to the other two, then it would suggest that all this talk of pressure, grind and so on was just nonsense, and basically coffee is coffee.

Each single espresso shot was brought out so that each of the four tasters – a café owner, a ten-a-day customer, a coffee nerd and a friend of mine – tasted them in a different order, to counteract any effect that primacy might have on appreciation. They scored without talking, taking notes as they went. I also tasted, but did not add my marks to the final tally since I had blown my own blindness in the process of making sure Bruno knew exactly what the tasting procedure was.

When we totted up the scores, the 'wrong' coffee I had brought did indeed come a distant third, and the winner was the Nespresso, which was also the favourite of two of the tasters. This was only the verdict of four people, of course, and the whole process of assigning numerical scores to such a complex experience is problematic. But it just underlined the conclusion any impartial observer must reach when surveying the evidence: like it or not, the multinationals have worked out how to make coffee at least as good as, and often better than, all but the best artisan coffee. That shatters the dogma that the handmade and artisanal always results in a superior product to the mass market, machine produced. It's also a reminder that, even if there are reasons not to embrace this particular innovation, one should resist a knee-jerk rejection of technology. After all, what we now think of as a 'traditional' espresso machine was first patented in 1938 by Achille Gaggia and was a pretty complicated piece of machinery that must have seemed just as radical at the time.

The comforting conclusion for traditionalists would be to back-peddle in the same way as artificial-intelligence sceptics did when Deep Blue check-mated Kasparov: coffee is a special case of creativity, just as chess is a special case of intelligence. It just so happens there are a few things that can be done by mindless algorithms, but most of human intelligence and creativity just isn't like that. There will never be a Nespresso equivalent to the chef's job.

Won't there? For evidence to the contrary, you only have to look at the very cutting edge of fine dining. Molecular gastronomy is premised on the idea that scientific and technical understanding can help us to create new flavours and combinations, and bring out the best in old ones. At the moment it is almost entirely the preserve of the artisanal restaurant led by a creative genius. People paid €285 per head to eat at Ferran Adrià's El Bulli before it closed, and still hand over £195, without wine or service, at Heston Blumenthal's Fat Duck. They are prepared to pay for such unique experiences, created by rare culinary geniuses at the very peak of their profession.

The logical consequence of the molecular approach, however, is haute mechanisation. If the best way to cook meat, for example, really is to vacuum-seal it with some herbs and spices and cook in water at 55 degrees Celsius (130 degrees Fahrenheit) for 48 hours, then as soon as a suitable cheap sous-vide cooker is available, there is no reason why a novice chef in a local pub, or anyone, for that matter, couldn't collect it from the butcher and do as good a job as anyone else.

The likes of Adrià and Blumenthal may become less like cooks in the traditional sense and more like designers. They will be the Henry Fords and James Dysons of gastronomy, designing dishes that others can assemble by following strict rules. If that seems far-fetched, consider that Blumenthal has already created a range of dishes that are mass produced for the supermarket chain Waitrose. For even more compelling evidence, watch the documentary *El Bulli: Cooking in Progress.* Adrià did not cook in his restaurant. His main role was to develop new dishes, especially during the six months the restaurant was closed for a form of gastronomic R&D. Even then he was mainly telling people what to try and providing feedback on the results of their experiments. The restaurant kitchen itself was really just a very fancy production line. In one scene, he said to the kitchen staff at the start of the season, 'You have to function like perfect machines.' If that's true, then it may just be easier and more reliable to use perfect machines in the first place. The parade of sous-chefs, chefs de partie and commis chefs in the kitchen might come to be seen as outmoded as human beings on car production lines where we now see robots. At least mechanised production can be extremely democratising, making luxury, bespoke goods into things anyone of average income can afford.

Fans of the artisanal might console themselves with one further thought. Maybe Nespresso machines and vacuum-packed meats can indeed bring excellent food and drink into anyone's homes. The mechanised might beat the average, or even the vast majority, but the very best still requires that human flair, creativity and passion.

A related argument is that mass production must appeal as broadly as possible, whereas the very best of anything is usually more individual, and will be loathed by some even if loved by most. Our coffee-tasting was a case in point. We all scored Nespresso within one point of each other and described it as 'smooth' and 'easy to drink', while the key message coming from restaurateurs was that they liked its 'consistency'. That does not mean it was bland, merely that it was not challenging or distinctive. It is impossible not to like, hard to truly love.

In contrast, our second-place coffee had more of a kick and depth, with that little bit of bitterness that many don't like but which for me is part of the taste of an espresso. Although it was the favourite of myself and the ten-cup-a-day connoisseur, one of the panel really took against it. That taster was the writer Tom Chatfield, who made the acute observation that what Nespresso had really done was to take the coffee-making process and systemically remove all that is problematic in it. For instance, while the much sought-after crema on a traditional espresso lasts only two minutes, the one from the capsule system will still be there a quarter of an hour later, if for any bizarre reason you like cold coffee. The result may be something flawless, but it also points to how it is possible to be better than perfect. A perfect bottle of Coke is not as good as a meal at El Bulli, even if they mess up one of the forty dishes. There are peaks above perfection that can only be achieved by accepting a certain amount of imperfection.

These considerations go some way to explaining why it is we still have good reason to value artisan-produced goods, foods and drinks, but they do not provide an in-principle argument as to why we always must. In effect, they simply issue a challenge to the mechanisers: don't just produce the highest common denominator; come up with a way to produce things that delight some and disgust others.

Indeed, this is just the route that mass production is going down anyway, as Malcolm Gladwell has brought to the public's attention in one of the most viewed TED talks. Gladwell points to how manufacturers have moved away from making one-size-fits-all ideal products in each category, such as a spaghetti sauce, which customers consistently rate, say, eight out of ten. Instead, they are giving customers a choice of products, a range of different sauces, the average rating of which is lower, but the peak ratings for which are higher.

The next stage of this process, much heralded but not yet a reality, is bespoke mechanised production on demand, gathering enough information on the client to produce mechanically the coffee, the pasta sauce or the meat marinade that is just right for each individual. That is surely something a chef could never do. To defend the artisan on the basis of idiosyncrasy is therefore to be a hostage to fortune, because mapping our individual preferences and tailoring products accordingly is the next phase of mechanised production.

There is, however, a way to defend the artisan that is more robust. The problem with the argument so far is that it has rested on the implicit assumption that the test of what is good is how it seems to you at the moment of consumption or appreciation. What is given pride of place is a decontextualised experience. That's why blind testing is considered so important, and yet is fundamentally distorting, for what really matters to us are not just the isolated facets of the experience, but how it fits in with everything else.

The point is one made by Brillat-Savarin, which is that the pleasures of the table are not identical to the pleasures of eating. Taste alone does not dictate what we want to eat. If it did, anyone who likes espresso should go out and buy a capsule system because it will almost certainly be better than an alternative domestic machine. The reasons not to, however, are not purely about flavour. First, there is the environmental impact. Sure, drinking capsule coffee is not going to make the already over-sized carbon footprint of a typical Westerner perceptibly bigger, but there is something gratuitous about embracing a technology that depends on a constant turnover of plastic, even if the company has in place systems to recycle it (ones that inevitably use up yet more energy). Not using the capsules in the first place won't save the planet, but it does mean living by and expressing good values.

Similarly, the machines, in a domestic sphere at least, represent a kind of excess: expensive kit that requires an expensive supply of capsules for a marginal improvement in the quality of your coffee. And it may indeed be no improvement at all, if you consider the whole coffee-drinking experience. Capsule coffee produces less of a smell when you make it, and we know that odour is important for the enjoyment of food. That is especially true of coffee, to the extent that many people like the aroma but hate the taste, or at least find that what delights the nose disappoints the mouth.

This leads to another point. Part of the pleasure of food is in its preparation, and for coffee drinkers, brewing can be a kind of sacred ritual. Popping a capsule and pushing a button therefore diminishes the whole coffee making and drinking experience; it doesn't enhance it.

Then there are socio-political considerations. When you buy a capsule system, you are in effect signing a contract with a large multinational company to supply your coffee. That does not necessarily mean you are exploiting farmers unable to earn a living, but you certainly lose the opportunity to help rebuild a global food economy that restores more personal links between producers and consumers. You can't buy directly from cooperatives and single estates. You can't yet (at the time of writing at least) choose Fairtrade. Much more often than not, you can't even buy the capsules from your small, local independent grocer.

In all these ways, the capsule system is an alienating technology: producers and retailers become anonymous, while the coffee-making process is hidden inside plastic casing. One of the things that makes the artisanal so valued is that it requires a personal relationship between maker and object, hands and materials, and, to some extent, creator and consumer. As I argued earlier, it matters for us to feel that at least some of our commercial transactions are part of a truly human network of relationships. Many a pub–goer, for instance, laments the decline of the owner landlord and the rise of the hired manager. Landlords tend to have a different kind of relationship with their customers, which is reflected back in the attitudes customers have to the pub.

This sense of personal relationship is reflected in one of the strangest features of restaurants. Although you pay for everything, often quite a lot, you are not just a customer but a guest. If you have a great meal, you thank the chef; she doesn't thank you. It's not just a cheesy bit of corporate jargon that restaurants are part of the 'hospitality industry'.

Ironically, perhaps, it is the corporations themselves who most appreciate what a handicap their colossal anonymity is, which is why they will often use a kind of bogus personalisation to make their products seem more appealing. One advertising campaign for Ben & Jerry's, for example, gave the impression that it was down to the whim of an individual as to what exactly went in their ice cream, with slogans like 'One man's imprecision is another man's extra marshmallow' and 'We usually try and put a handful of walnuts in every tub. How many you get depends on who makes it.' All this was after the company had been sold to the multinational giant Unilever and so the need to try to preserve the down-home brand of the company was more imperative than ever.

I came across another example at the small Boston chain b.good, whose slogan was 'real.food.fast. And food made by people, not factories.' On its tables were cards profiling suppliers. 'This is Frank,' one said, next to a photo of a blue-shirted, middle-aged, rustic-looking man whose 'family has been running the potato fields of western Massachusetts for a hundred years'. He and his three brothers are 'the guys who grow and pick the potatoes we're hand-cutting into fries every day this fall' and so on. The image it creates is folksy, but for all we've been told, this family farm might be a huge enterprise, over-reliant on chemicals and underpaid migrant labour. It certainly isn't a small cottage industry. The farm's website says, 'Szawlowski Potato Farms, Inc. is now the largest potato farm in New England.' It cultivates 2,500 acres and has a 'state-of-the-art packing plant and cooling facility'. As for Frank, he has 'left the fields to market and manage the business in the office-warehouse complex in Hatfield'.

We do not need to know every farmer who grew every vegetable or raised every cow, and nor need we oppose all forms of industrial agriculture. But if we have no links with any of the people producing our food, we become alienated from one of the most central things in our lives. That is one reason why we are not foolish to pay a little more to enjoy the beautiful or delicious things human beings can still make by hand. We want to maintain a society in which people can dedicate themselves to arts and crafts, in part because we just do, and also because the world is a more interesting place when people are engaged with interesting things. Making life easier and cheaper does not always make it better, if the price we pay is a loss of agency and creative expression.

We are knowing as well as sensing beings, and knowing how things are made does and should affect how we feel about them. Once you accept this fact, received wisdom about value and efficiency is overturned. The right way to assess agricultural production, for example, is not just by the measurable, objective metrics of yield, water usage, carbon footprint, soil erosion and so forth, important though they are. We also have to think about how different modes of production affect our landscape; our connection with farming and nature; and the links between farmer, land, animal, retailer and consumer. In short, technophronesis requires us to think holistically, rather than atomistically breaking down what is good into a checklist of desiderata, ticking them off and choosing the one with the highest score.

Too many opponents of industrial agriculture have been drawn into playing that game, only to find that they are sometimes defeated on just the criteria they put forward as important. Far from providing a fatal objection to industrial agriculture, it simply becomes a challenge for it to improve its performance against the measures chosen. Take polytunnels, the bête noire of the countryside lover. Charlie Hicks points out that they work fantastically well. They cut down on chemical use and on weather damage. When Hicks started out in the 1970s, for example, one big overnight rainfall could decimate a strawberry crop. 'If we didn't grow using polytunnels, we'd be importing more food,' says Hicks. Let's not forget that polytunnels are really just versions of greenhouses, which we've been using for centuries, and outdoor growing isn't best for everything. Take forced rhubarb, which is grown in dark sheds, a process discovered in 1817 by accident, when a plant buried in soil was found to be tastier. It's an artificial method of production so long established that it has become officially traditional: Yorkshire forced rhubarb has EU PDO status.

On the checklist approach, polytunnels win out on all but one criterion: they're ugly, although as Hicks says, 'The countryside is not a theme park.' Think holistically, however, and it seems clear that even if polytunnels have a large role to play, we would lose other things we value if we let them carpet too much of the land. Technophronesis in this case means allowing the new technology to play its role without allowing it to take over completely, reducing the countryside to a faceless, impersonal, ugly food factory.

Technophronesis means wanting the artisan to continue to thrive, even when machines can match or improve what she can make, because it understands that what matters is not just the result, but the process by which you get there. There is plenty that we will happily allow to be mechanised, for the obvious benefits it brings, but there are plenty of other things we will continue to prefer to be handmade, and food is one of them. We will appreciate the skill of the chef, baker or cheese-maker even if the results are not consistent. As Roger Longman, maker of the seasonally variable White Lake cheeses, puts it, 'If you want the same cheese every day, go to a supermarket.' We will understand the overworked host who has ordered a takeaway or heated up a ready meal, but we will appreciate more the one who has cooked for us, even if the results are not entirely to our taste. Even at a restaurant, where you pay for your food, the ethos should be one of hospitality, of the chef inviting you to enjoy what she has gone to much effort to prepare. The exchange of food is a human relationship, and humans are imperfect, so a world of technical perfection that denies the human element can never be truly perfect after all.

MACHINE BREAD

Just because you use a machine, it doesn't mean that everything you do must therefore become strictly mechanised. Bread machines come with recipe books, and you can buy others, but these should be used as a basis for experimental development, not as bibles.

For instance, my standard loaf was a combination of 5 flours in different proportions (about 30 per cent rye, 30 per cent spelt, 20 per cent wholewheat, 10 per cent oatmeal, 10 per cent white), which differed depending on what I had run out of. In some breads I put more olive oil than is suggested, which gives a different texture and flavour. I also used malt extract instead of sugar, as it adds another layer of flavour.

Machines can also make just dough, of course, which leaves you free to improvise what you do with it. I've found that a basic pizza or focaccia dough, for example, also works rolled thin and cooked in a pan as a flatbread.

I was a bit embarrassed when people complimented me on my bread and I always said, 'It wasn't me – it was the machine.' That's not quite right, though. It's the machine *and* me. Technology at its best does not take away all creativity and judgement, but allows us to extend those virtues to spheres where we would otherwise exercise none at all.

11

Don't be bored by routine

HEXIS

The Austrian philosopher Ludwig Wittgenstein was not exactly a bon viveur, and when it came to food, it seems he was particularly austere. It is perhaps revealing that in his masterwork, *Philosophical Investigations*, he uses three food examples, and one of those is of a cow munching grass. The other two both concern eating at the right time: 'I was thinking about my breakfast and wondering whether it would be late today' and 'Now, if I tell someone: "You should come to dinner more punctually; you know it begins at one o'clock exactly" – is there really no question of exactness here?'[63]

This sounds very much like the Wittgenstein portrayed by the economist John Maynard Keynes, who in a letter in 1929 wrote of his new acquaintance, 'My wife gave him some Swiss cheese and rye bread for lunch, which he greatly liked. Thereafter he more or less insisted on eating bread and cheese at all meals, largely ignoring the various dishes that my wife prepared. Wittgenstein declared that it did not much matter to him what he ate, so long as it always remained the same.'[64]

For those of us who really enjoy our food, this sounds somewhat dull and puritanical. Nevertheless, routine has its attractions. Wittgenstein is often described as being somewhat monastic in his single-minded dedication to philosophy, and it is a feature of life in a monastery that mealtimes are rigidly set, so you don't have to think about what and when you're going to eat. If you're a Benedictine, you'll have a choice of two hot dishes at every meal, as prescribed by the rule of its founder, but that's about as much thought as you'll ever need to put into it.

That is, of course, the point. If you are trying to serve God twenty-four hours a day, it is important that you do not get waylaid by relatively trivial questions such as whether the pesto will go better with orecchiette or spaghetti. For the same reason, wearing a simple habit every day means you don't have to think about whether to wear jeans or chinos. All that is inessential is codified into a routine so that your mind is free to focus on what really matters.

If you're neither a monk nor burdened by what Wittgenstein's biographer Ray Monk called 'the duty of genius', you might not think this applies to you. But surely we all suffer distraction from what is most important to us. In my case, I fight a constant battle against the entropy of my desk, the ever-rising tide of the inbox, commitments I stupidly agreed to months ago when I forgot yet again that it is never the case that 'Things should be quieter by then', domestic tasks, shopping and claiming refunds for late-running trains. Given most of these are unavoidable, the less I need worry about the avoidable, the better.

Having routines around food therefore makes perfect sense. Yet 'routine' has become something of a dirty word in a consumerist world where the only routine is the constant production of novelty and where stimulation is never more than a screen-tap away. We suffer from the wonderfully named thaasophobia: fear of boredom. Wittgenstein's 'the same thing every day' sounds like a modern idea of Hell. No wonder 'routine' has become a standard, dismissive adjective used by restaurant critics who can't fault the food but whose overstimulated palates can't be excited by it either.

There is, however, a good and useful form of routine that can be applied to various aspects of life, not just eating. It is captured in Aristotle's use of the Greek word *hexis*, usually translated as 'disposition' but sometimes as 'habit', since disposition and habits shape and reflect each other, two sides of the same coin. However, in English 'habit' has the unfortunate connotation of something you do thoughtlessly. You take the wrong exit on the motorway or pour milk into a guest's coffee when she wanted it black 'out of habit', because you weren't thinking about what was needed at that time.

This is not, however, what Aristotle meant at all. *Hexis* for him was an active condition, not a passive one. 'Mindless habit' is not a tautology, since habits can be mindful and deliberate. The monks provide a good example of this. It would be very easy for them to follow the strict timetable of the day in such a way that it became mechanised, just as at school we used to recite morning prayers like mindless robots; but it is not inevitable. What they aspire to is a mindful awareness of why it is they do what they do, so each repetition becomes not just a thing that happens but a reaffirmation of their commitment to God. Similarly, each meal is not something simply to be eaten, but a chance to thank the Lord for His bounty and to reflect on how the pleasures of the flesh are to be appropriately appreciated without their becoming objects of worship in themselves.

In order for non-believers to make good use of what Christianity has to say about food, we need to apply a kind of reverse transubstantiation and turn the body and blood of Christ back into bread and wine. Monastic life provides a helpful model of purposeful, mindful routine that secular life can mirror in several ways. After all, even foodies have routines. A few years ago a minor commotion was started when a survey revealed that a third of Britons ate the same lunch every single day, but this would not have been news if, instead of lunch, the survey had been about breakfast. For some reason, it is acceptable even for gourmands to have more or less the same breakfast every day, whereas routine in lunch and dinner is considered unimaginative and dull. Trying to make all three meals different from the ones you had yesterday would not only be burdensome, it would require devoting an inappropriate amount of mental energy to menu-planning. A healthy interest in diversity becomes an unhealthy neophilia if it is not balanced by some routine.

Since we all have a certain amount of routine in our lives, what matters is that we make sure we have chosen the right kind. Habits are only bad when we fall into them unthinkingly, and this is too often exactly what we do. In contrast, *hexis* is about freely and con-sciously choosing which routines to follow, regularly thinking about whether we ought to maintain the habits we have developed and being open to new facts or changing circumstances that might mean we ought to abandon or modify them.

Routine need not mean literally the same thing every day. It might mean the same excellent sandwich shop or café. Or it might mean the same basic thing, with variation. Even if you are literally having the same meal on a regular basis, such as curry on a Saturday night or a roast on Sunday, that does not mean it has to be eaten or prepared thoughtlessly. We are fortunate that whereas there are some foods we easily tire of, most people have a range of dishes they could happily eat regularly, if not for their whole lives, then at least for decades at a time. It is not just their familiarity that is reassuring – we really do enjoy them as much as surprising new dishes we might try at a restaurant. You'll have your own list. Mine includes pasta all'arrabbiata; risotto; cheese, bread and tomatoes; fish and chips; mar-mitako; eggs and mushrooms on toast. Their regularity on my table is not the product of laziness or unthinking habit. Rather, it is because they are perennial favourites that I prepare and eat them with care and relish.

The most positive exemplar of routine in food comes not from the cloisters of monasteries, but from the kitchens in countries with good food cultures. It is ironic that British and American foodies wax lyri-cal about the superiority of everyday Mediterranean cooking, yet those same *mammas* and *nonnas* they venerate are much less adventurous than their worshippers. For example, I ate several fantastic regional special-ties and Italian classics at a small family-run hotel in the Valle d'Aosta, but the cook told me she had never made a single foreign dish in her life. Similarly, when I visit family in Italy, I know that I am going to be fed one of a quite limited range of dishes by my relatives, the same ones that their mothers taught them. (The men of my aunts' and uncles' generation have been largely untouched by feminism.) Whereas in Britain people worry about serving guests the same thing they have made even once before, in Italy it is often the special of the house that you look forward to. There's a lovely example of this in Gianni Di Gregorio's wonderful film *Pranzo di Ferragosto* in which an elderly woman repeatedly goes on about how people always want her to make them pasta al forno. When my grandmother was alive, I would have been horrified not to have been given her fabulous home-made ravi-oli at Easter, and even today it would be disappointing to come home not having had a plate of risotto that remains inexplicably superior to any I've had elsewhere.

Even more extreme is the case of Jiro Ono, one of Japan's most feted sushi chefs, a true craftsman, a *shokunin*. A documentary film about him shows his obsession with routine, even to the point of always stepping onto his train to work from the exact same place on the platform. 'The way of the *shokunin* is to repeat the same thing every day,' says one of Jiro's former apprentices, Mizutani. And when Jiro's son goes on to open his own restaurant, the father's advice is, 'He should just keep doing the same thing for the rest of his life.' But of course this requires mindful attention, the opposite of mindless repetition. Perhaps this is connected with Zen Buddhism, which the film's director, David Gelb, suggests permeates the approach of all *shokunins*. It contains the idea that 'There are no large tasks and no small tasks; they're all of equal importance', so whatever you do in life, you must dedicate yourself to doing it as best you can. Routine is thus the path to excellence, not a dead end to sterility.[65]

The idea that novelty is a cardinal virtue in food can only emerge in a culture where the food tradition is weak and the daily menus not packed with favourites passed down the generations. Routine need not lead to boredom, but ironically, the constant pursuit of novelty can. There is nothing more tedious than culinary innovation for the sake of it. Every restaurant trend of recent decades, for example, has ended in a giant yawn, as yet another surprising savoury ingredient is put into an ice cream; food is delivered to the table in a tin pot, a brown-paper bag or anything other than a plate or bowl; dishes like lasagne arrive 'deconstructed', their various parts served side by side, not mixed.

The same thing every day may be too much, although for the small minority of 'fuelists' who simply get no pleasure from food, that probably sounds like heaven. But a measure of routine is good, for deepening our appreciation of the simple food we have and of those who have passed it down to us, as well as guarding ourselves against the avaricious, frantic pursuit of the next new flavour hit. The knack is not simply to fall into routines and be limited by them, but to choose them well, know why we're following them and hence be enriched and liberated by them.

SUGO DI POMODORO

There are as many ways to make a basic pasta sauce as there are pasta sauce-makers. The reason why Italians say no one makes a sugo like their mothers' is because this is literally true: everyone does it a little differently.

The principles are, however, simple: use good ingredients and ideally give the sauce plenty of time to concentrate. Two hours is not an unusually long time to allow a tomato sauce to simmer down.

The basis of any sauce is the sweating of some garlic and/or shallots or onions in some oil, not too hot. (I make no apology for so many of my suggestions starting this way. As Denis Cotter, the acclaimed head chef of Cafe Paradiso in Cork, has pointed out, this is how recipes 'almost always start' because 'a lot of the time it does contribute a lovely background mellow flavour.'[66]) Some add finely chopped celery. Before they have browned, add the tomatoes. A tin will do nicely. Fresh tomatoes, by themselves or as an addition, make for a different flavour, not necessarily better or worse. To peel them, score the flesh and plunge into just-boiled water for a minute or two and the skins will simply fall off.

From this base, the variations are almost endless. Dried oregano can be added early; fresh basil is best torn up and mixed in immediately before serving. Chillies, dried or finely chopped fresh, can be added just before the tomatoes. Anchovies should be gently dissolved into the warm oil right at the start. Chopped olives can be added with the tomatoes. Add tuna if you like, giving it time to break down and form an almost mince-like sauce. Or brown some minced lamb, beef or pork with the onions or garlic before adding the tomatoes for a meaty ragù. Try other things: some may work better than others, but unless you have no feel for food at all, you're unlikely to make something that isn't at least palatable.

Staples like these can become part of a routine that need not be unthinking. The possibility of endless small variations and the need to monitor each stage means that making a simple pasta sauce can become an always satisfying and never dull habit.

12

Add a generous pinch of salt

SCEPTICISM

> A few decades ago, the medical establishment told us that margarine was healthier than butter, eggs were bad – they raised cholesterol levels – and we should brush our teeth vigorously, especially after fizzy drinks. Now we know margarine is full of hydrogenated fats, the cholesterol in eggs has negligible impact on serum cholesterol levels, and brushing your teeth vigorously, especially after acidic drinks, erodes tooth enamel, and your gums. Thanks to the medical advice of the 1970s, I now have furred arteries, receding gums and I missed out on many fine omelettes.[67]

You often hear versions of this complaint by journalist Clint Witchalls. What you never hear is, 'Official advice on healthy eating is clear, consistent and makes perfect sense to me.' Yet this scepticism sits side by side in our culture with a remarkable willingness to buy into the latest health fads uncritically. The idea that carbohydrates are bad for you, for example, has quickly spread from faddish diets to the mainstream, with 'low carb' now being a key selling point for many products, whether buyers are trying to lose weight or not. Vegetable spreads that claim to reduce cholesterol fly off the shelves; a label pointing out the presence of omega oils boosts sales; and when something is declared a nutrient-packed 'superfood', consumption rockets.

It seems our scepticism is selective but not sufficiently discriminating. So what kind and degree of scepticism should we bring to the health claims made for food?

I'm not an expert on health, and I make no confident claims about what precisely we should eat or avoid, but given that the issue is in part about how much we should trust 'experts', I can't help but tread on their toes. So perhaps it is worth starting by sticking up for them a bit. Expert opinion on healthy eating actually tends to shift very slowly. In 1933, for example, the British Medical Association advised that we should obtain 12 per cent of our calories from protein, 27 per cent from fat and 61 per cent from carbohydrates.[68] Current official UK dietary advice is very similar: we should get 10 to 15 per cent of our calories from protein, 33 per cent from fat and 50 to 55 per cent from carbohydrates,[69] while the World Health Organization recommends a more elastic split of 10 to 15 per cent, 15 to 30 per cent and 55 to 75 per cent.[70]

The general message about eating plenty of fruit, vegetables and whole grains, while avoiding too many saturated fats and refined carbohydrates, has also been more or less the same for years. If the advice appears inconsistent, it is only because whenever a particular study suggests that part of the orthodoxy might be wrong, the media leaps on it and says, 'Scientist now say X is good/bad for you after all!' The scientists rarely say any such thing. What they almost always say is, 'This is a surprising result. More research is needed.' So it's the media, rather than health professionals, we should be most sceptical about.

Having said that, the health establishment can get it wrong, as it did horribly in the case of margarine. The consistent message for years, and still maintained by most today, is that saturated fat is a major cause of several health problems such as heart disease, whereas mono- and polyunsaturated fats, as found in vegetable oils, are much better for you. As a result, people were advised to cut down on butter and eat more vegetable margarines instead. From a culinary point of view, this was always a mistake. Butter is to margarine what a 2005 Château Lafite is to a 1979 Blue Nun. If it really was bad for you, then the answer would have been to eat less and spread thinner, not swap it for margarine, which tastes like a weak, viscous saline solution with an oily mouthfeel.

But it turned out the health advice was wrong too. The problem with margarine is that it is made from fats that are liquid at room temperature. In order to make them solidify enough to spread, they had to be subjected to an industrial process known as hydrogenation. This changed the chemical structure, creating trans fats, which are if anything more unhealthy than naturally occurring saturated fats.[71] Nowadays, almost all vegetable spreads do not contain these trans fats. Nevertheless, the margarine debacle has left me wary, so when I see adverts for olive-oil-based spreads showing vivacious Italian pensioners, I don't accept the assumption that because liquid olive oil as an integral part of the Mediterranean diet is good for us, so must be the solidified version spread willy-nilly over the British diet. Let's see. Or rather, let others see, because I'm not buying it. And I'll be similarly suspicious of any new foodstuff that contains apparently healthy ingredients that have been processed in novel ways.

The fundamental mistake with margarine was to make health claims based on too narrow a focus on a few known factors, considered in isolation. This tendency to home in on certain key nutrients also creates problems when assessing any data on the relationship between diet and disease. One example of a recent controversy around this concerned salt. The case for reduced sodium intake has been almost universally accepted, with manufacturers cutting down the amount they add to processed foods and many people avoiding sprinkling salt at the table. On the face of it, the evidence seems very clear. Salt raises blood pressure, and higher blood pressure leads to a higher incidence of cardiovascular disease. Case closed. Except that it isn't.

The problem is twofold. First, high blood pressure is not the only risk factor for cardiovascular disease. So we need to know whether reducing salt increases some of the others, and by how much, and it is not entirely clear how this all balances out. As Dr Michael Alderman, editor of *The American Journal of Hypertension*, says, 'A reduction of sodium by half will also increase sympathetic nerve activity, it'll increase aldosterone secretion, increase insulin resistance, and activate the renin-angiotensin system, another enzyme system in the body. All of those things are negative, [and] increase the risk of cardiovascular events. The health effect of reducing sodium is going to be the net impact of all of those factors.'[72]

Second, cardiovascular disease is not the only thing that kills you, and sodium is important to the proper functioning of the body. So what you really want to know is whether reducing salt in your diet is going to improve your health outcome overall and whether it might increase other risk factors for other diseases. Some studies have suggested that on balance, reducing salt intake does not reduce your health risks more generally.[73] Even if these findings turn out to be false, the general point remains: just because something decreases the risk of a particular condition, or one risk factor for one condition, that does not automatically mean that it improves your health or life expectancy overall. It's often unclear what unforeseen effects a dietary change might have that, in the round, might cancel out any benefits. So a good rule of thumb is that unless you have a specific condition or are in an identifiable high-risk group, there is little or no point in making significant adjustments to your diet on the basis of a general link between a certain food and certain conditions.

But what if you are in an at-risk group? In that case, the advice is '*Sapere aude*': check the evidence out for yourself. It is sometimes surprising how flimsy it is. The clearest example of this is official guidance on healthy weight, which is generally agreed to correspond to a body mass index (BMI) of 20 to 25. BMI is calculated on the basis of your weight proportionate to your height, age and gender. This is a proxy for body-fat ratio, the most accurate way of determining whether someone is carrying too much weight or not, but it is an imperfect one, since bodybuilders, for example, often have a high BMI, even though they are as lean as skinless free-range chicken breasts. It has been proposed that waist–height ratios are a more reliable indicator of body-fat ratios than BMI.

Even if BMI is a less-than-perfect tool for any given individual, it should, on average, be a decent indicator of what is healthy. So you would assume that when experts claim that 20 to 25 is ideal, there would be good solid evidence for that. As it turns out, it really doesn't seem that there is – quite the opposite in fact. A huge study of Canadians showed that if you plot a graph of BMI against mortality rates, the line forms a U shape, with the very underweight (BMI <18.5) and the very overweight (BMI >35) most likely to pop their clogs. So where would you expect the U to bottom out? Around 22 to 23, in the middle of the 20-25 range? Wrong. 'Overweight (BMI 25 to <30),' the authors of the study concluded, 'was associated with a significantly decreased risk of death.'[74] In other words, the people most likely to live longest are officially a little overweight. This finding is not a one-off. Other large-scale meta-analyses have concluded the same thing. As I was writing this chapter, another was published in *The Journal of the American Medical Association*, and once again the reaction of many was disbelief.[75]

And it gets worse. It is now widely agreed that unless you are severely over- or underweight, far more important than what you tip the scales at is whether you are fit. It also seems likely that it is better to be overweight because you eat too much of a good diet than to be at your ideal weight by eating the right amount of the wrong stuff. So people who eat well and are physically active with a BMI of 27 are generally healthier than those who maintain a steady 22 by leading sedentary lives but eating little more than processed, low-calorie foods.

And, of course, the thin smoker or slim heavy drinker is dicing with death far more than the slightly chubby, clean-living tennis player.

In this case, it is hard to avoid the conclusion that scepticism means never taking expert advice at face value. Again, however, in practical terms that doesn't leave us hopeless. The same general advice applies as it did to the cases of salt and butter. That is to say, if you're not at particular risk – in this case severely obese or underweight – don't worry too much about changing your ways to fit the official ideal. If you are considered at risk, however, check out the facts for yourself. And when you do, always remember to question advice that is based on looking at one variable and one variable alone. Find out what other variables, if any, the studies control. If, for instance, research shows that people who are officially overweight are more likely to suffer strokes, that could be because if you divide the population into those with BMIs over 25 and those with BMIs under, the former group will tend to contain more older people, people who eat badly or people who are inactive. Unless these variables have been controlled, the findings may show nothing about BMI per se at all.

One of the ironies of nutritional science is that the more we discover just how complicated it is, the simpler the principles we should use to eat become. I've called this Pollan's Paradox after the writer Michael Pollan, who reduced dietary advice to the now famous maxim: 'Eat food. Not too much. Mostly plants.'[76] Pollan realised that more complicated recommendations were based on the hubris of thinking we could know just how much of each specific nutrient provided the optimum nutrition, but trying to micro-manage a system we barely understand is hopeless. Just cook proper food from good ingredients and stop worrying.

Almost as simple is my recipe for a healthy scepticism about nutritional claims, which can be summed up in three principles: look for Moderation, Interrelation and Substantiation, which can remembered by the admittedly cheesy mnemonic 'Don't MIS the point.'

First, moderation. Away from the extremes, you don't have to worry too much. Even when things really are good or bad for you, the difference they make to your health only usually becomes significant when they are present in excess or hardly at all. If something is a natural foodstuff that has been eaten for centuries, that doesn't mean it's good for you, but it probably does mean that it won't do you much harm in moderation.

Second, interrelation. With some rare exceptions such as smoking, very few things either significantly help or hinder us in isolation. You can't just break down food into its component parts – fats, minerals, vitamins, carbohydrates, et cetera – and say, 'That is good. That is bad.' Foods don't kill us; diets do. You have to look at the whole package, including the way it fits together, rather than particular items in it.

Third, substantiation. You don't have to take things on trust. It's not as difficult as it might seem to check out the facts for yourself. Just look for reliable primary sources, not certain tabloid newspapers whose whole *raison d'être* is to scare their readers to death, or Internet chatrooms where conspiracy theorists, hypochondriacs and the worried well gather to convert the tenuous into received opinion.

Perhaps the most important thing of all is the nature of the underlying scepticism itself. Scepticism is often thought to be negative, and is often confused with cynicism. The scepticism I'd recommend, however, is the mitigated variety of David Hume. Hume realised that if you used reason to push any evidence-based belief hard enough, it would eventually fall down, and so 'We could never retain any conviction or assurance, on any subject.' No one can or should live like this. So scepticism requires a 'counterpoise', in the form of 'the more solid and more natural arguments derived from the senses and experience'. This is not quite common sense, but rather the things that experience has shown us to be true time and again. These can often be summed up in general rules of thumb, such as the fact that natural foods are healthier than highly processed ones, and that if a society has developed an eating tradition, it is probably basically sound. These are not by any means absolute truths and they will have any number of exceptions. The point is not to take them as unchallengeable dogmas, but simply to use them alongside what the harder-nosed use of reason suggests is true, but which we have not yet had time to test. In combining sceptical reason and knowledge from general experience, 'The one has no more weight than the other. The mind must remain in suspense between them.'[77]

That is a healthy scepticism, and one that will serve us well, though not infallibly, when we sit down to eat. It captures the most important form of scepticism of all: the belief that everyone is fallible and that even the surest knowledge might turn out to be false. It is also the logical consequence of taking the injunction '*Sapere aude*' to heart. If you dare to know, you soon discover how much you don't know. You also find that there is often no infallible logical, scientific or experimental method for determining with certainty what the truth is. Practical wisdom requires the use of judgement and so you end up with a somewhat sceptical view of our powers of reason and our capacity to know. But this is not a nihilistic, absolute scepticism, since the intellectual journey that has brought you to this point has shown that there is still a difference between better and worse arguments, robust inferences and fallacious arguments, uninformed opinion and justified belief. Embracing uncertainty is therefore not a recipe for despair but for holding more finely calibrated degrees of conviction. And if you do feel the need for a rock-solid certainty at the table, there is at least one. As Descartes might have put it, if I think I'm enjoying it, therefore I am.

CHARCUTERIE

If you're looking for the traditional foodstuff that most flies in the face of current health advice, head to the charcuterie counter. Red-meat consumption has been linked with colorectal cancer, while meats that are cured contain a lot of blood pressure-raising salt, and most contain the preservative sodium nitrite, associated with chronic obstructive pulmonary disease. In the UK over recent years we've been advised to eat no more than 70 grammes of red and cured meat per day,[78] and yet the best charcuterie is a pride and joy of the countries whose great Mediterranean diets we are supposed to emulate. Think of pata negra, chorizo and Serrano ham from Spain, or mortadella, salami and Parma ham from Italy.

Of course, there is absolutely no need to avoid these foods, not for health reasons at least. If you don't waste money eating a lot of cheap processed meat, you can just enjoy the best from time to time. I recently brought back a pack of pata negra de bellota from the great ham-producing town of Trevélez in Spain. Bellota is produced from the pork of pigs who spend most of their lives grazing freely in oak forests, eating lots of acorns. The pack weighed 100 grammes, and I ate half of it, which meant I was well under the daily recommended maximum – and I don't eat red meat regularly anyway.

The problem with ham, like cheese, is that the abundance of cheap, mass-produced varieties means that the quantity consumed has risen as its quality has fallen. We are then told we are eating too much and the good stuff gets tarred with the bad: sufficient grounds for scepticism about the idea that good charcuterie should be avoided.

Too much received wisdom about good eating is based around a list of foods we should avoid. Knowing how to eat, however, requires knowing about how, rather than what, not to eat, as I hope to show in the next section.

PART III

Not eating

You are what you don't eat too.

13

Resist the breakfast buffet

CHARACTER

Perhaps the strangest item in my biography is that I have made two cameo appearances in Alexander McCall Smith's The Sunday Philosophy Club series of novels. It all started when I interviewed him for *The Philosophers' Magazine*. We talked about his books' concern with issues of everyday ethics, like civility, consideration and honesty. It seemed to both of us that these were unjustly neglected by moral philosophy, which tends to focus on big issues like euthanasia, global poverty, war and climate change. I told him about the quotidian issue I would write about if I were to submit a paper to *The Review of Applied Ethics*, the fictional journal edited by the novel's protagonist, Isabel Dalhousie. 'Why don't you write to her and suggest it?' he asked. 'I might be able to get it into the next book.' So that's what I did.

23 September 2004

Dear Ms Dalhousie,

I am writing to see if you would be interested in a paper for your journal entitled 'The ethics of the breakfast buffet'.

I take as my starting point for this paper the observation that many people think it is acceptable to surreptitiously take items such as rolls and cheese from a hotel breakfast buffet in order to make a packed lunch for later. Others view this as not just a breach of etiquette, but as being in some sense morally wrong, even though they recognise that if it is indeed wrong, it is one of the least serious wrongdoings imaginable.

The question that interests me is whether these sometimes strong feelings of approbation are justified, and if so, why? My argument is that we take such small wrongdoings to be indicators of general ethical attitudes, and that these may indeed be morally significant. The person who steals from the breakfast buffet, for example, has an unhealthy degree of concern about maximising their own selfish interests, revealed by the fact that any small advantage they can gain is seized. Thus this tiny moral indiscretion reveals a more important character flaw.

I would be interested to hear whether this paper would be of interest.

Yours sincerely,

Dr Julian Baggini

Editor, *The Philosophers' Magazine*

Sure enough, in *Friends, Lovers, Chocolate*, McCall Smith has Dalhousie open her post to find a submission from me. Given that the subject concerned the importance of small matters, it is to my great shame that it took me six months to get round to writing to thank him. He then had Isabel think of me again in *The Careful Use of Compliments*, when she decides to invite me to join her editorial board.

I'd happily have accepted the invitation because I believe very strongly in the project of putting the quotidian at the heart of ethics: the question of how to live well. So far this book has attempted to demonstrate the importance of the everyday act of eating for ethics by focusing mainly on issues of interpersonal morality (Part I) and the use of reason and judgement (Part II). Arguably, however, the core of ethics is much more personal. It concerns our character, the ways in which everything we do, small or large, reflects values and virtues that are conducive to a good life, both for ourselves and those we interact with.

Character is related to, but not the same as, personality. Your personality is largely given to you by some combination of genes and environment. Personality traits are generally speaking ethically neutral. Introverts are not better than extroverts or vice versa. People who are more emotionally open do not necessarily behave better than those who keep their feelings more to themselves.

Character, in contrast, is ethical through and through. It is an ethical question how generous you are, for example, and it is not simply a matter of whether your personality disposes you to give more or less. Indeed, a person who is instinctively free and easy with her resources may be a poor exemplar of generosity, if she does not distribute it wisely.

To say character is ethical is not to say it always has a clear moral dimension. Ethics concerns everything about how to live well, and morality – which concerns our treatment of and obligations to others – is just a subset of that. So, for example, if you are not sufficiently discriminating in your choices of pleasures, that may not harm anyone else at all, but it will diminish your capacity to have a full, good life. In that sense, discernment is an ethical issue but not usually a moral one.

Character can also be built and developed, whereas your personality is generally stable and hard to change. So, for example, although your personality might make you flighty and impulsive, you may nonetheless develop the character to be able to make more reflective judgements about important matters before acting on them. A person who has worked on her character knows that some things are 'just the way I am', but will not see that as the last word, an excuse for behaving in whatever way comes most naturally.

As Aristotle first recognised back in Ancient Greece, if we want to live well, it is not enough to know how to treat others or to master the proper use of reason and judgement. We have to work on our characters, to become the kinds of people for whom doing the right thing becomes more natural than not. The everyday is not just the best domain for doing this; it is really the only one. You cannot establish good habits and settled dispositions in occasional short bursts; you have to work on them on an ongoing basis. That's why the whole idea of a 'character-building weekend' doesn't make much sense. Character cannot be erected in forty-eight hours; it has to be built day by day.

If that is so, then almost everything we do becomes a potential source of ethical insight. Your own ethical character is reflected in how you treat strangers or whether you drive courteously or selfishly. The ethical structure of society is reflected in what is sold by whom for how much; or by the extent to which citizens respect laws, traditions, social norms or religious injunctions; which pleasures are approved of or frowned upon.

Although there are innumerable potential sites of ethical insight in ordinary life, the breakfast buffet turns out to be a particularly rich source of reflection, as I was reminded when I negotiated one at a large corporate hotel hosting a conference. The buffet there was in many ways a microcosm of much that has gone wrong in our dealings with food. As is now usual, it offered a wide choice, but in this context more usually means worse. Eat what you like (or 'as much as you can', as many seem to interpret it) at low cost is only economically viable if you use the cheapest ingredients, or else trenchermen will scoff all your profits.

It also offered the convenience of being able to eat as soon as you liked, but all good food takes some time, even if it's only ten minutes. Not a single item in a cooked breakfast is improved by spending half an hour on a hot plate. I had to ask if the pot full of a greyish sludge the consistency of chicken stuffing really was porridge. I also saw dried-out, shrivelled sausages and trays of scrambled eggs, the edges of which had formed a kind of proto-crust.

Yet even those of us who know the food is going to be poor are to a certain extent sucked in by the promise of plenty. All-you-can-eat plugs into the primitive hunter-gatherer urge to stock up on calories while we can, for tomorrow we might starve. This is perhaps also why the majority have both the cooked and the Continental selection if they are included in the price, no matter how bloated they feel as a result. Indeed, it seems that for many there is no greater compliment you can pay a hotel or B&B than to report on how you could hardly walk after its breakfast. In all these respects, the breakfast buffet betrays all the vices of modern food shopping. Choice, quantity and convenience all trump quality, creating an illusion of value that in reality fails to appreciate the true value of food.

However good a cooked breakfast, and wherever it is served, there is also something revealed by the order in which it and the Continental selection are taken. When a breakfast is cooked to order, what is expected, and what almost always happens, is that guests help themselves to the Continental selection while waiting for the hot food to arrive. But why? Generally speaking, people eat savoury before sweet, yet at breakfast they will have sugary cereals and pastries before eggs and meat. Besides, you never know how large the hot breakfast you order is going to be. It would therefore make sense to wait and see before deciding how much other food you want to put into your stomach. But no, people dive in to the help-yourself cold selection before they've even seen their cooked breakfast. This order is so ingrained that where there is a hot buffet, and so the order of eating is not pre-determined, most people still have the cold items first.

I think all this reflects an excessively functional, distinctively Anglo-Saxon attitude to eating, which means spending no more time doing it than we need to. It is more efficient to use the time waiting for the hot food to get the cold stuff down us, even if that means guessing how much is enough and reversing the usual savoury-before-sweet preference. Convenience trumps all again, even the desire to feel comfortable. I really can't make sense of this in any other way: I have yet to hear another good reason why people should eat breakfast in the order they do.

I have got into the habit of eating the hot food first and only then deciding what else, if anything, I still want. The result is that the days of belt-busting mornings, made worse by the knowledge that what was eaten was not even that good, are long gone. I am so unusual in this respect that one B&B host told me she had literally never had a guest eat in this order in all the years they had been running the place. That is a frightening reminder of how unthinkingly we tend to follow convention.

Finally, there is the issue raised in the letter to Isabel Dalhousie. Many people can't see the problem. So much of a buffet gets wasted anyway that surely, if anything, it is wrong *not* to take some with you? At a very small hotel, what you don't eat may not get thrown away, but in any case, that's not the point. On a purely utilitarian calculus, I agree there is nothing or little wrong here: the direct consequences are probably, on balance, good, since the benefits to the pilferer are much greater than any cost, probably negligible, to the pilfered from. Nevertheless, to think about ethics purely in these terms is too restrictive. We need also to think about how our actions and attitudes shape who we are.

My concern is that by stealing from the breakfast buffet, we nurture characteristics of ourselves that are far from attractive: petty acquisitiveness, deceitfulness, satisfaction at getting one over on others, excessive concern with small material rewards. We do not become better people by having our self-interest radar on constant alert, always ready to take advantage of an opportunity. We may not harm others by acting on such grounds, but we harm ourselves, becoming diminished by our focus on trivial gains.

This argument is an Aristotelian one. As has already been noted, his key idea is that we become good people by cultivating habits of virtuous behaviour. Given that opportunities for great heroism or terrible vice are limited, the way we do this is by being good in myriad small, everyday ways. Although I'm broadly persuaded by this, I would add two large caveats. First, there is research in psychology that suggests character traits can be very situation specific. Someone who is very kind when times are easy may become a selfish egotist when his back is to the wall, for example. Similarly, the scrupulous respecter of the rules of the breakfast buffet may be less able to resist greater temptations.[79] So the point is not that doing the little things correctly guarantees we will become good people, but at the very least it helps. As long as we back up habit by regular reflection on why we continue to follow it, it can serve as a practical reminder of the virtues we want to uphold.

The second caution is that although in ethics the large may be written in the small, translating one from the other is a very tricky business. In the case of the breakfast buffet, for example, the secret hoarder may be motivated by perfectly respectable thrift or hatred of waste, or it might not have crossed his mind that an unauthorised takeaway raised ethical issues. We should not jump to conclusions about people's moral laxity on the basis of one or two little things they do that we think are wrong. After all, one negative character trait is being too judgemental of others, and that should not be fostered by small daily habits either.

In practice, deceit at the breakfast buffet is not necessary, since it usually turns out that just being honest has the same result. In a small hotel, if you ask if you can take some leftovers with you and they really are surplus to requirements, they'll probably let you. In a big chain, of course, the chances are they will follow company policy and much will indeed be wasted. In such circumstances, it may be that a little light-fingeredness is justified – I'm not sure.

Either way, the point is that how we behave at a breakfast buffet matters ethically, not because it presents chances for saintly or dastardly deeds, but because it is just one of the many little opportunities we get every day to exercise our virtues or nurture our vices. Attend to small and apparently insignificant actions and you'll often find something larger and more important lurking behind it: character.

GRANOLA

It is a source of too much pride to me that I eat hardly any prepared foods at home (with the caveat that, of course, basics like cheese and pasta didn't process themselves). One exception is granola. I once set out to remedy this, put off by the large quantities of sugar and vegetable oil found in many commercial varieties. Scouting for recipes, I found little agreement, and plenty that were as sugary and fatty as the shop-made varieties.

In the end I got quite close to making something good. I mixed jumbo oats, seeds and nuts with concentrated apple juice, enough to make it all stick together, but not in one gloopy mass. I then spread it out on a rimmed baking tray and cooked it at a very low temperature – around 140 degrees Celsius (280 degrees Fahrenheit, gas mark 1), but I think it should have been even lower. Every now and then I'd give it a stir to break it up. I took it out when it began to brown and left it on the tray to continue drying out. Once cool, it broke up even more.

That iteration was still, like ones I'd tried before, a little overbaked, especially the nuts: they probably need to be added right at the end. I didn't try again. I concluded that it was possible to be too keen to do it all yourself, and I had found two or three boxed varieties that were both very tasty and not too full of junk. Excessive rigidity about the desire to cook everything from scratch is not a character trait I wanted to reinforce. It would be wrong to become moralistic about what is in essence a luxury. Before the widespread use of domestic ovens, the poor did little home cooking as we would now recognise it. In the slums of the developing world, takeaways and simple restaurants are the cheap option, not an indulgence, since it is more expensive to buy the fuel to cook at home for a single family than it is for one person to cook for many. In the modern West, doing a lot of home cooking is the privilege of the time-rich, or at least time-flexible.

I've had one or two excellent home-made granolas elsewhere, so I'm not saying that you can't beat pre-packaged. All I am saying is that it's not always worth trying, if ready-made is already more than good enough.

14

Lose weight

WILLPOWER

'You're in denial, Jules.' The soundman was right. Strapping a microphone radio pack to my waist, he could see my stomach was too big for the trousers he was hooking them to. I had been determined not to go up (another) trouser size or a belt notch, but my resolve only involved compromises to my sartorial comfort, not my diet. My waistline had been expanding very gradually for several years, the millimetres becoming centimetres, then inches, and I wanted to stop the rot before it became a serious health issue. So I bowed to the seemingly inevitable and set out to lose weight.

Within six months I was more than 2 stone lighter. I now consider that a disaster, for reasons I'll come to in the next chapter. Nevertheless, it wasn't a complete waste of time. I did take some important lessons about willpower away from the exercise. In some ways I prefer the term self-control, because willpower can suggest that 'will' is some kind of special faculty we call upon when really it is no such thing. On balance, however, willpower is the term that most clearly identifies what I mean in this context: the ability to do what you have resolved to do even when you feel inclined not to.

This ability is something it seems the vast majority of dieters lack. Some lose their way by a thousand small violations. For instance, they will dutifully go to weigh their morning cereal portion, but while doing so, slip a mouthful or two extra straight into their mouths, kidding themselves it doesn't count. Dinner may be what they planned, but feeling they deserve a reward for their efforts, they have a glass of wine with it. Others go off the wagon in more extreme style. Mid-morning the dieter eats a whole, large bar of chocolate or two. Guilty, they will then miss lunch, but are ravenous again by mid-afternoon, when another calorific binge-snack is consumed. Others give up completely, throw off all restraint and spend days or weeks eating what they hell they want, as often as they want.

Why do we so often lack resolve? Often it appears to come down to impulse control: you may really, really want to lose weight, but faced with the temptation of a chocolate brownie, your desire only needs to overrule your resolution for a minute or two and your good intentions are vanquished. Experiments with toddlers show that even at a very young age, some people are able to resist or defer gratification better than others. This matters for more than just weight loss: it turns out that having good self-control is a very strong predictor of academic and career success. Psychologists Angela Lee Duckworth and Martin Seligman have conducted experiments that suggest that the ability to delay gratification predicts academic performance much better than IQ.[80] (Whether it is the *cause* of this success, however, is less clear.[81])

What makes the difference between those who have this control and those who don't? Brain scans will, of course, show differences in which areas of the brain light up, but this doesn't necessarily mean that it is all biologically determined. If I ask Fred to think of an image and Judy to think of a piece of music, their brain scans will show different patterns, but clearly my instruction is the main explanation for why they thought what they did, not anything inside the brain. There are some people who simply lack the right brain circuitry to exercise impulse control, but they are a small minority, not typical of the general population.

The key, it seems, is how much we are able to think about our thinking: 'metacognition', as it is known. In a classic experiment, children who resist taking a marshmallow that others gobble up don't desire it less; they are simply better able to distract themselves, or think of something else.

The importance of metacognition rings true in my own case. I really, really like food. If you think the reason I stayed on my diet wagon is that I just don't get tempted, you don't know me. I was able to resist partly because of a particular piece of metacognition known as an 'all-things-considered judgement'. The reason why many people fail to stick to their resolutions is that they think they have a clear goal, but they haven't actually thought about it enough, and are in reality much more ambivalent than they believe they are. So, for instance, they think they have decided definitely, clearly not to eat any sweet things, but they haven't fully taken into account the fact that they also believe, of any given cake, that it really wouldn't be so bad if they ate it after all, or that it is wrong to deny oneself too much, or that being good means giving yourself some reward. So when faced with temptation, one of these reasons becomes the basis for the judgement 'Go ahead.'

This also points to the importance of what in the addiction field they call bright lines: limits that you just don't cross, not even with a toe. The importance of bright lines is to eliminate discretion. The moment you give yourself options, the possibility of weakness of will forming a coalition with self-deception becomes too high. Take the rule 'Don't drink too much.' How much is too much? Not one more, surely? Not one more after that? You can see where that is going. The same applies for too much cake. A little bit? A little bit three days in a row?

When you have bright lines, it's easier because you know exactly what you have to do and you don't have to think about it. No alcohol today is pretty clear. If you are offered a drink, you know the only way to stick to your intention is to say no.

There are problems, of course. First of all, if you don't sincerely believe the bright lines matter, when it comes to the crunch, you may be willing to cross them. So, for instance, if you really don't think one drink makes any difference, then the bright line may not do its job in stopping you having one. So it's not enough to draw a bright line; you have to believe in respecting it.

The other main problem comes if the line is in too restrictive a spot. Trying to lose weight is not a life-or-death matter, and if everywhere you see delicious food there's a line saying 'Do not cross,' life can become miserable and claustrophobic.

So how do you draw bright lines that work? First of all, it is important to remember that, in a strange sense, they are always drawn somewhat arbitrarily. Take the intention to quit smoking. It will always be true of any given cigarette that it doesn't matter if you smoke it. It makes no difference if this fag is the last one, or the next one is, but, of course, if you had that thought every time you had to decide whether to smoke or not, you'd never give up. What you have to realise is that it is arbitrary which cigarette is your last, but one has to be. You then pick the arbitrary one and stick to it.

Losing weight is similar. It is always true that it doesn't matter whether you have any given drink or slice of cake. It won't make a difference to whether you ultimately lose weight or not whether you use oil in the particular dinner you're making. Any individual choice is too small to matter, but in order to stop the small choices accumulating, you need to just say, 'These are the rules and I'm going to stick to them.' Taken individually, each choice is arbitrary, but it is not arbitrary to say that you will allow yourself no discretion in any individual case, because that is the only way to make sure that the plan works.

It does, however, help to remember the arbitrary nature of each individual prohibition if you lapse. Then it really can help to say, 'That doesn't matter, just as long as I don't do it again.' Unfortunately, people often get so convinced that they have to follow the rules that they feel one lapse has ruined it, so they may as well smoke the whole packet, drink the whole bottle or eat the whole cake.

As well as the idea of bright lines, the addiction field also bequeaths us another technique for exercising willpower: urge surfing. As I discovered, although there are strategies for reducing the hunger caused by losing weight, there is no safe way to avoid it. In dieting, there's no such thing as a free skipped lunch, but you can 'surf' the urges hunger induces. The first time I did this was completely accidental. Travelling to a meeting, I was feeling so hungry I thought I'd have to have a banana, but I didn't have one on me, and by the time I had the opportunity to buy one, my pangs had abated a little and it was getting closer to lunch, so I didn't. Something similar happened a few days later and I learned the simple lesson that sometimes you can just ride out desires and they pass. A craving that is not satisfied will often give up and go away.

I've been urge-surfing ever since. It doesn't mean never acting on hunger, but simply giving it a chance to ease of its own accord. And if it doesn't? The back-up comes from mindfulness meditation. The idea, applied to diet, would be that you observe your hunger in a somewhat detached way. The thought 'I am hungry' is not usually experienced as a mere report. It has the implied corollary that I should do something about it. The challenge is simply to allow the thought be a thought. 'I'm hungry.' Well spotted! And your point is? Nothing. Just that I'm hungry. It's OK to be hungry. People get used to much worse chronic pain. It sounds obvious: just as you don't need to have sex or masturbate every time you feel a bit aroused, you don't have to eat every time you feel hungry. Just accepting that – really accepting it, believing it – makes a lot of difference.

Perhaps one of the most important lessons psychology teaches about self-control is that conscious willing has a rather limited role to play, sometimes even a counterproductive one. This has been a recurring theme of work on appetite, which I got to discuss with three leading researchers in the area over a suitably modest lunch: Jeff Brunstrom, Peter Rogers and Charlotte Hardman from the University of Bristol. 'From a psychologist's perspective, it's a mistake to say that control has to be conscious,' Brunstrom told me. There is such a thing as effortful deliberative cognition, 'where we battle and wrestle with our own appetite perhaps and then reach a point where we decide, almost against our will, to stop eating'. But he thinks it is 'a mistake to assume that when we don't do that, there's a lack of cognitive control' or 'to think that automatic behaviours are somehow bad and conscious controls are somehow good'. Consider, for example, driving. Obviously you are controlling the car – what else could be? But at any given moment you are often not conscious of what you are doing, and it would be odd to conclude that therefore your mind is not engaged in the task.

When it comes to appetite and eating, Brunstrom and others have found that 'There isn't a very strong relationship between capacity to engage in dietary restriction – to consciously restrict intake – and [low] BMI. If anything, it's the opposite: people who are heavier tend to engage with that kind of behaviour.' Why that should be so is not entirely clear, but work by Brunstrom's colleague Peter Rogers suggests that the constant engagement with the effortful mental activity of restriction could result in degraded cognitive performance. In effect, you're expending so much energy making one kind of mental effort that you don't leave yourself enough for others. This suggests that although metacognition can be useful in impulse control for one-off temptations, relying on it as a medium- or long-term strategy may not work.

It also turns out that what we judge to be 'enough' has little to do with how the food physically affects us. 'With a typical meal you're getting nowhere close to maximum fullness,' says Rogers, 'so the change in bodily sensation is relatively small.' That's why amnesiac patients who soon forget they have eaten a full meal will happily down another. 'They don't feel fullness,' says Brunstrom. 'They just feel discomfort.' Similarly, people given bowls of soup that are, unbeknown to them, being constantly refilled from a hole in the bottom will end up eating much more than they ordinarily would, because in their heads it's just one bowl.

What is going on in these and similar cases is that there is what Brunstrom calls 'a fine-tuning of feedback from the gut', which can be based on a memory of what you've eaten, beliefs about how filling it is or perceptions of how big it is. The good news is that if you do want to control what you eat, there are plenty of things you can do to affect all these and pull the unconscious levers of appetite. One of the simplest is planning. People tend to eat what is in front of them and, as long as it is not too meagre, be satisfied. Cook or order the right amount and you're less likely to over-eat. What you need to counter is the natural evolved tendency to play safe, which in this case means erring on the side of too much rather than too little. This leads to what I call the tapas paradox: when ordering in tapas bars, people almost always ask themselves, Will that be enough? and order one more plate just in case. Yet this is just the rare kind of restaurant situation in which under-ordering is no problem at all, because you can always order more later. The little rule we should internalise here and at all times is that when you ask, Will that be enough? assume that it is, knowing that it is almost always possible to get a little something else after if it isn't.

Attention also matters. People eat more when distracted, either by other people (the more people around a table, the more people eat) or by the television. That's why Brillat-Savarin was right to say, 'Gourmandism is the enemy of overindulgence,' because the gluttons are the ones who just munch what is in front of them while their minds are elsewhere.[82] Similarly, the philosopher Barry Smith told me, 'People who are bingeing are the people who are not getting enough pleasure and enjoyment from their food, so they're constantly seeking gratification: "That didn't work. Give me another doughnut."'

How filling you believe the food will be also affects how much you eat. That's why small plates are advised: the same amount of food looks like less if put on a large one. Brunstrom et al. have also shown that how meals are described can affect satiety. People felt fuller for longer if they believe they had eaten from Marks & Spencer's 'Stay Fuller for Longer' range, whether they had done so or not.

All this work underlines the idea that we are creatures of mind and body, conscious thoughts and unconscious processes, and these can only be separated somewhat artificially. We quite literally think with our stomachs, since we have around 100 million neurons in our guts.[83] This is known as the 'enteric nervous system', dubbed by some researchers our 'second brain', and it affects the way we think and feel. Brunstrom says that it is not helpful to conceive of our psychology and physiology as two different systems. 'You have to treat the person in the round.'

Willpower thus turns out to be a complicated, many-faceted thing. Increasingly, however, people are looking to lose weight by medical interventions instead. Chief among these is bariatric surgery, which covers a range of procedures, divided into two main types. The first is aimed at increasing malabsorption, meaning it prevents the body from properly digesting foods and so means more is excreted as unprocessed waste. This is what happens after a gastric bypass. The second reduces the size of the stomach, by stapling it or inserting things like gastric bands.

Researchers have found that 12 months after such operations, patients had lost on average 58 per cent of excess weight, and recorded improvements in hypertension, dyslipidaemia, type-2 diabetes and sleep apnoea. It sounds less impressive when you realise that this vindication of bariatric surgery comes courtesy of the National Bariatric Surgery Registry (NBSR). Nevertheless, the study appears to be reasonably robust and broad, based on data from eighty-six hospitals.

One doctor, commenting on the website of the GPs' magazine *Pulse*, captured a very common reaction to this kind of news: 'I've a better idea – and can prove it works. Eat less – move more . . . It's a sad reflection of today's society's increased learned helplessness that people don't take responsibility for their own health. There's almost no excuse for being fat.'[84]

He has a point, although it has to be remembered that a significant minority of the obese have real physiological problems. One should not dismiss psychological causes of over-eating either. Many pile on the pounds when depressed or stressed, and telling such people they just need to get a grip is rarely effective. Nevertheless, it is surely true that some, if not most people are severely overweight simply because they have eaten too much due to lack of self-control.

Whatever the causes of obesity, why is it that so many people feel indignant when it is treated by surgery? Why do people seem to think that people *ought* to lose weight by willpower alone? There is certainly no general principle that says we ought to do nothing that reduces our reliance on willpower. We may admire people who come off drugs by sheer determination, but if there are medicines people can take to reduce their cravings, we generally think it is right and proper they should take them. When people try to lose weight, we think they are wise to avoid having temptations around the house. We'd think someone foolish, not virtuous, for filling their fridge with cakes and cheese in order to test their willpower to the limit. So why should we object to surgical procedures that make losing weight much less reliant on willpower?

I struggle to find a good answer to this. Sure, it would be wrong simply to give surgery to people as a first option. We want to encourage people to eat well, and surgery always carries risks. But no one is seriously proposing bariatric surgery as the first response to being overweight. Its effectiveness is being championed for people who are morbidly obese, not just fat. If surgery helps them, and reduces the cost of dealing with the ongoing health problems they will have if they remain obese, it would seem to be a good thing. And if the whole point of exercising willpower is to do what you have resolved to do even when you feel inclined not to, then changing your inclinations seems to be a sensible way of achieving the same result.

Willpower may not always be the best form of self-control, but it is nonetheless a capacity we should prize. Even if your only motivations are hedonistic, you often get more pleasure if you have the ability to exercise some measure of restraint. Most obviously, your medium- to long-term happiness is not served by pleasurable actions with serious negative consequences down the line. The clever hedonist takes into account future pains and pleasures, not only those right in front of him or her.

Even if there is no long-term harm caused by an indulgence, there is still the possibility of what economists call opportunity costs: the loss you suffer because an alternative option might yield even more benefits. Kierkegaard illustrated this brilliantly in his *Diary of a Seducer*. The seducer is the epitome of someone who lives in what Kierkegaard calls the aesthetic sphere. His life is dedicated to immediacy, the thrill of the moment, but as a connoisseur of the sensual world, he appreciates that the best such moments require preparation, and so taking more pleasure now may deny greater pleasure in the medium term. He could sate his lust easily with prostitutes or women as loose as he is, but his seductions are all the sweeter for being hard won.[85] I should point out that Kierkegaard doesn't advocate this kind of life. Ultimately, he thinks living for moments of pleasure only satisfies the part of our nature that is trapped in the present, not that other part that is extended over time. Nevertheless, his account does show how the heights of aesthetic experience are not gained simply by always acting immediately on the desire we feel. Willpower is as useful for aesthetes as it is for ascetics.

It is not simply that the longer the deferral of pleasure, the greater it is. Rather, for every kind of pleasure, we have to balance the benefits of delay and gratification. Take the simple example of cake. Eat it every day and (for most people) it ceases to be such a wonderful pleasure, but that does not mean that if you eat it only once a month, you'll get more than thirty times the satisfaction from that one slice. I think I'd get optimal hedonic value out of cake by eating it two or three times a week, which is sadly a couple of times too many for my lifestyle and metabolism.

Having said all this, we should be careful to distinguish delaying gratification from denying it. The desire not to act on desires can morph into the puritanical belief that all worldly pleasures are in some way distractions or traps. We do not want to become like Francis of Assisi, who, according to a contemporary biographer, believed, 'It is impossible to satisfy need without yielding obedience to pleasure.' On the rare occasions on which he 'allowed himself cooked food', he 'would often mix it with ashes, or quench its flavour with cold water'.[86] For me, self-control is not a way of avoiding the evil temptation to enjoy yourself. Rather it is simply a means to enjoy oneself more deeply, and to keep in mind the fact that enjoyment is not all there is to life.

I certainly learned a lot about how willpower works when I lost weight, and the combination of setting fairly clear bright lines, formulating all-things-considered judgements, being mindful of hunger and practising urge-surfing were sufficient to do the job, in the sense that I stuck to my plan and hit my target weight ahead of schedule. Unfortunately, it turned out to be a pyrrhic victory. I had successfully stuck to an ultimately unsuccessful plan.

SOUP

Soup has been a dieter's weapon of choice for decades. Being virtually all water and vegetables, there's almost no limit to how much of it you can eat without consuming too many calories. It makes you feel full, so you don't notice the calorific deficit too much, and it also has the advantage of being very tasty indeed.

For many years soups were somewhat unfashionable, perhaps because of their association with the banal 'soup of the day' (almost invariably cream of tomato) offered at local bistros in the 1970s. More recently, food writers and home cooks have come to love them again. Specific soup recipes, however, are completely unnecessary. All you need to know are how soups in general are made, have an idea of what would make a good combination of ingredients and then experiment away.

Although there are some exceptions, almost all soups start with the slow softening in a pan of aromatic vegetables like shallots, garlic, onions, celery or peppers. It's trial and error to discover which soups you think work best with oil or butter. A general rule of thumb I've heard, which works more often than it doesn't, is that if it's dug out of the ground, it loves butter, whereas if it grows on a vine, it loves oil.

Towards the end of this softening, you can add spices. If using meat, you'll brown it quickly in the pan at this stage too. Then you add your main chopped vegetables, beans and pulses if using and a stock. All the chefs will tell you to make your own stock, but although I cook almost entirely from raw ingredients, I fear life is too short for this, so most of the time I simply use a good bouillon. I also use enough spices, herbs and aromatic ingredients to ensure I'm not relying on the stock to give all the flavour. How much stock you add simply depends on what kind of soup you're after: a liquidy, brothy one or a thick, almost stew-like one.

Add dried or robust herbs as you bring it to a simmer, and more delicate ones like fresh basil or parsley at the end. Herbs often make the difference between a good soup and a bland one. Once again, you have to experiment with combinations, but rosemary works very well with many vegetables and white beans. More variation comes from the addition towards the end of rice, pearl barley or small soup pasta. One final option is whether to then make a smooth soup with a blender. I sometimes like to use a potato masher to make it smoother without turning it into a purée. Or you can remove half, blend that and then return it to the rest.

How long do you cook a soup for? Again, it varies, but many soups really benefit from a good, slow simmer of up to two hours, which is how my Italian grandmother made her minestrones. It allows the flavours to really concentrate. Most also taste better the next day.

The beauty of soup is that the principles are easy, but they allow for so much variation and experimentation. Some of my favourite combinations are: a simple minestrone, with carrots, celery, potato and oregano; a clear broth with cannellini beans and rosemary, perhaps poured into a bowl with some wilted spinach and drizzled with lemon juice and olive oil; and my smooth, thick 'red soup' of tomatoes, sweet potato, red pepper, red lentils and carrot with pimentón and cumin.

15

Keep weight off

HUMILITY

Even as people were congratulating me on my new svelte shape, I was reminding them, and myself, that losing weight is, relatively speaking, the easy bit. The really hard thing is keeping it off. Even when people who follow a diet succeed in losing serious weight, almost all put it back on again, often within a year, and many end up heavier than they started.[87] The depressing conclusion reached by Janet Tomiyama, co-author of a UCLA analysis of thirty-one long-term studies of dieting, is that 'One of the best predictors of weight gain over the four years was having lost weight on a diet at some point during the years before the study started.'[88]

Of course, I didn't seriously believe I would be one of these recidivists. For one thing, it had been such an effort that I was determined not to let all that hard work go to waste. But at the time of writing, here I am, eighteen months later, my weight (but oddly not my waist) more or less back to where it was. That is not, however, the most humbling aspect of the entire experience.

I have discovered things about myself over the last few years that have not made me proud. Feeling hungry and low on energy day after day often badly affected my mood. The best way I can describe it is being short: short of energy, short of patience, short of temper and short with people. None of this should be surprising since my blood was often short of sugar. Unfortunately for my partner, the main manifestation of this was domestic. She knows me well enough to have learned that, for me, the equation 'tired x hungry = grumpy + irritable' is pretty much an inviolable law of nature, so this wasn't so much the discovery of a shocking new side of me as more frequent visits from my least noble side.

More troubling, perhaps, is how I sometimes behaved out and about. I found myself being visibly irritated in queues, even though it was not the fault of the person serving me. My elbows came out in crowds, even though other people were as stuck in them as I was. Worst of all, I once stuck two fingers up at an officious woman directing us at a car-boot sale. I meant to do it behind the car door, out of sight, but I'm pretty sure she saw me. This is shaming and pathetic stuff.

I also found myself being more forceful in discussions and less tolerant about slips in time schedules. 'Being on a diet has made these failings more obvious, regular and acute. But they always existed,' I wrote in a journal at the time. 'My hope is that I have been prodded to address them so that even when the diet is over, I will be something of a reformed character.'

You may well laugh. Even as I was apparently humbly accepting my failings, I hubristically believed that I could readily correct them. But ending the diet did not mean instant reversion to my previous, more placid self, let alone the birth of a new, improved one. I picked up bad habits that I think I still have not entirely shaken off. What losing weight exposed is nothing other than a slightly exaggerated version of my normal self. I have witnessed *in fames veritas*, the truth in hunger, and it is not flattering.

There is some reassurance in the fact that many of my weaknesses are just general human failings. For example, psychologists have identified a phenomenon known as ego depletion.[89] It is as though we have a finite supply of willpower, so if we use it up on one thing, we have little or none left for anything else. That's why you shouldn't try doing two things that require a lot of application at the same time. And that's probably also why although I got quite good at accepting and observing my feelings of hunger during the afternoon, I had run out of patience by the time dinner was late.

This is just one of the ways in which losing weight made me realise how much I was in hock to biochemical processes that I could not control. To take another example, psychologists have also shown that our ability to stick to a resolution depends a lot on blood sugar level.[90] So in a kind of evil trick played on dieters by nature, eating less makes it harder for you to resist eating more.

Becoming aware of how much the state of my mind depended on the state of my body was disconcerting for several reasons. First of all, it was a striking reminder that, however much a person may try to live the life of the mind, or even of the spirit, we are very much animals. Whether we are good or bad depends on many things, but at any given point one of those reasons may simply be that our body chemistry is a certain way. You may say, given the relative mildness of the changes that came over me, that I could be overstating this. On the contrary, what is troubling about my case is that if simply eating less can noticeably change how I am, then how much could more serious bodily imbalances transform a person? You may think that Geraldine is a nicer person than Gerald, but it may just be that Geraldine's body provides a more benign environment for gentle feelings, while Gerald's is creating emotional turmoil.

That invites questions about the extent of our free will. Free will is a notoriously difficult issue, but we can park the deep, metaphysical question about whether all we do is ultimately the effect of physical causes acting on and in the brain and body, beyond our control. Whether or not we are 'ultimately' free in this sense, there is still a difference between acting freely on the basis of decisions made by ourselves (albeit operating purely according to the laws of physics) and being forced to act against our wills by someone else. Similarly, there is still a difference between choice when sober and actions made under the influence of a powerful drug.

In some sense, this must be true, but my dieting experiences and the psychological research I have read raises the worry that the difference is not as clear as it might seem. Perhaps more choices and actions than we'd care to think are in fact a direct result of nothing more than hidden processes in the blood: we are as much puppets of hormones and blood sugar as drunk people are of alcohol, or potheads are of marijuana. We only notice this when our body chemistry changes. But if it is true that I was being short only because of the way my body temporarily was, isn't it equally true that I am not usually short only because of the way my body normally is? Someone who is crabby most of the time is not a worse person than me – they simply have the kind of system that I, fortunately, only have to put up with during and after dieting.

There is one potential consoling thought here. As I've said, it is not as though I am totally out of control. I can catch myself, apologise and adjust to some extent. Perhaps this is what free will, for want of a better name, is really about. How we feel, think or act immediately is too automatic for us to be blamed for. Maybe you can't help a stab of *Schadenfreude*, a snort of derision or a pang of envy, but you can help what you do with that feeling. You can choose to act on it or not, and you can also choose how you act in the future to minimise or reduce such feelings. The paradox is that in order to be more in control in this way, you often have to accept the many things you cannot control. Free will is not, then, about our ability to be right or wrong first time. It's about our ability to correct ourselves.

Seeing my worst side, recognising how feebly I am able to resist small biochemical changes, coming face to face with the limits of my free will, I've had to eat so much humble pie it's no wonder my waist has expanded again. What is most frustrating is how close I was to knowing all this when I started. It was there in the fundamental principle I based my regime on, if only I could have seen it.

The basic insight is that the reason most dieters piled the pounds back on after they had lost weight is that what people do while they are dieting is not sufficiently continuous with what they do afterwards. To work, losing weight has to be continuous with keeping it off. This is something Aristotle would have understood. Aristotle argued that knowing rules is not good enough, because we are creatures of habit and cannot always (or even mostly) stop and think about what the right thing to do is when confronted with every single choice.

Dieting usually works against the grain of habit at both ends. When you go on a diet, you are asked to radically change what you eat from day to day. This makes sticking to the rigid new regime very hard. And once you've stopped it, the diet you go back to bears little relation to the one you've been on. This means you have learned next to nothing from losing weight about how to keep it off.

Some diets recognise this and try to address it. These are the ones that advocate changing the way you eat for the rest of your life, but almost always this ends up making unrealistic demands, especially if you're the kind of person who enjoys food, and life. The GI diet, for instance, classifies as red-light foods – things you should almost always avoid for ever – cheese, full-fat yoghurt, bagels, gnocchi, pizza, melons, tortillas and more than one alcoholic drink per day. I'm sorry, but that ain't gonna happen. Similarly, I'm sure that most people evangelical about one of the various fasting diets fashionable as I write – in which you severely restrict calorific intake anything from one to three days a week – are not going to carry on with such a disruptive practice for the rest of their lives.

So the core principle for dieters is simple: don't change your diet; make changes *to* your diet. Simply start with what you normally eat and make adjustments. Easiest of all is reducing the extra, empty calories, such as alcoholic drinks, cakes and sweet treats. I say reduce, not eliminate, because weight loss takes time, and it is not realistic to expect people who enjoy wine and cake to have none at all for six months or more.

I remain convinced that the principle is right, but my execution of it was completely wrong. Although I did not radically change the kind of thing I was eating, the difference in quantity between the diet and normal life was too great. Losing over 2 stone in 5 months sounds great, but the golden rule of dieting is always that the more gradual the weight loss, the more sustainable it is. Being as severe as I was messed me up, psychologically and probably physically. Apart from provoking the negative changes in temperament, it encouraged me to be far too fixated with the next meal. Consequently, even when the diet was over, I carried over some of the mentality of thinking about when I was next *allowed* to eat. This is very different from the genuinely healthy attitude to quantity, which is to think, When am I *ready* to eat next? At the time of writing I am still trying to shift these habitual attitudes, I would say with some success were it not for the fact that I remember saying similar things about other changes I thought would do me good.

The evidence seems overwhelming that five months of consuming fewer calories than I expended led to metabolic and hormonal changes that didn't help once the diet was over. If our bodies do not get enough food, they find ways of slowing down so that they need less. As one recent study summed it up, 'Caloric restriction results in acute compensatory changes, including profound reductions in energy expenditure.' These changes persist even when you stop dieting: 'A disproportionate reduction in twenty-four-hour energy expenditure persists in persons who have maintained a reduced body weight for more than a year.' So if, when you've finished your diet, you go back to eating what used to be enough to keep you at a steady weight, it will now make you fatter. The same study established that the hormones regulating appetite also get out of kilter, making you want to eat more than you need, again for up to a year after you stop dieting.[91] In my case, I am convinced such a change must have occurred, because I definitely did not go back to old habits and yet

I was still putting on weight much more quickly than before. It took about a decade of marginal over-eating for me to put on about 10 kilos; it took a year of more moderate eating to put back on 10 of the kilos I had lost.

It may be the case that even reducing weight gradually often won't work in the long run. Many researchers are persuaded by the evidence that the body is a kind of homeostatic system that regulates its calorific intake to remain at a steady weight, one set by a combination of genes and environment, particularly childhood experience.[92] The most intuitively plausible evidence for this is that the difference between over-eating and under-eating seems to be too marginal for it to be the result of conscious choice. Take my example. In total, I had put on about 15 kilos in 15 years. That's an average gain of 1 kilo per year, which according to nutritional orthodoxy means I had been eating 7,700 calories more per annum than I expended in energy. In weekly terms, that's just under 150 calories. So for all the preachy comments I might get about eating too much cake and drinking too much wine, by standard measures my 'over-eating' amounted to the equivalent of one large banana a week. Or to put it in terms of under-exertion, I was not doing enough exercise by about four minutes of normal-speed walking a day.

But if such small margins really made a difference, and since we have no instinctive idea how many calories foods contain, you'd expect weight to yo-yo considerably. Yet it doesn't. Why not? Because the body is good at regulating itself. It's only if we massively over- or under-eat that we blow up or whittle down to something far from the 'set point' weight our body decides it wants to be. The biology of this turns out to be very complicated, but in general terms there are hormones that the body produces, most notably leptin, that tell the brain whether it needs food or not. This is what determines whether you feel hungry. In everyone there is a time lag, which is why it is advised that if you still feel hungry after having cleared your plate, you wait at least twenty minutes before eating more. But it also seems to be the case that some people's appetite hormones are better calibrated than others.

Knowing this can be a terrible excuse, of course. There are people who have put on weight simply by eating much more than they knew they needed, and that error can be corrected, as long as it is done gradually. In my own case, the fact that I feel hungry quite a lot does not mean I am compelled by my body to satisfy the craving. I also think there is a difference between hunger – the feeling that you need to eat – and appetite – the feeling that you want and are ready to eat. I have sometimes thought that the difference between my actual weight and my ideal one is no more than the difference between my appetite and my hunger.

So I sit here now humbled by both my personal failings and the inherent difficulties all humans have in taking charge of the one thing of which they are supposedly sovereign: their own bodies. My only consolation is that humility, so long as it does not descend into pointless self-loathing, is a virtue. No one becomes a lesser human being by becoming more aware of their limitations. While it would be wrong to become apathetic in the face of them, it is only by fully knowing the limits of our powers that we can make the most of the ones we have, and perhaps even learn how to increase them.

TRUFFLE OIL

Peter Sanchez-Iglesias of the Michelin-starred restaurant Casamia in Bristol told me that there is an easy way of making very good, expensive food: use very good, expensive ingredients. For a chef, however, this is boring. 'You can get a tin of caviar, open it, serve it,' he says. 'If you do anything else to caviar, you ruin it.' Other very expensive ingredients like foie gras (if you believe there are genuinely ethical versions) and lobster are also spoiled by being prepared in overly fussy ways.

For that reason, I would nominate truffle oil as an unlikely vehicle of culinary humility. What the oil shows is that for all you think you may be a great cook, sometimes it really is just the food, not you. Oil infused with truffles (not truffle flavourings – beware cheap imitations), for example, will lift virtually any egg dish: try it with scrambled eggs or in a frittata. It also goes wonderfully with mushrooms, so a risotto con funghi can be made that bit better by a drizzle of the wonder oil.

You might wonder how on earth such a luxury ingredient can be presented as a paradigm of humility. Actually, given you use only a few drops, it's no more expensive per serving than a large dollop of ketchup. More profoundly, humility is not about self-denial, hair shirts and asceticism. Humility is just about accepting your limitations, and often it is the very best that induces this feeling in us. What makes me most humble as a writer is the genius of others, and one of the things that makes me most humble as a cook is knowing that it wasn't because of me that the meal was so good; it was just a few drops of a fantastic ingredient.

16

Fast

AUTONOMY

I have never tasted polenta or cauliflower like it. Credit is due to the cook, my friend George, but perhaps not all, for this is the meal that has broken a ten-day fast, and the cheese and butter it contains have both been forbidden ingredients. Absence makes the tastebuds fonder.

If you say you are fasting today, people tend to assume that you are doing it for either religious or health reasons: detoxing your body or soul, purging sins or fat. They might also assume you are eating nothing at all, although traditionally most fasts have imposed selective, not global, restrictions on eating. I've had to throw the *Oxford English Dictionary* at more than one person who has misunderstood this: 'To abstain from food, or to restrict oneself to a meagre diet.' The recently revived Catholic Friday fast, for instance, simply requires followers to 'abstain from meat, or some other form of food' as penance.[93] During Ramadan, Muslims only restrict the time of day they can eat, and several studies have suggested many gain weight during the fast.[94]

But I am not religious and nor was I trying to lose weight or flush out toxins. I was fasting because I think it is a religious practice that retains a great deal of value even in a secular context. Indeed, it might be better without its religious baggage.

Virtually all religions place some restrictions on eating, in the form of prohibited foods or periodic fasting. This is especially evident in monastic life, where food is usually simple and eaten only at set times, in moderation. That's not to say all orders are terribly austere. The Rule of Benedict allows monks half a bottle of wine every day, and at Buckfast Abbey, the brothers are still provided with beer or cider at every meal, should they choose it. After all, the Benedictine Dom Pérignon played a key role in the development of champagne, while St Thomas Aquinas was notoriously corpulent. Fat friars may not be the norm today, but having visited several monasteries, I know they aren't unheard of either.

Irrespective of *what* they eat, monks regulate *when* they eat. But why? Christopher Jamison, the former abbot of Worth Abbey, says that in the contemporary world, we have become used to acting on our desires almost automatically. If you want something and you can get it, you do. Hence the bored snack and the peckish peck. Similarly, the Buddhist abbot Ajahn Sucitto says that too often eating becomes just one of those 'compulsive activities which on a functional level are not necessary. We do it just because of a psychological habit.'

Perhaps one reason we do this is that we think being able to act on our own desires, unencumbered by others, is what being free means. But this is not the kind of autonomy valued by philosophers or theologians. Autonomy literally means self-rule. Unthinkingly acting on whatever desire you have is not to govern yourself, but to allow yourself to be governed by your impulses.

True freedom therefore requires the ability to exercise self-control rather than simply being carried by whatever desires and impulses arise in you. Only eating certain things at certain times, as monks do, is a way of countering our tendency to slavishly follow our desires, breaking the link between desire and action, impulse and acting on it. As Jamison put it, 'It's a way of exercising choice very knowingly.'

In secular life, we don't have the monks' strict daily routine and it would seem too austere to try to impose it. Periodic fasting, however, is one way in which we can practise this proper kind of autonomy and break the lazy habits that make us slaves to our desires.

It was primarily for that reason that I thought I should introduce regular fasting into my life. I also thought it would be a good way to foster appreciation of meals, by being more mindful of what I was eating, putting a brake on my tendency to shovel food into my mouth faster than I know I should. At the same time, I did not want my fast to be anything to do with mortification of the flesh, or making life unpleasant for no good reason. My purpose was not to suffer, but merely to be spurred to attend to what is important.

Looking for a model, I came across the Hindu feast of Navratri, dedicated to the worship of Shakti, the deity responsible for Creation, the agent of all change, the primordial cosmic energy. Navratri literally means 'nine nights' in Sanskrit. (*Nava* means 'nine' and *ratri* means 'nights'.) When and how the feast is practised varies, but in essence it is nine days and nights of some kind of fast, ending with a feast on the tenth evening.

I gave my own fast the almost homophonic name Novrati. It takes its meaning from the Latin *ratio*, meaning 'thought'; *novus*, meaning 'new'; its verb form *novare*, 'to refresh'; and *novem*, meaning 'nine'. It is ten days (nine nights) to refresh the way one eats and thinks about eating. I decided to celebrate it twice a year, around the spring and autumnal equinoxes. That way, it would also provide a reminder of the passing of time, the cycle of life and the impermanence of all things. Although I did think it would help my ongoing attempts to curb excessive eating, I was very keen that the week itself should not be turned into an exercise in weight loss or detox; it was to be, for want of a better word, a spiritual rather than a physical exercise. I was also keen that it should be a kind of celebration, a festival as well as a fast.

A fast like this requires rules, although I think that if anyone else wants to adopt something like Novrati, they should find their own way to apply the general principles to their situation. These rules should require sufficient effort to achieve the desired goals but not so much as to create real hardship.

My own rules were that I would eat three meals a day, with no snacking in between of any kind. I would restrict my diet to ovo-vegetarian (no milk or dairy, only eggs) and would not drink alcohol or eat sweets or cakes. I would strive to eat each meal mindfully and thankfully. On the last evening I would share some kind of feast, not an excessive gorging, but a celebration of the pleasure and variety of good food. In summary, the idea is to counter the bad 'A' of automaticity with the three good 'A's of right appreciation, right autonomy and right action.

This may all sound very well, but there would appear to be a big problem. If you make up your own rules, who says you must stick to them? Isn't the whole exercise undermined by its self-directed nature? Traditional fasts work because the restrictions are imposed from outside. If I, however, decided I felt like having a bar of chocolate, what would there be to stop me saying, 'Sod it,' and tucking in?

However, this is in fact what makes Novrati in some ways better than religious fasting. It is a practice of the purest kind of autonomy precisely because the only person prescribing your action is yourself. The highest kind of freedom is to be able to control and regulate your own behaviour simply because you have realised that it is good to do so. In contrast, to follow a fast because your religion demands it is merely to submit your will to that of another.

There are, however, different ways of being in control. One is by use of *phronēsis* – practical wisdom – which we have come across already. To recap, to have practical wisdom is not to have a piece of theoretical knowledge or a technical skill. It is to have good judgement, based on reason and experience. The vital thing to recognise about *phronēsis* can be summed up in what I have come to adopt as a bit of a motto: there is no algorithm. Good judgement cannot be reduced to a set of rules, a formula, a procedure. It is not that it is mysterious and intuitive – there is plenty one can rationally say about it. But reason cannot generate the correct solution in some formalised way, with a guaranteed correct outcome.

Practical wisdom has declined as we have come to rely more on measurements, rules and procedures. We prefer the comfort of following officially sanctioned prescriptions to the responsibility of allowing ourselves and others to decide what is best. The rule-based approach has its attractions. Diets that require weighing and measuring, counting calories or sticking to colour-coded food groups make life easier in the sense that you have fewer decisions to make. You just have to follow the rules and wait for the magic to happen.

But I think the short-term gains of such an approach are outweighed by the way in which it undermines practical wisdom in the long term. You may be able to lose weight by counting calories, but this develops none of the good judgement needed to sustain sensible eating over the long term. Either you become an obsessive life-long calorie-counter or you carry over nothing from your weight-loss phase to your keeping-weight-off normal life. So, in a sense, control that relies on micromanaging every detail is not really control at all, because it can't be sustained. The calorie-counter can't cope in the restaurant where menus don't list the calories or all the ingredients. The strict procedure-follower doesn't know what to do if a step is missed, messed up or forgotten. True control requires an ability to accommodate what you can't completely control, and true autonomy means living life according to your own judgements, not controlling everything that happens in it. That's as true of eating as it is of any other part of life.

Perhaps that's why I felt fasting was a better exercise in autonomy than dieting, which is much more narrowly about resolution than about self-governance in the wider sense. That is perhaps also why, despite a nagging awareness of the artifice of the fast, I found the ten days of Novrati extremely worthwhile. It did achieve its goal of breaking habits and encouraging me to stop and think before automatically filling up. At ten days, it also seemed about the right length: long enough to require genuine effort but not so long as to make me feel on a leash, which would encourage a bingeing excess on release from the discipline. It was obviously no panacea for greedy and thoughtless eating, which is why I thought I really should do it twice a year. I've since decided to go further and am experimenting with a weekly fast day, following the same rules but adding eggs to the prohibited list. A more regular practice helps because old habits die hard and it doesn't take long for them to reassert themselves.

I wouldn't go so far as to say that everyone should try fasting. Some may have no unhelpful eating habits to counter. And as I have argued throughout this part of the book, the project of character-building is one that involves almost all our everyday actions, from the perennial routines of life to projects like losing weight. Fasting is just one of many practices that, if undertaken in the right spirit, can help us to develop virtues such as autonomy, willpower and humility. However, I suspect most of us could benefit from some kind of regular systematic practice of restraint and reflection, whether that revolves around food or something else we do without enough thought and appreciation. If autonomy really is about more than just doing what we want, then we need to take time to work on our powers of self-governance. How we eat – and don't eat – is a good place to start. And so, finally, it is time to turn to eating itself.

PORRIDGE

Porridge made with water is my staple fast breakfast. Although recently fashionable again, porridge has suffered over the years from its reputation as a virtuous, worthy dish. It is indeed worthy, but not in an austere, joyless way.

Assuming you make it properly, and don't simply add boiling water to an instant preparation, porridge has the great advantage of allowing a slow, thoughtful start to the day. I have come to really value the quarter of an hour I spend stirring in the mornings that I make it, without the radio on or any other distraction. I often use that time to ponder the day before and the day to come, a kind of meditation or even prayerful reflection. Fifteen minutes of cooking first thing in the morning may seem too much for some, but if we only have five minutes for breakfast, that is because we have only given ourselves five minutes, not because the gods have set our timetable.

Porridge is one of those SIVs – simple but infinitely variable dishes – I described earlier. In its most basic form, it is nothing more than water, oats and salt, heated and stirred. What could be easier? Yet it turns out that no two people make porridge in exactly the same way. Do you soak the oats overnight? Do you use oatmeal (pinhead, fine or medium ground?) or oat flakes (small or large?)? Do you add any milk to your water, and if so, when? Do you add the oats to the liquid at the start or only when it has come to a simmer? How long do you cook it for? How gloopy or runny should it be? What, if anything, should be added at the table? Dried fruit? Honey? Brown sugar? Treacle? Do you stir constantly or merely quite a lot? This may seem a rather modest set of options, yet from this small range of variables infinite variety is made possible, in part because so many of the choices are a matter of more or less, not either-or, which allows for any number of gradations.

Except during Novrati, the way I usually make it is to slowly bring one part oats (half jumbo and half standard porridge oats) to the boil with three parts semi-skimmed milk and then just stir and simmer until it's the consistency I like, which is thick but not yet gluey, adding a pinch of salt towards the end. Less liquid means quicker cooking but a less creamy consistency. I find a heaped espresso cup of oats about right for one person: 50 grammes is often recommended.

I sometimes put in blueberries when the porridge is nearly cooked, serving it just when the fruits start to burst. Ground cinnamon is good, especially when cranberries are added. Dried fruit, nuts and toasted seeds also work, either stirred in or sprinkled on top. During the autumn I sometimes serve it with a compote of apples and blackberries, simply cooked in a saucepan with a little honey or nothing at all added, the eating apples providing all the sweetness needed.

However you make it, porridge is proof that with a little effort what is simple can be immensely rewarding, and that what appears to take time can give time back, in the form of space to think, reflect and prepare to meet the world. And what that means is that what is wholesome can also be pleasurable, and so virtue is more than just its own reward.

PART IV

Eating

Animals feed; man eats; only a man of intellect knows how to eat.

Jean Anthelme Brillat-Savarin[95]

17

Say grace

GRATITUDE

Although I'm an atheist, I have always tried to acknowledge the genuine merits of religious life that are lost along with faith. One of the great advantages of religion is that by ritualising certain practices, it stitches them into the fabric of daily life. It can do this well or badly, of course. Prayer can be a daily time for reflection on self and others, or it can be the mindless reciting of empty words. Weekly services can be positive times of coming together, or a kind of mass hysteria where the main role is to distinguish the saved 'us' from the wicked 'them' out there.

There are more people than you might think who take the benefits of a religion but who don't really believe in its tenets. Daniel Dennett and Linda LaScola even managed to find, without too much difficulty, a number of pastors who had lost their faith but not their jobs.[96] Personally, however, I can't bracket off the belief and embrace the practice. I've been to church as an ex-Christian and there's just too much said that makes me have to stare at my feet and shut my mouth.

Religion is also unsatisfying because, generally speaking, it has a mistaken anthropology. It recognises that we are more than just simple animals who live entirely in the moment. We have a highly developed sense of past and future, our own and that of the world we live in. But religion fails to accept fully that we are nonetheless still mortal animals, creatures of flesh and blood whose bodies are neither left behind by our souls at death nor resurrected by some divine miracle. We are neither pure beasts, trapped in the moment, nor angels, tuned in to eternity. We are fully biological creatures, but ones who, through the amazing way in which our minds organise our experiences, can live for more than a moment, but less than an eternity.

As I have put it in more detail elsewhere, we are no more than, but more than just, matter.[97] We have souls, but only in the ancient Greek sense of *psuchê*. This is not a spiritual, immaterial entity, but the individual consciousness that results from the ordering of physical matter in our brains and bodies. We are then what I'd call 'psuche-somatic' creatures: souls that are fully bodies (*soma*). The question of how to live is therefore a search for a properly psuche-somatic ethics, one that fully accounts for our animality and personhood. Although I haven't used this term until now, that psuche-somatic understanding of human nature has been implicit in everything in this book. It is because we have pasts and futures, but not an infinity ahead of us, that we need to respect the needs and welfare of each other in our interpersonal morality. It is because we are capable of reflection and rationality but are all too limited in our intellects that we need an understanding of reason that accepts the imperfect, sometimes imprecise nature of the judgements it yields, both factual and ethical. And as we try to build essential character strengths like willpower, autonomy and humility, we need to fully acknowledge the limits our bodies place on us, as well as the ways in which we can be more than just slaves to them.

Eating is the ideal domain in which to consider our psuche-somatic nature because there is no denying our animality when we ingest. And although religion fails to fully accept our physicality, that is not to say it has nothing to teach those of us who do. Some religious practices around food can be borrowed, even if something is lost in the translation to secular life. We have already considered fasting, but perhaps more instructive still are the rituals of gratitude, expressed in prayer. We in the developed world are extremely fortunate to be able to eat as well as we do. Through the eyes of most of human history, and much of the world today, our main nutritional problem – how to avoid eating too much – is an enviable one. Isn't it appropriate to regularly remind ourselves of our good fortune?

If so, there are more ways of doing this than saying prayers. One possibility is to say a secular grace before meals, inwardly if not out loud, and in our daily reflection give thanks. When I've suggested this in the past, many people object that secular grace makes no sense because there is no one to be grateful to. I entirely agree that believing that there is a single divine entity who is responsible for all that is good does make gratitude easier to express. (Although you may be troubled by the thought that if this God is responsible for the good things in life, He might shoulder the blame for the awful stuff too.) The obligation for your grace and daily prayers is bestowed on you from without, and having a being to address directly provides a clear focus. The rituals are also ready-made for you, with guidelines for their observance sanctioned by the religion you belong to.

However, although religion makes expressions of gratitude a more natural part of life, it is not indispensable. Feelings of gratitude or thankfulness need not be directed at anyone in particular. The thought is simply 'I am fortunate, and I do not want to take that good fortune for granted. For what fortune gives to one, fortune denies to another. What fortune gives, fortune can take away.' It is a reminder that what is good in life is to be appreciated all the more for not having eternity to catch up on what we have missed, and so if we do not savour it now, we never will.

The linguistic fact that 'to thank' is a transitive verb that grammatically implies an object misleads us into thinking that thankfulness requires someone or something to be thankful to. But surely we can understand what it means to be thankful without feeling there is anything in particular to thank, just as we can understand what it's like to feel bored when there is no one or thing we are bored by. Those who insist on denying the atheist's genuine feelings of thankfulness are, I think, not trying very hard to understand what is really quite simple.

Because thoughts of thankfulness nonetheless arise more easily when there is someone to direct our gratitude towards, some atheists or agnostics might prefer to find something non-divine to thank. When the philosopher Daniel Dennett survived a heart attack, for example, he thanked 'goodness': the goodness of doctors, nurses and scientists who had made successful treatment and rehabilitation possible.[98] Bhai Sahib Bhai Mohinder Singh, the chairman of the Sikh Guru Nanak Nishkam Sewak in Birmingham, suggested to me that, in addition to God, the long list of people we should thank for just, say, a chapatti, is almost endless: the farmers who sowed the seeds and cut the harvest, the miller who ground the wheat, the cook who made the bread, the person who served you. But since food producers are not doing their work for any altruistic reasons, it's not clear to me that regular, deep thanks are in order.

The main problem for atheists and agnostics is not that we have no one to thank, it's that we don't have a ready-made framework for doing so. After I once talked about issues like these, a woman came up to me and said she had tried to start a secular grace in her home, but the rest of her family just thought it was silly. It isn't, but a kind of self-created mini-ritual can feel forced and artificial. What's more, the only reason you have to continue doing it is that *you* think you should: there is no sense of an external force imposing some sort of obligation on you.

For reasons like these, much as I commend grace in its religious and secular forms, I do not actually say one myself. However, I do think I have inculcated more general habits of gratitude. I may not say a prayer when I sit to eat, but I often, perhaps usually, feel silently grateful for it. Indeed, if you can foster such habitual responses, it can have advantages over said prayers, which can become mechanical and empty. I can still remember, for example, the words of the grace we had to say at my Catholic primary school, recited in a monotonic staccato bounce: 'Thank-you-Lord-for-these-Thy-gifts-which-we-are-about to-receive-from-Thy-boun-ty-through-Je-sus-Christ-our-Lord-Aaaaa-men.' Not only did we not mean it, we had no idea what 'from Thy bounty' meant. For me, 'Bounty' was a coconut-filled chocolate bar that I didn't much care for. And at the end of the meal we were forced to lie: 'Thank you, God, for a lovely dinner.' However lucky we were to have eaten, there was nothing lovely about stewed gristle and lumpy mashed potato.

At the other extreme, the Georgian essayist Charles Lamb felt uncomfortable giving thanks at the tables of the rich, because they had 'too much, while so many starve'. Lamb believed, 'Gluttony and surfeiting are no proper occasions for thanksgiving.'[99] I see his point, but it is precisely the habit of reflecting on our good fortune that should prevent us from entering into gluttonous excess in the first place.

My suggestion, then, is that in a secular context we need something other than prayer around which to foster appropriate feelings of gratitude. The best candidate for this is, I believe, waste, the inevitable by-product of surplus. By nurturing awareness of this and trying to minimise it, we can provide a practical channel within which to keep feelings of gratitude salient.

Reliable data on food waste is surprisingly hard to find, but one typical, recent report by the Institution of Mechanical Engineers contained the estimate that 'Thirty to fifty per cent of all food produced on the planet is lost before reaching a human stomach.' The reasons for this vary enormously. In the developing world, the problem is mainly one of 'inefficient harvesting, inadequate local transportation and poor infrastructure', meaning that 'Produce is frequently handled inappropriately and stored under unsuitable farm site conditions.' In some South East Asian countries, up to 80 per cent of the total rice

crop never makes it to the table, much of it spilled from badly maintained vehicles or lost to bruising, mould and rodents.

In the developed world, it is claimed that 'Up to 30 per cent of
the UK's vegetable crop is never harvested', because 'Major supermarkets, in meeting consumer expectations, will often reject entire
crops of perfectly edible fruit and vegetables at the farm because they
do not meet exacting marketing standards for their physical characteristics, such as size and appearance.'[100] Less publicised is the fact that
supermarket contracts often require suppliers to have a certain quantity of produce available but don't oblige the supermarket to take it
all. Charlie Hicks offers as a symbol of this 'the pallet of iceberg let-
tuce with the Tesco labels torn off (not very successfully)' that appears
at the wholesale 'dump-markets' on a Friday, after an optimistic
weather forecast earlier in the week caused the supermarket to over-
order. 'As the risk lies entirely with the grower, supermarkets do tend
to habitually over-order, then cancel or reduce,' he says. The supplier
has no choice but to try to sell the surplus off cheaply.

Finally there are consumers, who simply buy too much. The
IME claims, 'Of the quantity that does reach the supermarket shelves,
30 to 50 per cent is thrown away by the final purchaser in the home.'
For instance, 680,000 tons of bread, around a third of all that bought
in Britain, is thrown away every year.[101]

There are good reasons to be offended by much of this. Those
who lived through times of restricted food supply, such as the Second
World War, feel this instinctively and they tried to pass down their
distaste for waste to their children, insisting they finished their plates,
saying, 'Think of all the starving children in Africa.' The impertinent
reply of many an unconvinced child, more often thought than
spoken, was, 'Why don't you send it to them, then?' The response
misses the point. Throwing food away wastefully is not usually bad
because someone else could literally have eaten it. Irrespective of any
practical consequences, it is bad because it fails to show appropriate

respect for the value of the food, both in nutritional and hedonic terms. If you know what this value is, you can no more throw food casually away than you could toss a copper coin down a drain, even though a penny buys you virtually nothing these days. In both cases, what matters is not what could otherwise have been done with the money or food. It's simply that no one who has any respect for money and an appreciation of what poverty means could treat it so disdainfully. When you see the value of something, you always treat it with respect. You don't just think of what practical benefit it might have on any given occasion.

Of course, the feelings of respect are not disconnected from the practical benefit. It is simply that the relation is at the general, not the particular, level. You respect all food because of what food does for people, rather than respecting that bit of food for what it can do for a particular person. This might seem irrational. If food is good because it is nutritious and enjoyable, then why show respect to some small bit of food that you don't fancy eating, the nutrition of which you don't need, and from which no one else can benefit? The answer goes back to Aristotle's insight that we are creatures of habit. We do not and cannot live our lives assessing every individual situation on its own merits. We need rather to inculcate certain patterns of response that incline us to do what is right most of the time. A habit of wastefulness will lead us to waste too much, while a habit of thrift will lead us to waste less, even if it sometimes makes us too unwilling to let something go in the bin.

Nevertheless, the fact that the right dispositions are the ones that incline us to do the kinds of things that have the best outcomes points to the need to think very carefully about what sorts of actions do have good results and which are just empty gestures. Waste is an excellent example of this. It is good to encourage intolerance of waste as a means of developing gratitude and pushing us to take the kinds of actions that actually mean some can benefit from what would otherwise be thrown away. The trouble is that the anti-waste impulse can morph into a kind of quasi-religious cult, or a blinkered ideology that can exert a pull on us that may do nothing to achieve the outcomes we want.

Here's an example from close to home. Eating out in the café-bar of a cinema with my partner, it became clear that her plate contained more than she had anticipated and she wasn't going to finish it. Seeing me eye it up, she said, 'You don't have to eat it.'

'True, but in some sense I really think I ought to,' I replied, at least in my half-imagined reconstruction of the conversation. What I meant was that I felt an almost moral obligation not to let the food end up in the bin. In some ways, I feel that obligation holds even if I don't particularly like the food or eating it would make me too full. Certainly, if it's nice and I've got room, it would feel disrespectful of food's value to let it go in the bin. Even if it's too strong to say I am obliged to finish it, it would certainly be good if I did.

However, there is also a good reason to feel in such situations that you ought *not* to eat it, one that shares the same basic motivation: a distaste for excess. Excessive consumption could reflect an indifference to those who don't have enough and hence a lack of respect for the value of food as deep as that shown by wastefulness. Equally good values can lead one person to feel uncomfortable about letting food go to waste and another to feel uncomfortable about saving it from the bin. What this shows is not that fostering habitual responses is useless, but that they are rarely enough by themselves to tell us what we should actually do in a given situation. We have to use our trained impulses as warning lights, alerting us to the presence of something ethically salient, not as infallible road signs, pointing us in the right direction.

It was my partner who pointed out that if we are not attentive enough to what our impulses are telling us, they can also become Trojan horses for other vices. So, for instance, the justified distaste for excess can be hijacked by a puritanical rejection of the pleasures of hearty eating, perhaps connected with an ingrained fixation on calorie control as the primary food virtue. In my own case, my rightful regret at good food going to waste could be marshalled by my greedy impulses to justify extra helpings. The dilemma I have is whether food is better going to waste or my waist.

How do we deal with these potential tensions? By becoming aware of our own weaknesses and biases. So in my case, I should stop and think, Yes, there is something lamentable about good food being wasted and it's good to avoid it if possible, but it's also good that I don't get into the habit of giving in to my greed. If I'm not sure which impulse should prevail, then I should choose to counter the one that is more self-serving.

Getting the right attitude to waste is also difficult at a social and political level. Recycling, for instance, can easily become a free-floating fetish that neither serves as a reminder to be grateful nor helps the planet. I'm as guilty of this as anyone, even taking home the cardboard sleeves around takeout coffee cups rather than putting them in the bin, which is a little absurd when the non-biodegradable plastic lids are just thrown away. Good though it is to be in the habit of not mindlessly binning things, it's not much use if it doesn't nurture gratitude or drive changes in behaviour, such as taking a flask in future.

It is also possible to be too vexed by the sight of inevitable waste, which I often find I am. For example, one late October I remember being surprised at how many almonds were still on the trees in Andalusia after the harvest had been completed. But I reminded myself that no means of harvest is 100 per cent efficient and what you often find is that however much time and effort it takes to gather the 90 per cent of the crop that is most accessible, it takes as much again to collect the remaining tenth. Since no farmer would ignore what he could profitably harvest, the reason for the surfeit of almonds was obviously that what was left was not worth the effort of collecting, either because it was not good enough or it had ripened later than the rest and in insufficient numbers to justify a second harvest. Ironically, it could well be a manifestation of urban ignorance and an internalisation of the values of mechanical efficiency that makes us unable to accept that some waste is a natural part of the food production cycle.

Connecting distaste for waste with gratitude can help temper the simplistic tendencies to attribute all waste to the failings of modernity and business. We are able to waste as much as we do only because modern agriculture and retail distribution have made food cheap and plentiful. That generates real problems that need to be tackled, but unless we balance our concern with thankfulness for what is delivered, we are not going to address the right problems or come up with the right solutions.

Feeling appropriately grateful therefore turns out to be a complicated business. Although gratitude might come more easily to those with religious traditions, perhaps that ease has its own drawbacks, as it can mislead us into thinking all we need do is thank our creator. A deeper sense of gratitude needs to be embedded in the habits of daily life, expressed in our attitudes to waste as well as our frame of mind when we sit down to eat. It also needs the input of constant intellectual interrogation to make sure that it is more than just a knee-jerk feeling and that it leads us towards what is good. It's easy to say thank you, and to mean it, but true gratitude is expressed by how we live, not just by our words and feelings.

EGG-FRIED RICE

The careful use of leftovers is one practical way to manifest appropriate gratitude and respect for food. Rice probably tops the chart of foods most frequently cooked or ordered in excess. One of the best things to do with it the next day is to fry it with eggs and whatever else is around that might add some flavour. So, heat some oil and put in one or more of garlic, shallots, red peppers from jars, albacore tuna – just see what's in the fridge and cupboards that might work. Beat an egg or two, depending on personal taste and quantity of rice, and add it to the mixture, at a low heat and stirring reasonably vigorously to stop it congealing into pieces of omelette. Whether you eat when the egg is still a little soft, when it has started to crisp or anything in between is a matter of preference. In any case, you will not just feel virtuous for not having thrown the rice away, you will have had a good and easy lunch.

18

Know more than what you like

We live in an age when hardly anyone knows what '*De gustibus non est disputandum*' means, but almost everyone agrees it's true. There's little disputing the claim that 'There's no disputing taste.' If someone only likes simple, plain flavours, what's wrong with that? If one person likes avant-garde modern orchestral music and another throwaway pop, then you might say the first has more *sophisticated* tastes, but you must not call them *better*. When it comes to aesthetic judgement, there is no objectivity, only subjective preference.

I don't think this is right, and there is more at stake in understanding why than the relative merits of Mahler and Motörhead. There is widespread misunderstanding of what 'objective' means, which leads people to doubt that there can be objectivity in ethics, or even in history and science.

To build a defence of objectivity around food and drink might appear to be perversely quixotic. What could be more subjective than culinary preference? You can't be wrong if you don't like strawberries, or prefer fish and chips to *bacalao al pil-pil*. It is, however, the very obviousness of these statements that points to the root of the mistake. 'Often people don't distinguish between something being good and them liking it,' says the philosopher Tim Crane. 'I think there's lots of music that is good, even brilliant, that I don't like.' That is surely true. I don't like much Bob Dylan, Coldplay or Jedward, but I believe Dylan is some kind of genius, accept Coldplay have some talents and maintain Jedward simply are without any redeeming qualities. Even if these particular judgements are wrong, there surely are differences between the good and bad things I don't like. The same goes for food. As the chef Björn Frantzén told me, even after he has eaten at the best restaurant, 'I can leave and say, "It's not actually my cup of tea, but they're fucking great."'

Once you reject the simple equations of (like = good) = (don't like = bad), the next step is to accept the obvious fact that works of art, pieces of music, food and drink all have objective qualities that our tastes respond to. Wine is a very good example. 'Part of the interest in wine is thinking about what *it* is like, not just what it's like for *us*,' says the oenophile philosopher Barry Smith. For all we might endorse the view that taste is purely subjective, we do not usually talk of food as though its flavours are only in us. When we try something delicious and we say to a friend, 'You must taste *this*,' we are referring to the food, not what is going on in our mouths. A good croissant really is buttery; it doesn't just seem buttery to us.

When we taste food, we can fail to notice flavours it has, and this would not be possible unless they were there to be missed. Smith gives the example of drinking a wine. 'I say to you, "Did you get the mint? Did you get the pear?" and so on. The experience is gone, but you think to yourself, Hang on, yes.' It is true that we are sometimes suggestible and will, if prompted, 'detect' flavours that were never there, but we should not confuse our capacity to be misled with an absence of any ability to accurately spot flavours at all. 'People are really quite resistant if you suggest, say, green pepper and you didn't get that,' says Smith. Try it. People will not just agree with any suggestion about what flavours are in a food or drink. When we do say, 'Yes, I get it,' Smith claims that 'The "yes" is matching a judgement against something that was in the experience but which was not noticed at the time. There's having the experience and there's the attention to the experience.'

It is therefore evident that taste is not purely subjective, in that it involves discerning qualities that are there in the objects themselves, not just in us. We can also be more or less attentive to these real qualities. Most of us, most of the time, simply drink our wine and find it pleasant. With a little effort, we start noticing more. The wine connoisseur simply takes this attentiveness further, noticing all sorts of features that completely pass the causal drinker by.

Not so long ago, if someone was sceptical of the wine aficionado's ability to discern what philistines missed, the most he could say was, 'It all tastes pretty much the same to me.' Now, he is more likely to say, 'Have you heard about the study . . .?' You probably have, although you may mix it up with another similar one and forget the details, but you remember the upshot, which is that people who claim to be able to distinguish the excellent from the poor or mediocre repeatedly fail to do so in blind tests. To run through a few of the most famous examples, at the University of Bordeaux, Frédéric Brochet got all fifty-four oenology students he tested to think white wine was red, simply by adding a flavourless dye to it. He also got them describing cheap wine as rounded and complex, and expensive wine as weak and flat, simply by switching the labels.

Similarly, anyone who keeps chickens will tell you how much tastier their super-fresh, hen-friendly eggs are. But when researchers have tried truly blind tastings, comparing these with ordinary supermarket eggs, a difference in flavour is almost never found. One smart food writer, for instance, conducted an initial experiment in which half the tasters did prefer the backyard hens' eggs, but he realised they could have been responding to a visual cue, since those eggs had a darker yolk and so made for a richer-coloured scramble. When he repeated the experiment using a green dye to make all the samples look the same, the preferences disappeared for all but one taster.[102]

And so on. Nevertheless, the idea that there are no differences in taste or quality between foods and wines is clearly absurd. Whatever these experiments show, it cannot be that we lack all discernment. Sure, wine-tasters can be fooled, but they can also be very good at telling you what grape variety a wine is made from, and from which country it comes. It's their taste telling them that, not psychic powers. If you try a variety of restaurants and foods, you will come to have preferences that do not always conform to mere appearances: some you will like despite your prejudices ('The atmosphere and service are awful, but you can't fault the food') and others you will really want to love but will find you can't.

There is no mystery as to what is at the root of this. It is part and parcel of being psuche-somatic creatures: minds that are fully embodied, animals permeated by mentality. Experience is never simply something that goes on inside our brains, and nor is a physical experience unaffected by what we think and believe. In the case of food and drink, the upshot is clear: there is no such thing as tasting, smelling or enjoying food in a way that sidesteps our past experience, prejudices, expectations and beliefs. All of these things interact, and sometimes our expectations, prejudices and beliefs are so strong that they lead us to err.

The world we experience is therefore neither a pure human construct nor objectively independent of us. The quality of a wine, for instance, depends on characteristics it has, whether we perceive them or not, but wine is only palatable in the first place because of the ways in which it reacts with the human digestive and nervous system. Our human psychology and physiology frame the way wine is experienced, and that is normally unproblematic. We only lose touch with what is real when that framing distorts the experience, so there is no longer a good fit between the objective properties of things and our sense perception.

What the wine experiments therefore show is primarily that 'The judgements that people come out with are partly the function of their expectations,' as Smith's fellow philosopher and partner in wine Tim

213

Crane put it. This merely proves we can be tricked, not that in an ordinary situation our judgements mean nothing, and nor does it show that 'There's no way of telling the difference between red wine and white wine.'

You might think this is true, but still object that it doesn't justify the value judgement that one wine is better than another, merely that people who get into food and wine will judge both according to more sophisticated criteria than those who don't. Once you accept what connoisseurship really entails, however, it seems perverse not to acknowledge that it can lead to a superior ability to discern quality. Almost everyone has had the experience of coming to see that some products or restaurants are simply better than others, and there are some you would only recommend to your worst enemy. To take another example, my wine knowledge is rudimentary, yet I often now notice that cheap wines, although perfectly pleasant, are rather flat, one-dimensional and uninteresting compared to many that are a price bracket up. There seems to be no truthful way of describing this other than to say that those more expensive wines are better. Since that does not entail that we should all prefer the better wine, why would I want to resist making that judgement? Only because, I think, we fear it elitist to suggest that all tastes are not equal, even though the evidence suggests otherwise.

The suspicion of claims to superior taste is not entirely unfounded. The historian of food Massimo Montanari claims that in the Middle Ages there was no idea of some tastes being more refined than others and people believed in 'the same legitimacy for all tastes determined by the natural instinct of each individual'. The shift to the notion of good and bad taste had two elements. First, as Count Giulio Landi said of Piacento cheese, 'However much the populace may recognise its goodness, not for that can they provide the reason why it is so good.' The distinction opens up between the universal capacity for taste and a more elite ability to understand the grounds of good taste, *why* some things are better than others. This, for the first time, attributes to taste a cognitive element, the role of rational judgement and deliberation. This led the way to the second stage, which was to maintain that good taste, 'a cultivated knowledge filtered by the intellect', was different from and superior to a vulgar, untutored taste.

The progression can be summed up by an example: first, everyone could straightforwardly perceive that Piacento was good; second, everyone could perceive it was good, but only some understood why; third, only those who had cultivated their good taste could really appreciate the superiority of Piacento, and those who had not were likely to be just as happy with an inferior cheese.

The reason to be suspicious of this is that Montanari and others believe that the motivation for this progression was at least in part the need for the elites to distinguish themselves from the masses. Taste becomes 'a mechanism of social differentiation', which arises from 'the need of the elite to reaffirm at all times their difference, attributing to it a "rational consciousness" which they do not recognise in the peasantry'.[103]

There can be little doubt that notions of taste and right ways to eat can be used in this way, and often are. It's the reason why Steven Poole wrote his invective against the current foodist trend, *You Aren't What You Eat*. 'Food has become a way of showing off, a fashion,' he told me in a fashionable London gastropub serving 'British tapas'. It's the 'moralistic aspect' of this that bothers Poole, the attitude of 'I understand so much about food: I'm better than you. Look at you. You're eating crap. You're eating really badly. You need to be educated about food.'

Poole is right to be suspicious. The food world is full of bluff, pretension and pure bullshit, as both Tim Crane and Barry Smith accept, but Crane insists that 'Suspicion has to be based on knowledge. I don't respect people who say things are bullshit if they don't know what makes it bullshit. It's like saying philosophy is bullshit.

There is a lot of philosophers' bullshit, but you've got to know what's bullshit and what isn't.'

There is also a great deal of snobbery too. 'Snobbery is valuing something that shouldn't be valued,' says Crane. 'It has to be some kind of mistake. I think there is genuine wine snobbery, which is making judgements by reputation or price.'

The fact that some, perhaps many, claims about the superiority of certain foods, wines and restaurants are based on little more than fashion, snobbery or status does not mean that all are. And even if it is true that the rise of the notion of a discerning palate owes more to the need for social distinction than aesthetic judgement, that does not mean there is nothing to it. Bad ideas often sprout from grains of truth, and many a good thing grows in manure.

If you accept that liking is not the same as judging to be good, that aesthetic objects have objective qualities, that some people can discern these better than others and that the existence of these qualities provides grounds for claiming that some things really are better than others, then you cannot but accept that taste is not purely subjective. Still, this leaves us a long way from what is usually assumed to be full objectivity: the final, authoritative, single truth, as perceived from a godlike perspective. That still seems impossible, especially for food. Can it really be an objective fact, for example, that the best wine in 2012, as *Wine Spectator* claimed, is Shafer Vineyard's Relentless 2008, and that it is better than the second-placed Château de Saint Cosme Gigondas 2010? Of course not. But not even the people who create such rankings believe that. To think that objectivity requires such absolute judgements is to misunderstand its nature.

The biggest mistake people make about objectivity is to think it stands in an either-or relation to subjectivity; that either there is a simple fact of the matter or it's a matter of opinion; that there are facts, which are true or false, or there are opinions, and there is nothing in between. As Thomas Nagel argued so persuasively, 'The distinction between more subjective and more objective views is really a matter of degree, and it covers a wide spectrum. A view or form of thought is more objective than another if it relies less on the specifics of the individual's makeup and position in the world, or on the particular type of creature he is.'[104]

The application of this to food is clear. The experts who chose *Wine Spectator*'s best wines of 2012 were more qualified to identify and assess the qualities of the wines than the casual quaffer. With their practice in discerning the real qualities in the wine, plus their knowledge of what makes the difference between a wine that really works and one that doesn't, they have a more objective view than those who know little more than what they personally find pleasant. The most objective views involve much more than just the experience of eating and drinking. Knowledge of how foods are produced, the science of agriculture and food production, the biology of taste, the role of food in the global economy and society – all these things take us beyond how we subjectively feel about food to what it objectively is.

That does not mean there is a kind of 'view from nowhere', as Nagel put it, from where all the world's wines could be placed in strict order of merit. Objectivity has great limits with food, largely because you are never strictly comparing like with like: how would you even begin to say which was better of an excellent claret and a fine Rioja? But except for the artificial distinctions of awards and competitions, the aim of greater objectivity in food is not to reach such a ranking, but simply to appreciate more fully the qualities of what we put in our mouths.

Properly understanding the nature of objectivity helps us to avoid the kind of shoulder-shrugging relativism that has poisoned contemporary culture. This is most vital in the sphere of ethics. As long as we think that moral judgements are either clear facts that are true or false, or 'mere' preferences, we're going to end up either leaning towards a probably theological absolutism or unable to condemn anything at all.

The mature view is to accept that moral judgements can be more or less objective. Good ethical judgement requires all sorts of facts about how things really are, such as whether animals feel pain, what the consequences of free trade are, how different farming systems impact on the environment and so on. These facts do not generate moral truths as experiments generate scientific truths (although even that is not quite so straightforward), but they do constrain what is morally plausible and defensible.

In the case of food, it would be especially misguided to think of the fully objective view from nowhere as the ideal. Rather, just as our psuche-somatic nature requires an integration of mind and body, so it requires the bringing together of the subjective and objective perspectives, so that what we know can change the way we experience the world. As well as expectation and belief blinding us to real differences, they can make us perceive differences that our senses alone cannot detect.

Think, for example, about how ideas of healthiness might affect taste. I think I prefer wholemeal pitta bread to white, but this could simply be because I have come to associate white flour with unhealthy blandness. Similarly, fat has come to be seen as a bad thing, to the extent that people will often claim to be disgusted by the very same food that others lapped up with delight only a few generations ago. Familiarity is part of the explanation, of course, but so surely is internalised revulsion at the thought of artery-clogging fat. Even the kind of fat you're used to makes a difference. I had a friend once who ate lots of cheese, chips and other foods high in solid fat, but he found pasta coated in liquid olive oil far too greasy.

If ideas of healthiness do alter our appreciation of food, however, it does not follow that we should we try to overcome our 'delusions' and make more 'objective' judgements. If our experience of the world is fully psuche-somatic, then it is natural, right and proper that beliefs and expectations should colour it, if they are appropriate. If believing that certain foods are good for us helps us to enjoy them more, and they really are healthier, then that is a good thing. Similarly, if we are put off foods by thoughts of what they might do to us, that might be a good thing too. Our goal should not be to separate out the cognitive from the biological, the objective from the subjective, but to integrate them, bringing our minds as well as our mouths to our appreciation of food.

This relates to an important insight of the Slow Food movement. Slow Food insists that eating should be a pleasure, but that does not mean it should only be about what happens between food, nose and tongue. Slow Food claims that proper enjoyment of food requires understanding where it has come from. In that sense it advocates a kind of higher gastronomy, in which pleasure involves not just the senses but the mind. And in that respect it captures perfectly our psuche-somatic nature and shows how the experiments that many claim debunk gustatory discernment actually merely point us towards what discernment in its full sense means. Food really does, and should, taste better when we believe it has been prepared with love, purchased at a fair price, grown sustainably and so on. We literally develop taste for what we should enjoy more, and a distaste for things we should not.

Go back to those backyard eggs. The sight of the deep-yellow colour tells you something about how the hens have been living that should make you better disposed towards them. Knowing that they did not come from caged birds makes the pleasure deeper. So, of course, if you are eating in a position of true knowledge, backyard eggs really do taste better. As was the case with the coffee-tasting earlier, it is the blindfolded scenario that is less real: robbed of all the important information about the provenance of your food, your judgements are less reliable, not more so, as they depend simply on taste and smell, when the proper enjoyment of food requires all our senses and mental faculties. We are not simply hedonic machines who thrive if supplied with things that tick certain boxes for sensory pleasure, aesthetic merit and so on.

Knowing how much belief and expectation help form our food preferences, we have more reason than ever to make sure those beliefs and expectations are justifiable. If eggs taste better because we believe the hens are living better, we had better be correct. We would indeed be deceived if our judgements were based on things that simply weren't true, if we allowed an illusion of virtue to colour our taste palates, masking what should be the bitterness of vice. Too often, I think that's what happens. We buy into currently fashionable opinion about what is good for us, what is ethical, what is sustainable and so on.

So we have nothing to fear from the claim that what counts as 'good food' is more than a matter of opinion, just as long as a self-appointed set of experts don't use that fact as an excuse to lecture the rest of us about what we ought to eat. Increasing our knowledge of food can and does change our preferences, but they remain our own, and if they sometimes lead us to foods we know are not objectively good, that is fine, just as long as they are not ethically unsound or medically ruinous. It's easy to know what you like, more difficult to know what is good, but finding out can make you appreciate what you like even more, and maybe even make the things you like better.

WINE

You don't need to become a serious oenophile to develop a deeper appreciation for the objective qualities of wine. You can go a long way simply by attending to the three phases of the drinking experience. First, there is the aroma on the nose before you taste. Second, the 'attack' as the wines enters your mouth, which is often when the fruit flavours hit the 'mid-palate', when the different parts of the tongue respond to sourness and bitterness, and the mouthfeel of the wine becomes apparent. Finally, there is the 'finish', which is how the different flavours come together on swallowing, and in the after-taste that remains.

Barry Smith, who drew my attention to these aspects of tasting, says he has 'great faith in people's ability to be changed for ever by having their epiphany with an experience of a wine that is so compelling, complex, balanced and beautiful. At that moment they think, I'm not just attending to something going on in me, personal and private. I'm taking cognisance of something with extraordinary beauty.'

This level of appreciation is not of course limited to wine. People are increasingly coming to realise that any quality drink – including beer, tea and coffee – can have a complexity that rewards attention. You don't get that from the cheapest, blandest varieties, of course, and there is a risk that if you find yourself getting seriously interested, you'll be drawn towards ever more expensive brews. 'Getting into wine financially ruins you,' Tim Crane once warned me, embracing his fate with another sip. But if you have the means, the interest and the capacity to truly appreciate it, fine wine can be worth the expense. 'The point about high-quality, very fine, handmade wine,' says Smith, 'is that it gives me the opportunity to exercise my capacity for sensual pleasure and my intellectual powers of discrimination.' Spoken like a true psuche-somatic man.

That is not to say more expensive wine is always better. Smith advises, 'You should not buy a £200 wine if you cannot discriminate in the class of wines between £25 and £200. You should buy the best wine in the class within which you can discriminate.' Whatever you pay, the main thing is not to allow it to go from glass to stomach virtually unnoticed.

19

Let the performance begin

AESTHETIC APPRECIATION

If someone were to tell you that among the most incredible experiences of her life were watching Cecilia Bartoli sing the title role of *La Cenerentola* at the Met, seeing Diana Rigg play Medea at the Wyndham Theatre, hearing Alfred Brendel play Schubert's Piano Sonata no. 21 in B flat at the Niedersachsen in Hanover and spending an afternoon walking around the Prado Museum in Madrid, you might not share her tastes, but unless you thought she was bluffing, you'd probably respect her selections. If, however, she were to say that none of these compared with dinner at the three-Michelin-starred L'Arpège in Paris, your opinion of her might go down. Even the restaurant critic Jay Rayner told me, 'You can't compare the experience of standing in front of a Rothko and sitting down at a top restaurant, and I'd be very suspicious of anyone who thought you could.' Food can be very good. It can even be extraordinary, but surely it can never be put on the same footing as art.

But why not? The most obvious objections don't stand up to a moment's scrutiny. Some say a meal just comes and goes, while true art endures, but all performances are experienced in time and once finished cannot be exactly replicated. An audio or video recording does not recover an identical experience. In the same way, you can only eat any given dish once, but a chef can create it again and again, each a slightly different 'performance' of the same recipe.

It might also be objected that food has no 'cognitive content', no truths – moral or metaphysical – to take away and think about, but nor does much art. There are those who will always try to extract 'meaning' from a dance, an abstract painting or a piece of music. Usually that meaning is the least valuable part of the experience, or just not there. Many a time I've read a curator's caption for a work of art or programme note for a dance and found that it reduces what is visually amazing into something philosophically banal. The world is full of works that 'question the distinction between illusion and reality', but few do so more penetratingly than an undergraduate essay. As aesthetic objects or performances, however, they can be brilliant.

Finally, it might simply be said that a meal cannot move you as deeply as the best art. The only way a meal can reduce you to tears is if the chef has used too much chilli. Here we might have alighted on a genuine difference. But rather than showing why food cannot be art, it might point to the way in which food is its own kind of art.

Of all the questions in philosophy, 'What is art?' is one of the most interesting but also the most tiresome. To me, it has seemed obvious for years that there simply is no one answer to this. The arts vary too much for there to be one single thing they have in common that distinguishes them all from non-art. The genius of Picasso's cubist works is to be found in their pure form, the genius of Jane Austen in her psychological insight. The greatness of *Kind of Blue* is in large part down to Miles Davis's playing, whereas for Beethoven's String Quartet no. 14, it is all in the composition. There are things you can say about art that apply to many instances of it, but how important each thing is depends on the work in question, and none apply to all. So if you believe there is a sense in which food really can be seen as art, there's no point trying to make it exactly fit the mould cast from other arts. You need to explain why it is its own art, and why it should be valued alongside the others.

The strongest case for food as art that I have come across was an evening at Frantzén/Lindeberg in Sweden, which in just two years had gathered two Michelin stars and shot to number twenty on the most authoritative list of the world's best restaurants.[105] I went only because I thought I couldn't write about food without some experience of the very peaks of fine dining, and I had never been to a Michelin-star restaurant before. I chose this one because I knew I would be passing through Stockholm and the chef, Björn Frantzén, agreed to a request for an interview. Unfortunately, it was, in Frantzén's words, 'the most expensive restaurant in the Nordic region', with an average bill of €350. There's no limit to what you can spend in a restaurant if you order the finest wines, but it is impossible to pay more than this for your food at any British restaurant unless you're eating for two. I took a deep breath, told myself it was research and that I'd try to recoup the cost by writing about it.

It was a totally different kind of experience to an ordinary dinner out. A good restaurant is normally one where eating and drinking very well in a comfortable environment enhance the pleasure of the company. At Frantzén/Lindeberg, sociability takes a back seat as the diners become engrossed in the performance that is the nineteen-course tasting menu, and 'performance' does seem like the right word. Even the menu – a handwritten calligraphic parchment, rolled up and tied with string – resembles a programme, dividing the meal up into a prologue, two chapters and an epilogue. As Frantzén told me, going to a really good restaurant is 'like going to the theatre. Nowadays it's a lot more than just what's on the plate; it's a lot of other things: storytelling, ingredients, where they're coming from, how you present it, the look and feel of the restaurant.'

The performance begins when you take your seat and see on the table before you a small baguette-shaped piece of dough still proving in a glass-topped wooden box. This is then taken away and cooked over an open fire. When it comes back, nine dishes later, the maître d', Jon Lacotte, brings with it a kind of pestle and mortar in which he churns the butter there and then. As in a good play, this is not performance for the sake of it: the action moves the plot forward and adds to it. It's not the cheap theatricality of banging plates or chubby chefs tossing pasta. Proof of that comes when you bite into what is the very quintessence of warm buttered baguette.

Then there is the 'coal-flamed veal "tartar"', which Lacotte brings as a raw whole piece to our table and blowtorches, the flame hitting the meat only after being bounced off a piece of coal. Again, it's not just a theatrical flourish. It means that when the meat returns, chopped and served with tallow from an eleven-year-old milk cow, smoked eel and black roe, you understand better what you're eating. That's also why Lacotte explains a little about each dish as it is brought to us, while never making the fatal mistake of some pretentious restaurants of giving you something that takes longer to describe than to eat.

Like any performance, it's not just what you do, but in what order and at what pace. 'When you're having a tasting menu, it's a lot about the rhythm, and the speed you're serving things,' says Frantzén. 'It's also a lot about where in the menu you put a dish. Sometimes we have a dish on the menu that I think is fucking brilliant, but I ask the service and I talk to customers and no one's mentioned that dish and I wonder why. It might be because it's in the wrong place on the menu. So you swap plates with something else and then they start talking about it.'

Frantzén/Lindeberg got the pacing and rhythm just right. I subsequently went to a more modest – in relative terms at least – one-star Michelin restaurant in Britain, and although some of the food bore comparison with Frantzén/Lindeberg's, there were longueurs between courses, glasses left empty. Without the seamless flow, it was simply a very good meal, and that alone is not what you pay exceptionally high prices for.

Tellingly, when Frantzén compared going to his restaurant with the theatre, he prefaced his remarks with the confession that it may sound pretentious. He's right, of course, and you may have found some of what I've written a bit pretentious too. Other chefs and food writers also seem unwilling to compare food to art too explicitly, even though they don't reject the parallels outright either. The chef Fergus Henderson, for example, told me, 'Appreciation of food can be as strong as that of art and have much more effect,' but that 'To call it art doesn't really add up,' saying only that 'It brushes shoulders with art.' The reason Henderson gave for his reservations was that 'Food is quite grounded,' but that, I think, is the first clue as to what makes culinary art distinctive and in some ways even superior. Similarly, Frantzén says, 'At the end of the day, let's not forget, it's a restaurant, you go to a restaurant because normally you're hungry, and it's just food.' In one sense he's completely wrong. Of course you don't decide to go to Frantzén/Lindeberg because you're hungry. Rather, you make sure you are hungry because you decided to go to Frantzén/Lindeberg and having booked weeks or months in advance, you want to make the most of it. There is, however, a sense in which 'It's just food.' When the medium of your creativity is something so visceral, you are never allowed to forget that you are an animal. As Henderson suggested, it keeps you grounded, which is why it is so easy to sound pretentious when you intellectualise about food.

This is very different to many other art forms, which can create a sense of transcendence, a feeling that you are somehow transported beyond the merely mortal realm to taste something of the divine. Indeed, that is precisely why some people believe art is so important. I would argue the other way. The problem with art is that it can fool us into forgetting that we are mortal, flesh-and-blood creatures. The advantage the culinary arts have is that even as they delight us with creations no other animal could ever produce, they remind us that we are psuche-somatic creatures of bone and guts. Fine food is about the aesthetic of the immanent, not the transcendent. A mouthful of Björn Frantzén's bone marrow with caviar and smoked parsley transports you to a kind of Heaven that you cannot forget is a perishable place on Earth.

Through experiences like these you come to acquire a kind of direct knowledge of the potential intensity of being alive, what it means to 'suck out all the marrow of life', in Thoreau's evocative phrase.[106] This again is a familiar aspect of aesthetic experience. I find one of the most powerful feelings art can induce, especially music, is a sense of the poignancy of being alive. The beautiful intensity of the experience is accompanied by an acute sense that it is rooted in time, and so shall pass, and that one day such experiences will be no more. If food delivers this feeling less intensely, it also does so more truthfully. Eat something delicious in the right frame of mind and you get a similar feeling: both that this is wonderful and that it belongs to a life that is mortal. And it is precisely because the experience comes from eating, a daily part of mere existence, that this message comes through so forcefully.

Downplaying the animal part of aesthetic experience is, I think, part of the appeal of Kant's theory that the pleasure we get from art is of a particular, disinterested kind, meaning it is not connected to any instrumental goal. So, for example, pornography is not art, because its aim is arousal, whereas Michelangelo's *David* inspires a kind of awe. We talk of a 'beautiful goal' in football, but it serves the purpose of winning a game and is not just beautiful in itself. On this account, food is not a pure aesthetic pleasure because it is inherently tied to the satisfaction of desire or appetite. Similarly, Aristotle thought the sense of touch and taste were 'servile and brutish' because they are 'pleasures as brutes also share in'.[107]

Kant and Aristotle are on to something here, for sure. It is true that when pleasure is all about satisfying some immediate, physical need, it tends to be shallower and less meaningful. But the distinction between interested and disinterested pleasure is neither as sharp nor as obvious as Kant's theory suggests. Art is rarely completely disinterested.

Artists often want to make a living and achieve recognition, while opera-goers, readers of literary fiction and the like can be seduced by the glamour and status of ostentatious cultural consumption. Both the National Gallery and British Library in London are well known as places for like-minded singles to meet as well as places to pursue the disinterested life of the mind. On the other hand, it seems a pure prejudice to assume that sport and food don't have their own disinterested elements. There are moments of breathtaking brilliance in sport that leave every spectator astounded, whether they favour the team or player they want to win or not. And the delight I experienced when I popped Björn Frantzén's oyster, frozen rhubarb, cream and juniper into my mouth was not because I was pleased to be sating my hunger.

Kant's insight was, I think, that the most profound aesthetic experiences are not *purely* instrumental, but that does not mean that instrumentality is a kind of aesthetic contaminant and that the more disinterested a pleasure, the better. Indeed, I think a clear trace of traditionally baser elements makes an experience more, not less, profound. As we eat, we experience at the same time the disinterested pleasure of sheer wondrous enjoyment and the instrumental need to fill our bellies. As a result, we live as fully rounded human beings, aware of the totality of our complex psuche-somatic nature.

In one way, as the statement issued by four of the world's leading chefs – Ferran Adrià, Heston Blumenthal, Thomas Keller and Harold McGee – put it, 'Preparing and serving food could therefore be the most complex and comprehensive of the performing arts,' because, uniquely, 'The act of eating engages all the senses as well as the mind.'[108] Sound, touch (texture) and sight all influence how we experience our food. The University of Oxford's Massimiliano Zampini and Charles Spence, for example, conducted a now famous experiment that showed that people thought potato crisps were crisper if the sound of their crunch was amplified.[109] So there is a sense in which the traditional arts seem superior in part because of their deficiencies: by not involving the senses of taste and smell, they remove the most corporeal elements of our experience, tricking us into forgetting their centrality.

Art flatters us into thinking we have depths that our animality cannot explain. This may make us feel like a better class of being, but the reassurance is false. I am always baffled by those who argue that art makes us into better people. You don't need to use the obvious example of the Nazis who wept at the opera to show that. People step out of theatres and over down-and-outs sleeping in the streets. They go to galleries with their mistresses behind their wives' backs. As for writers and artists themselves, egotists and monsters seem to be at least as common among them as in the general population. Art doesn't make us higher beings; it makes us *feel like* higher beings. Food doesn't make us higher beings either, but it can make us appreciate just how rich and valuable the life of a lower being can be.

You can get that feeling from something as simple as a plate of tomatoes with olive oil, basil and bread. What fine dining adds is another familiar element from our experience of art: a sense that an order or harmony has been created that lies just beyond our ability to grasp it, and certainly to create it for ourselves. Picasso's cubist works do this: there is a sense of coherence that seems to emerge inexplicably from their fragmented complexity. I think this is the truth behind the 'I could have done that' dismissal of certain art works. If there is nothing before you that strikes you as both extraordinary and outside your understanding or ability, you lack the sense that the art surpasses the ordinary. I say 'surpasses' rather than 'transcends' because, as I have already said, I think that term misleads. The incredible thing about art is that it is the product of human creativity. An artist has not risen above the human condition; rather she has extended its possibilities, shown how we can 'surpass ourselves'.

The very best cooking does exactly the same thing. You do not think, I could have done that at home. You think, It takes a kind of genius to be able to create such a fantastic combination of tastes and textures. At Frantzén/Lindeberg, one dish that did that is 'satio tempestas' (sowing season). On paper, it is literally incredible that it could be anything special at all. It's just a small salad of forty different ingredients, harvested that day from their two gardens, chopped finely and mixed so that each mouthful combines several incredibly fresh, vegetable flavours. Yet it is a signature dish, one of the most delicious on the menu. Making real the unimaginable is often part of the value of creativity, and cooking is no exception.

Indeed, some of the value of human creativity is independent of what sphere it is applied to. It is hubris to imagine that we can ever create eternal works of art. All is dust in the end: food just gets there quicker, which is again part of its honesty. The main goal of many creative people is to achieve excellence, and what medium they choose to express that in is secondary. For instance, before becoming a chef, Frantzén played professional football with the top Swedish club AIK Stockholm, before injury ended his career at the age of twenty. Having worked at the top of two very different professions, I asked whether it was the pursuit of excellence that really drove him, whatever sphere that happened to be in. He nodded. 'It happened to be cooking now; it could have been anything.' The great sushi chef Jiro Ono echoes this when he says, 'You must dedicate your life to mastering your skill,' whatever that skill might be.

But was my meal worth €350? Can I justify paying that much? The questions are slightly different. In some ways, it was indeed worth €350 because Frantzén says it costs the restaurant €349 to produce. 'Everything goes back to the customer. Everything. Our margin is almost zero.' The very best chefs pursue excellence first and work out how to handle the bottom line later. The other half of the partnership, pastry chef Daniel Lindeberg, told me that 40 per cent of the bill is accounted for by the price of the ingredients alone. The summer after my visit, to take the restaurant to the next level, they closed their small dining room to add an extra kitchen, increased the number of chefs to eleven and reduced the capacity to seventeen. Like an opera that requires an orchestra, a chorus and the world's best solo voices, it's this expensive because it costs this much to produce.

Of course, that is not the only, or even primary, meaning of worth. I think it was worth it because it was the experience of a lifetime, a revelation of the incredible heights culinary skill can soar to, but that does not mean I feel confident in saying I can justify going. For one thing, I was lucky. On the whole, I have not found the relatively few high-end restaurants I have been to worth the money, and I'm sure there are some I would actively not like. Going to a top restaurant is a very expensive gamble, and the fact that this time I won may not justify taking the risk in the first place.

Although I think Frantzén/Lindeberg was an aesthetic experience comparable in value to that of high art, opening my eyes to the wonders that can be achieved with food, I am not convinced that going again, or to other top restaurants, would have anything like the same effect. Every great artist enriches your imaginative and aesthetic horizons in her own way, and so every new work can open your eyes in new ways. Can food be the source of as much diversity and variety? The question is not rhetorical. I suspect the answer is no, but I'm not sure. Of course, cooking is constantly developing, and different chefs have different styles, and that is a reason to try the best more than once in a lifetime. But I do not think the difference in the kind of aesthetic experience given by the food of Ferran Adrià and René Redzepi is comparable to that between a Rembrandt and a Van Gogh. So it seems to me that although the aesthetic value of one visit to an exceptional restaurant might be higher than that of one particular visit to a gallery, you are much more enriched by ten good galleries than you can be by ten of the best restaurants.

Another reason why a world without fine dining would not be anywhere near as diminished as a world without the very best art is that if the value of the culinary arts is indeed connected to how they ground us in the immanent, then most of that value can be got by good, everyday eating. But fine art is in a completely different class to merely good art. A Rembrandt self-portrait gives a sense of humanity surpassing itself and an acute sense of the amazing potential of life that a merely competent portrait does not. With food, on the other hand, it does not take an exceptional genius to open us up to the wonder of being alive, and we can all buy a great cheese, salami or even loaf of bread that leaves us marvelling at what human ingenuity can achieve. That's why fine dining is dispensable in a way high art is not.

I do think, then, that a life without good food would be at least as impoverished as a life without good art, and that culinary art should indeed take its place alongside the other arts. But its value lies more in its daily practice than in the exceptional achievements of its finest practitioners. It is an art of the everyday, and all the better for that.

You might think the idea of food as the art of the immanent is like the unmentionable offal served by fashionable restaurants at sky-high prices: a load of pretentious bollocks. But even if eating is no more than a mere experience, some 'mere experiences' are so amazing they are worth it for their own sakes. Life is not just about such peak moments, but it is very much enriched by them. As Jay Rayner sees it, 'If it is OK to spend large sums of money watching your team play in the FA Cup final or see Eva-Maria Westbroek sing *The Ring Cycle* at the Royal Opera House – and we know how much that can cost – then there is no moral reason why it is wrong to spend that sort of money on a good experience. All it is about is how you wish to buy your memories and your experiences, and what price you attach to those experiences.'

If you do choose to spend some of your money on eating fabulously well, you can at least reassure yourself that many intellectuals have found great pleasure in good food too. Albert Camus' last meal, before he got into the car that crashed and killed him, was at Au Chapon Fin at Thoissey, then one of France's top restaurants. A. J. Ayer ate at the Ivy. David Hume claimed he had a 'great talent for cookery', boasting that when it comes to beef, cabbage, old mutton and old claret, 'Nobody excels me' and that one person who tried his sheep's-head broth couldn't stop talking about for it eight days.[110] Whether it is art or not, food is a perfectly respectable source of great pleasure.

Still, I can't shake the feeling that it is wrong to indulge in fine dining too often. The explanation for this came to me at the end of the meal at Frantzén/Lindeberg, with the petits fours that accompanied the coffee. I don't usually care much for macaroons, but these were ... the word that came to mind was 'extraordinary', but this must have been at least the dozenth time I'd used it. Does there not come a point at which to say yet another dish is 'outstanding' or 'extraordinary' becomes a contradiction in terms? How can more things stand out than not? Perhaps that's why it really would be wrong to do this kind of thing too often. Even Giorgio Locatelli disapproves of the customers who eat truffles at his expensive restaurant every day during the ten weeks or so of the autumn season. 'I have always thought,' he says, 'that you shouldn't eat them twenty times, just two or three times a year, because every time you taste a truffle, it should be a special thing.'[111] The extraordinary should not be allowed to become ordinary, no matter how good it is. Go to a really top restaurant, for the sheer pleasure and to expand your aesthetic sensibilities, but go rarely, and savour.

CHIPIRONES EN SU TINTA

Read almost any interview with a chef and they'll tell you that restaurant cooking is very different from home cooking. There are, however, certain things that have something of the glamour and exoticism of the restaurant but that can be made quite easily at home. One such dish is squid in its own ink, which I discovered while teaching English in Bilbao after university.

On return visits to Spain, I would sometimes buy a tin, as I did when they later became increasingly available in the UK. They were all very much second best. Then one day I came across an easy-enough-sounding recipe for them and I finally tried to recreate it for myself. The result was surprisingly delicious, all the more so because, I think, I had accepted that it was not going to be as good as the ones I used to eat and so was using my fond memory as a spur to try making something new rather than to exactly replicate the restaurant original.

The process is quite simple. Soften some chopped shallots and garlic with olive oil in a saucepan, and after they have sweated for a while, add the chopped baby squid, or another cephalopod such as cuttlefish. Then throw in some white wine and let most evaporate off, so there is not too much liquid. Add some chopped tinned tomatoes, lifting them from the can with a fork to leave most of the juice behind – draining is not necessary. Once it's simmering and it's not too liquidy, add some salt and the ink (usually sold separately in sachets – use about one per two servings), then cover and simmer for about forty-five minutes, until the squid is very tender. The sauce should be just thick enough that it won't readily run off the plate. If it isn't, blast on a high heat to boil some off or ladle some liquid into a separate pan and do the same, before returning. Best served with crusty bread. The same basic recipe, in lesser quantity and with the squid cut smaller, makes a wonderful pasta sauce.

Its colour alone makes it unusual and often leads people to be more impressed you've made it than they should be. Perhaps this is connected with the principle expounded by the chef in Peter Greenaway's film *The Cook, The Thief, His Wife and Her Lover*, which is that restaurants can 'charge a lot for anything black'. However, I'm not convinced by his rationale for this: 'Eating black food is like consuming death, like saying, "Death, I'm eating you."' That seems to be a classic example of the curator's note adding unnecessary pretension to what is simply a wonderful aesthetic experience.

20

Do lunch

RHYTHM

Imagine going to your doctor and being told, 'You're a classic case of early-onset Parkinson's.' What would be the best way to deal with such a shock, something you will later describe as the greatest disappointment of your life? Cry? Pray? See a therapist? If you're the chef Fergus Henderson, the answer is much simpler: 'I went and had a very good lunch and felt better.' Similarly, asked what he'd do if he lost everything tomorrow, he replied that although he would consider it 'a bit of a bugger', he would 'go and have lunch – that soothes everything – and think about how to readdress things'.[112]

If you think that all Henderson is talking about here is desperate 'comfort-eating', then you've got him, and lunch, wrong. Not that there need be anything wrong with comfort-eating. We are psuche-somatic beings, after all, so why shouldn't soothing our bodies soothe our souls? Although we sometimes simply seek a hit of fat, sugar and carbohydrate when we are down, often what we reach for has some emotional resonance: a taste of childhood, happier times, better places. Whether it has this quality or not, all good food has a remark-able potential to cut through our existential anxieties and remind us that even at the worst of times, normal, everyday life has been good and can be so again. As our hearts and minds tell us all is dreadful, our mouths can whisper, 'Yes, but pizza is still delicious.' Geoff Dyer cap-tured this experience perfectly when he wrote of an excellent plate of scrambled eggs, bacon and hash browns: 'I stifled my sobs and ate my breakfast, which did not taste any worse because I was having a nervous breakdown.'[113]

In any case, Henderson did not say he would go and comfort-eat a large chocolate bar, or more likely his favourite grilled tomato, cheese and ham ciabatta from Bar Italia in Soho.[114] He said he'd go for lunch, and lunch, like all meals, is not just an assembly of food. For example, food writer Seb Emina describes breakfast as 'a time of day, not just a meal'.[115] The same could be said of lunch and dinner too. If we only see breakfast as a means of putting some fuel in the tank to see us through until lunch, then a sugary cereal bar and a take-away latte en route to work might well be enough. But no matter how nutritionally adequate a breakfast on the go is, it sets the tone and rhythm of the day to functional and hurried. Eating becomes the first task on the agenda to be got out of the way as soon as possible, so that we can get on with being productive.

It's very different when you take the time to sit down and have a proper breakfast – not necessarily large, but eaten at a table over conversation, the radio, a newspaper or just our own thoughts. By starting the day with a pause, it asserts the value of pausing, so we keep things in focus and perspective and are not simply carried along with the treadmill of each day's obligations. It acts as a reminder that what is worth doing is worth the time it takes to do it properly, and that life is not just a to-do list to be ticked off as swiftly as possible.

As usual with good eating, many will protest that this is all very well but most of us just don't have the time to do it. Also as usual, the harsh answer is that it is rarely a brute matter of time availability but of priorities and time management. Giving yourself just fifteen minutes for breakfast means getting up, and so going to bed, a mere fifteen minutes earlier. I just cannot believe that most people couldn't do this if they wanted. If you feel you need that extra quarter of an hour sunk in your chair winding down with a glass of wine or three at day's end, that's probably a sign you need to make the change more than anybody. Obviously, when people have demanding lives, some such uncoiling is needed, but how much depends on how wound up you are in the first place, and I think that breakfast helps the day start with the coil as wound down as possible.

Lunch and dinner also help establish a healthy rhythm to life, and in this respect lunch might well be the most important meal of the day. In Britain and North America, lunch has largely become a cursory refuel, based in the UK around the standard combination of sandwiches – made from sliced bread, usually smeared with some kind of margarine and filled with cheese, ham or both – and a bag of crisps, of which Britons eat on average the equivalent of almost 100 packets per person per year.[116] I think it's telling that this basic formula is known as the 'packed lunch'. It's a starkly utilitarian phrase that has no proper translation in cultures where the midday meal is usually a more drawn-out, sat-down affair. Whether it's in a school lunchbox or a convenience store 'meal deal', the ubiquitous crisp-and-sandwich combination has standardised British lunchtimes with Stalinesque efficiency.

The Anglo-Saxon lunch, like breakfast, is thus something that is reduced to the minimum required for its eater to get on with pursuing the Protestant work ethic. In this culture, long lunches only ever have negative associations. 'Ladies who lunch' have nothing better to do, while business lunches are a perk of the salariat who down fine wine on company expenses. The 1980s notion that 'Lunch is for wimps' was not a weird aberration but an exaggerated version of the cultural norm. Only on Sunday is a longer, larger lunch valued, and that is because it is one of the last vestiges of the shared family meal.

How different it is in the Catholic and Orthodox countries surrounding the Mediterranean. Although Anglo-Saxon habits are establishing themselves there too, with France now the second-largest market for McDonald's outside the US, lunch is still largely a sit-down affair that lasts longer than many British lunch breaks, which for the average office worker is less than half an hour.[117]

Wanting to take more time is not the same as the romantic, hedonistic desire for the long, lazy, indulgent lunch. As Henderson understands, the main reason for valuing a proper midday meal is about the rhythm of the day. You've done your morning's work, and lunch provides an interval, a chance to recharge, take stock, get 'sorted and calm', setting you up for 'the potential of the afternoon'. To use another metaphor, the typical Anglo-Saxon day begins by jump-starting an already tired engine and then keeping it turning until it runs out of juice. The Mediterranean alternative is to give it a good check and top-up, get it going, then rest and oil it in the middle of the day so that it gets a second good run around in the afternoon and returns to the garage in decent nick.

This ebb and flow naturally leads to dinner, as the start of the slow-down before bed. Ideally, it shouldn't be too heavy: what you most want to be digesting as you prepare to end the day is what has gone on in it, not what you've just eaten. However, when we think of a special meal or eating out, dinner is still considered king, which is why if you do want to eat at a top restaurant, you can often do so considerably cheaper by going at the less popular lunchtime.

The way in which meals set the rhythm of the day is no trivial matter. The greater part of each waking day is spent working, and most of our days are workdays. We cannot have a good quality of life if these become joyless hours that leave us worn out and frustrated. We are not all lucky enough to find work that is richly rewarding, but if at least our working days follow a civilised routine and rhythm, one fit for psuche-somatic beings of body and mind, we can deal with them better and be left with more energy and enthusiasm for what matters most in the hours and days that remain.

RICE SALAD AND FRITTATA

In many cities and towns of the UK, it's not difficult to find a good soup or sandwich at a decent price, something that is, in terms of ingredients and freshness, close to the equivalent of home-made. No one should feel bad about eating this sort of thing rather than making their own. After all, the much-admired European lunch culture is not about do-it-yourself but eating at a modest restaurant or café.

When I do have to pack a lunch, I've got a couple of standbys. One is a rice salad, which can be made in bulk for a meal at home one day and another to go the next, or built around some deliberately leftover rice. For years I was very sceptical of rice salads, generally seeing them as dull affairs, padded out with flavourless store-cupboard standbys like tinned sweetcorn. But it doesn't take much to perk them up. Tomatoes and tuna are the most obvious ingredients to add, but capers, sliced boiled egg and chopped roasted red peppers can bring them to life, as does a generous amount of olive oil and a herb like oregano.

One thing to put between slices of bread that is more interesting than most is a frittata. What raises this from simply being a dull, cold omelette is the addition of plenty of strongly aromatic but unbulky ingredients, such as herbs, shallots, garlic, crushed chilli and grated Parmesan. These can be enough in themselves, or fry some vegetables, such as courgette or very small pieces of potato, in a pan first, then briefly add them to the beaten-egg mix before returning to the frying pan, which should be hot but not so much as to burn the underside before most of the rest has set. The knack is, I think, to avoid playing around with it too much. When you can see that the base has firmed up to the edges, lever up a bit to check it's done underneath, then lay a plate on top and invert the pan so the frittata is on the plate, uncooked side down, then slide it back into the pan to finish it off. There's no reason why the centre should not be a little runny, as it often is in its thicker Spanish cousin, the tortilla, although if you are eating it cold later, firmer may be less messy.

Of course, there's nothing to stop you wolfing down either of these lunches as hurriedly as any takeout sandwich. The how of lunch – and of life – matters at least as much as the what.

21

Eat alone

INTERIORITY

When I was a postgraduate student, I moved into a North London house as a lodger. My room was intended to be as self-contained as possible, being a decent size, with a shower in one corner and a sink, a fridge and two-ringed Baby Belling oven in another. There was just one thing it lacked and I asked the landlady, a university lecturer, whether she could get one or pay me back if I found a cheap one myself. The item in question was a small drop-leaf table, so I had somewhere to sit to have my meals.

Her reaction was not what I had expected. She seemed genuinely amazed that I – a young, single man – would want to eat at a table. Perhaps I was odd. The lodger before me didn't even know if the oven worked, because he ate only takeaways. It's not just young men either: one survey suggested that nearly a quarter of British homes do not have a dining table, and in those that do, fewer than half are used for eating meals.[118] That might be related to the fact that 7.6 million people (around 15 per cent of the adult population) in the UK live alone, meaning nearly a third of British homes have only one occupant.[119]

There is a strong cultural assumption that eating well and being single do not go together. Almost all the archetypal images of good eating are social: Sunday lunch with the family, a romantic table for two, a lively dinner party where wine and conversation flow with ease. Think now of the stereotypical images of solo dining: the miserable bachelor with his Pot Noodle, the spinster with her calorie-controlled ready meal, the lonely pensioner with her tin of soup. The only solo eating that is generally considered pleasurable is the guilty binge – with the emphasis firmly on 'guilty' – on whole boxes of chocolates or tubs of ice cream, and this is most likely to be seen as a sad, desperate means of suffocating sorrows. As for restaurants, people eating alone there are generally assumed to have been stood up or to be milking an expense budget on a business trip. Despite the avalanche of cookery books over recent decades, only one major volume has been targeted at the single cook, Delia Smith's *One Is Fun*. Its very title implies that most people think it is not.

I've spent more of my adult life by myself than in relationships, and having seen both sides of the coin, I wouldn't want to exaggerate the joys of living and eating by yourself. Some do actually prefer to live alone, while others find being by themselves so difficult that they'd rather live with almost anyone, no matter how unsuitable. Most of us are somewhere in the middle, and as I said when single and still say now, if you do happen to be alone, you don't have to pretend that it is the ideal to be perfectly content. For while the best may be a good relationship, or to live with people you get on with, the worst is to be stuck in a terrible relationship or to have to suffer intolerable housemates. Both Heaven and Hell are other people, while Earth has some perfectly pleasant desert islands.

When praising the virtues of the solitary life, people often talk about independence or self-sufficiency, but it seems to me neither of these is necessarily a good in itself. Make either a cardinal virtue and you deny yourself the greater rewards that come from a fruitful interdependence with others. There is also a whiff of virtue-from-necessity about this, since most people, if honest, would happily sacrifice a large part of their independence for the right life partner. The real virtue that solitude tests us for is interiority. Whether we live by ourselves or with others, we all benefit from having a rich inner life.

By this I do not mean only the things that require no external stimulus. If anything, I mean the opposite. To have a rich inner life means that you are able to take in what you experience and process it in your own mind, intellectually, aesthetically or emotionally. In the absence of such interiority, experiences just skim the surface and life becomes superficial. The person who lacks interiority can be amused, entertained, excited or soothed. But take away whatever is stimulating these reactions and they are left with nothing. The person who has interiority is able to extend and deepen such experiences, by memory, reflection, silent interrogation or using them as inspiration for some creative activity of their own. By such means, the person is not retreating more into themselves but becoming more actively engaged with what surrounds them. In a seeming paradox, it is therefore people who need the constant stimulation of others who are often most alone and least engaged with the world. Social activity is essentially a distraction from the existential challenge of confronting what is inside them. Hollow men don't sit and read.

For most people, cooking and eating do not greatly feed their inner lives. For some of us, they do. If you are remotely interested in food, however, then no meal is ever simply an opportunity to refuel. You will be attending to what is pleasant or unpleasant about the dish, how you might do things differently next time or how you might reproduce it yourself at home. These are not high-minded thoughts, but they have a role to play in a life that is enquiring and attentive to the richness and value of quotidian experience.

Singletons are as capable of such engagement as anyone, and of taking pleasure from what they eat. So why is it so many people talk and act as though eating alone can or should only be a form of refuelling? It is as though people implicitly assume single people *should not* or *cannot* take pleasure from cooking and eating. But why not? Hardly anyone believes no one should take pleasure from cooking and eating, so it can't just be an extension of that.

At times like these, when a rational explanation for an attitude seems to be lacking, I try out the suggestion of the philosopher Janet Radcliffe Richards, which is to ask, 'What belief would make it rational?' If there is only one plausible candidate, then no matter how crazy the belief is, you have good reason to think that is what lies behind it.[120] In this case, I think the only explanation is that food and eating are just two examples of a wider belief – implicit rather than explicit – that single people should not or cannot take pleasure from *living*. Of course, stated so boldly, few would assert such a thing, but if you look at how people talk and act around single people, that does indeed seem to be the working assumption. The self-professed happy loner is widely assumed to be either a freak or in denial.

The evolutionary just-so story for this prejudice would be that our pro-social bias is a product of our need to cooperate as a species. We are wary of loners because they spurn the sociability that we need to survive. That might also be why people who say they are happy not to have children are also often treated with some suspicion. Whether or not evolution is the cause, there does appear to be a sense in which the perfectly content singleton is seen as a threat. Their apparent lack of need for other people makes others feel needy in comparison. Their ability to be content with their lot makes our own desire for more seem excessive. Perhaps that view is so internalised that it explains why many single people don't actually take time to cook and eat as well as they might: the thought that they could be content to live alone scares them. Only freaks and eccentrics happily live alone, they assume, and I'm not going to become one of them.

These are somewhat speculative thoughts, but the main point should be uncontroversial. There simply is no good reason why we should not enjoy cooking and eating alone, if we have some interest in food. Almost everyone would agree in principle, but in practice the widespread prejudice against the lone eater is evident.

'Feeling comfortable alone in a restaurant is a real sign of being a grown-up,' the philosopher Barry Smith told me. 'You are the most comfortable person. You can survey the room, you can watch the married couples not speaking to each other, you can watch eager youngsters on a date and so on, and you're at ease: you can really savour the food, take your time.'

Although some may actively prefer eating alone, Smith, like me, prefers eating in good company, while eating in bad company is the worst option of all. Eating alone conforms to my own personal life motto: less than perfect, more than good enough. What's more, it provides an opportunity to nurture the kind of rich interiority that makes us more developed, interesting people when we do get to share the table with others.

CHILLI NON CARNE

There are plenty of things that can easily be cooked for one, and others that make a couple of portions, the second of which can be reheated the next day or, even better, served a second time with a twist. Vegetable chilli is one. There is no such thing as a traditional recipe for this, but I think I've developed quite a good one. At its base is chopped red pepper and garlic, gently fried in olive oil in a saucepan. If using fresh chilli, chop finely and cook together with these. It really is impossible to say how much: it depends on how hot the chillies are and how hot you like your chilli. Smaller tend to be hotter, so if cautious, start with a couple of any size and see how you like it.

When soft, add mushrooms, some in larger pieces, others very finely chopped. This gives an almost meaty, mincey texture and flavour. Next the spices: dried chillies if you haven't used fresh, or in addition if you like it hot; some cumin perhaps; and for me, plenty of pimentón to impart a deep, smoky flavour. Add some diced aubergine, frying until a little shrunk. Then add tinned, chopped tomatoes and tinned or precooked beans. People tend to go for red kidney beans, but for my money, mixed, pinto or black-eye beans are better. Now for the secret ingredients: a teaspoon or so of Marmite and a couple of teaspoons of cocoa powder, the latter an essential element of Mexican *mole*. The Marmite is already salty, so you don't need to add much more salt. You probably don't need much more liquid either, perhaps a little water. Then just gently simmer until the aubergine is as you like it.

This basic template can be adjusted by experiment to create your own perfect version, swapping vegetables, beans and spices as you prefer. It will taste even better the next day, when the flavours have fused. A good twist when reheating is to crack an egg and poach it in the mixture, serving before the yolk has set.

22

Share the joy

'Don't use that word in my kitchen!' Cat Gazzoli, CEO of Slow Food UK, loves her movement's ethos but can't stand its esoteric lexicon. Specialist local foods are gathered in a metaphorical 'Ark of Taste', protected by local *'presidia'* and celebrated on the annual 'Terra Madre' day. For Gazzoli, all this alienates potential British members who might be put off joining their local group, especially if it is known by its official Slow Food name – the one she has banned – a *convivium*.

With its roots in the Latin for 'conviviality', the word might simply evoke what Italians call *commensalità*, the companionship and sociability of the table. The combination of good food, good wine and good company is often and rightly celebrated. The risk, however, is that this is all *convivium* evokes, and so Slow Food, a campaigning NGO, is seen as little more than a middle-class dining club, which, in Britain at least, is precisely what it has sometimes become. Not that it is accurate to think of this kind of conviviality as an essentially middle-class pursuit anyway. For instance, in late-1970s France, the sociologist Pierre Bourdieu found that 'Peasants and especially industrial workers maintain an ethic of convivial indulgence', while those 'at the highest levels of the social hierarchy' had succumbed to 'the new ethic of sobriety for the sake of slimness'. So whereas at 'bourgeois or petit-bourgeois' restaurants and cafés 'Each table is a separate, appropriated territory', the working-class café is 'a site of companionship'.[121]

But conviviality could mean so much more than this. The etymology of the word shows it is a conjunction of the Latin *com* ('together') and *vivere* ('to live'). When these two words were conjoined, the result was something joyous: the verb *convivere*, meaning 'to carouse together' and the noun *convivium*, meaning a 'feast'. Conviviality is thus the art of living together, not in the sense of just rubbing along or mutual toleration, but with warmth and pleasure.

This conviviality should not be confined to groups of friends at table, but should extend even to strangers. Many people who have spent time in the poorer areas of the world have returned with stories of the hospitality of people they met, usually expressed by the offering of some kind of food. The sharing of meals has always been one of the simplest and most powerful ways of making someone welcome, signalling an assumption of benevolence rather than mutual suspicion.

One of the most impressive institutionalised versions of this kind of hospitality is found in the Sikh tradition of *langar*. All over the world, anyone can go to a Gurudwara, the Sikh place of worship, and be given a free meal, no questions asked. I saw one in action at the Gurudwara served by Guru Nanak Nishkam Sewak Jatha in Birmingham, which serves around 25,000 meals a week, all prepared by volunteers (*sewadaars*).

'*Langar* is a tradition that was started by our first guru way back in the fifteenth century,' the chairman of the organisation, Bhai Sahib Bhai Mohinder Singh – known as Bhai Sahib Ji, told me. 'His father gave him the equivalent of twenty rupees and said, "Go, child, and do some good business," and he served food to holy people who were very hungry. He came back and said, "I have done true business, Dad." The dad was not very happy.'

Given what business generally means, that's understandable. *Langar* isn't business, says Bhai Sahib Ji; it's service. 'There are people who go and eat out at McDonald's. The food may taste very nice, but there is something absent there: that is love and devotion with which it is cooked.'

The free offering of food allows us to relate to one another in ways that are not purely transactional or designed for the maximisation of self-interest. It is another example of how food is importantly grounding, bringing us all down to the same level. It does not seem a coincidence that '*Langar* is a Persian word also used for a ship's anchor', as Bhai Sahib Ji told me. 'There's equality to have everybody sit on the same level and be served the same thing, without exceptions. It's good for your ego, which is a bad human affliction. Even the Mughal emperor had to come and be served food just as ordinary people and that happens every day in the Darbar Sahib (Golden Temple), for example. About 130,000 people are served food every day there, and the people who are super rich and the people who are very poor, they're all sitting in the same way.'

This levelling is even more effective when everyone at some point is both the server and the served. Bhai Sahib Ji himself serves tea every afternoon he is at the Gurudwara. 'The fact is that you will not serve anybody food if you are not humble, if you do not have this love of the other, if you do not want to go beyond yourself.'

The mutuality of *langar*, that you can serve one day and be served the next, as well as the fact that it is for all, not just the hungry, means it has none of the feel of a charitable soup kitchen. 'Charity gives you a bit of this egoistic streak, that *you* are giving charity, whereas you should actually feel happy that you have been able to serve somebody,' says Bhai Sahib Ji. But being benevolent is not an optional act of kindness; it is a duty. He says, 'We feel an honour to serve people,' and the *sewadaars* I spoke to expressed the same sentiment.

The virtues expressed so completely in *langar* are found in other religious traditions too, which almost invariably recognise the important role the sharing of food has to play in bringing people together and getting them to relate to each other in the right ways.

For instance, I went to several Benedictine monasteries and found that the meals are seen as very important parts of the life of the community. The high value placed on meals, Father Christopher Jamison told me, 'is to do with the communion aspect. This is an opportunity for service; it's an opportunity to be together as a community, and to listen together, because the meals are in silence.' But during festivals, meals are also opportunities to express joy 'because you have special meals where you might have talking, and then you have a feast-day meal and so you choose to eat a lot and you choose to do that together'.

What is really important about this form of communion is that it is on a fully human plane. 'When we come together for the meal, we're together both spiritually but really physically as well, sharing food together, a very human thing to do,' said Father Joseph of Mount Saint Bernard Abbey in Leicestershire. Similarly, Downside Abbey's Dom David said, 'In the refectory, it's just human beings doing human things, like eating and helping each other and wiping up puddles of water and messes. Just very human things,' albeit done 'in order to cultivate at a human level a sense of God's presence in each of us and a sense of being together in Him'.

Joy, sharing, community, service, humanity. I think our approach to all food aid should express the same values. It should be seen not as a gift from the haves to the have-nots but as a sharing we do out of duty and fellow feeling. Nor is it just about providing nutrients, vital though that is. Conviviality, living together, is also about sharing pleasure. There's a wonderful illustration of this in the film of *Babette's Feast*. Babette, a French chef, has fled the Revolution and is the housekeeper for two ageing spinster sisters who are continuing the religious community started by their father. Babette prepares the soups and breads that the sisters take to the poor of the village, who are shown savouring the simple but delicious meals. When she temporarily leaves, however, the same people are shown frowning at the brown sludge the sisters have prepared in her absence. It is good to provide food so people can stay alive, but better if you can give them food that allows them to really live, not just exist. Survival is not the ultimate aim of sharing wealth and helping others; it is simply the means to the real goal of enabling more people to live a full life.

The true conviviality of food is not just to be found in its preparation and eating, but also in its growing. The Incredible Edible Todmorden project, for example, is 'not about vegetables', says activist Estelle Brown. 'It's about making the community stronger.' This is not primarily about the relatively few people who are highly active in the growing. It's about the way in which the simple act of cultivation seems to bring everyone together. 'People have started talking to each other. If you plant a carrot in a public place, everyone that comes past will have a better way of doing it, will know how their granny did it; maybe they won't know what it is and they'll stop to say, "What the heck's that?", so it gets everybody in one conversation.'

The project has certainly benefited more people than a small group of middle-class foodies. Realising that people in social housing or on benefit were less likely to come to meetings, the group set up camp kitchens on the housing estates and shouted to people to come out and get some free food. They also wheeled up barrows full of free tomato plants for the residents' gardens. The estates now have their own raised beds and the local housing association, Pennine Housing 2000, came in on the project, so all new tenants are issued with a grow bag, chitted potatoes and permission to keep chickens.

Across the town as a whole, vandalism and criminal damage have gone down by over a quarter since the project started. Even the drunks who sit under the canal's horse tunnel have stopped littering the towpath and water with their bottles. Brown says they were 'three sheets to the wind' at another of their favourite haunts, the bus shelter, the day the TV chef Hugh Fearnley-Whittingstall came to film his programme at the town's harvest festival. 'Hugh and his team went along to pick herbs from the bus station and they rushed out and said, "You bugger! You put them down! They belong to Todmorden!"'

There seems to be something about the cultivation of food that softens the edges of the built environment. That is perhaps most striking at the police station, which now has several raised beds outside the front, with quirky names like 'Sergeant Browning's Lonely Peppers Club Band', 'Pollination Station' and 'A Fair Crop'. 'It's a fun aspect of a place where someone comes to report bad things that have happened or where they want help and assistance,' the duty officer inside told me. 'It makes it more accessible.'

It's easy to get too romantic about the bonding power of food. As a counterweight, we should also remember that people have gone to war over land and water, and farmers across the world have always fought over accusations of sheep- and cattle-rustling. In some respects, how we do or do not share food is a kind of barometer of the strength of human relations. Withholding hospitality, refusing to share a table, these are the clearest signs of hostility. And this has a political dimension. At the moment, global trade rules do not reflect a healthy international conviviality. In place of sharing, there is a limited form of charity from rich to the poor. Instead of equality, rich countries make it harder for poorer countries to export produce by subsidising their own farmers and putting up trade barriers.

Conviviality is shallow, egotistical and purely hedonistic if it is confined to our friends at the dinner table. Real, ethical conviviality is about recognising our shared humanity, seeing that we are all in service to one another, and that by sharing what is good we can live together not just in peace but in joy. Food is the ideal vehicle for this, because when we break good bread, we can never forget that we are all, in essence, fragile, mortal, fleshy beings who have learned how to transform a means of survival into one of life's most satisfying pleasures.

MEZE

The Middle Eastern meze is perhaps the archetypal sharing meal, all the more so because it is a style of eating that the Ottoman culture it grew out of has shared with the world. Its typical components are also reassuringly earthy, simple dishes, whose flavours seem only a few steps away from the soil and the farm.

Hummus, which I covered earlier, is one staple component. Baba ganoush is another. All you need do to make this is split an aubergine and cook both sides under a hot grill until soft, so that the skin is charred – this is essential for the smoky taste. Scoop out the flesh and mix it with one or more of olive oil, lemon juice, tahini, a dash of yoghurt and cumin.

Tzatziki is made simply by deseeding and peeling a cucumber, grating the flesh and leaving it in a sieve with some salt to draw out the excess water. Then add to Greek yoghurt (which you can make simply by straining ordinary yoghurt through muslin for a few hours) with a generous amount of chopped mint or dill, lemon juice and olive oil to taste, and crushed garlic if you like.

Gigantes plaki is made by adding nearly cooked giant white beans to a basic tomato sauce, with dill or perhaps another herb added, then putting it in the oven for forty-five minutes to an hour – depending on whether you cook slow and low or at a higher temperature – until the sauce has thickened and the beans are cooked. If you can't get the giant beans, butter beans will do, and if you can't be bothered to prepare from dried beans, just reduce the sauce a bit before putting in the oven and don't leave it there too long.

A salad of tomato, feta and cucumber is always easy, but for something a little more interesting, grill or griddle thin slices of courgette, lay on a plate, sprinkle small pieces of feta and mint leaves on top, then dress with lemon juice, olive oil and salt.

For a simple flatbread, just mix ten parts plain flour to six parts warm water and a dash of salt, and knead well to form a dough. Cover and leave to rest for a while: different cooks advise anything between ten minutes and an hour. Divide into balls, roll out thin and cook one by one on a pretty-hot non-stick frying pan, dry or with a little oil or butter, turning once the bread has started to char. It only takes a few minutes each side, and if you get it just right, air pockets will form, lifting the top from the bottom.

The word 'companion' literally means those with (*com-*) whom we share bread (*pan*). Freshly baked bread is therefore one of the most fitting symbols for how we humans combine sensual pleasure, creativity, intellect and sociability. Making and sharing such a simple bread is thus one of the purest examples of psuche-somatic living.

23

Seize not the day

Nando Parrado and his friends have a motto: 'Eat every sandwich, kiss every girl.' It's a wonderfully down-to-earth version of the more familiar advice of Horace: '*Carpe diem*', or 'Seize the day.' Parrado's maxim was inspired not so much by a brush with death as a long walk with the Reaper. In 1972 he went on a rugby trip from his native Uruguay to Chile. The plane never landed, but slammed into the Cordillera de los Andes at 18,000 feet. Among those immediately killed were his mother and youngest sister. Incredibly, however, Parrado and sixteen others survived for seventy-two days, culminating in an eleven-day trek out of the high mountains.[122]

The experience was extreme, but many others have come close to death and the vast majority end up saying a version of the same thing: it has made me feel lucky to be alive and determined to make the most of every day. It is a sad but all too human weakness that often it is not until people stare death in the face that they realise just how valuable life is. Living with a heightened sense of the sheer wonder of being alive is something that seems hard to sustain, even after we have become acutely aware of our mortality. This is brilliantly satirised in an episode of *The Simpsons* in which Homer believes he has eaten a poisonous fugu fish and only has twenty-two hours to live. When the next dawn arrives and he realises he hasn't died, he exclaims, 'I'm alive! From this day forward I vow to live life to its fullest!' The credits of the show, however, simply show him sitting in front of his television, watching bowling and munching on pork rinds, completely unreformed.[123]

Homer may be an oaf, but none of us is immune from the pattern. Havi Carel is a philosopher who was diagnosed with a rare lung disease that threatened to end her life within a decade. Soon afterwards, she wrote how the resulting acute awareness of her mortality taught her to 'rejoice in small pleasures', be 'generous towards myself and others' and 'grateful for every moment that is not consumed by sorrow, pain or despair'.[124] A few years later, however, as her condition stabilised and the immediate threat of death subsided, she acknowledged that maintaining that same focus on essentials had become harder.

Making the most of each day is not easy for anyone. It is a kind of art, one that requires an understanding of the human condition as well as simple *joie de vivre*. Certainly the slogans used to implore us to make the most of life are not very helpful. Parrado doesn't literally mean 'Eat every sandwich, kiss every girl.' That's not a recipe for life but a manual for becoming an overweight, immature, lifelong singleton. The literal reading of '*Carpe diem*' is not much better. The one thing we cannot do with our days is seize them. Being fully aware of your humanity means also being fully aware of the extent to which you are a creature for whom time is always, unstoppably passing. Trying to seize the day is therefore like trying to stop the tide.

You could say that's the point. Life is absurd and the only way to deal with it is to engage with an heroic but ultimately helpless struggle to grab hold of it as hard as you can. It's a kind of twist on Camus's *Myth of Sysiphus*. Sysiphus is condemned by the gods for ever to push a heavy stone up a hill, only for it to roll back down to the bottom again every time. Sisyphus can only be happy if he embraces his fate, ultimately pointless though it is. The idea that we should seize the day sounds like an equally ingenious game of the gods. This time we are condemned to spend our lives in a pen trying to chase and catch a greased pig, one that we can get our hands around but never keep hold of for more than a few seconds, the length of the 'specious present', defined by William James as 'the short duration of which we are immediately and incessantly sensible'.[125] It's a futile game, but unless we play it, we're just left standing in the pen with nothing to do, and once the game is over, so are we. So play. It's fun and better than the alternatives. 'Carpe diem' is thus a call to hedonism, the pursuit of pleasure.

If you are just going to enjoy the ride as much as you can, the pleasures of the flesh offer the most obvious options, of which eating, drinking and being merry are the easiest. It's not as potentially complicated as the relentless pursuit of sex, and no one gets hurt – much, at least. You can also easily do it at least three times a day, something that, if we're honest, is much harder to keep up if you try the other alternative.

A vivid example of the cheery binger is Samuel Pepys, whose diary reveals a man who didn't just chronicle London; he ate it. A not untypical dinner-party menu for not more than a dozen people included: 'Fricasse of rabbets and chicken – a leg of mutton boiled – three carps in a dish – a great dish of a side of lamb – a dish of roasted pigeons – a dish of four lobsters – three tarts – a Lampry [an eel-like river fish] pie, a most rare pie – a dish of anchoves – good wine of several sorts.' This apparently gratuitous excess becomes a bit more understandable when you read the context in which the gorging took place. 'Above 700 dead of the plague this week,' Pepys writes at one point, almost as an aside, like noting the day's temperature reading. When the world around you is going to Hell, it's understandable to think, To hell with it. But still, this excess takes its toll, even on the crudest hedonic calculus. Pepys's diary is full of remarks like 'My head hath aked all night and all this morning with my last night's debauch' and 'When I waked I found myself wet with my spewing.'[126]

Even if the pleasures outnumber the pains, there is something unsatisfactory, profoundly sad even, about a life lived solely in pursuit of the next amusement. No matter how good a meal is, you sit satisfied by its warm glow for only so long, which is not very long at all. We can leave the table full, but at the same time empty, for we take away nothing but memories. The next day the chase has to begin again. Pleasure does not store well, so when you make it your quarry, you are condemned to constantly hunt to keep up the supply, and if it is cut off, then you are left with nothing.

But is there a better way? The traditional alternative seems even worse. It is to renounce the pleasures of the flesh, or at least reduce them to a minimum, and embrace the satisfactions of the soul. Instead of seizing the day, let eternity seize you. Turn to God, or the divine, transcend the pathetic limitations of our animal existence and seek instead the Kingdom of Heaven, a world without end, where there is happiness without limit.

If you believe that we have no immortal soul, that there is no Heaven and no God, that's obviously a non-starter. Even if you have a faith, it's not as simple as that. If life goes on after death, for instance, you will remain a person who lives across time, always in the present but also with a past and future, and that means you still face the same question of how to live. The greased pig still can't be caught, even if the game goes on for ever. If it's just the case that something of your essence returns to the godhead, or some such other vaguely comforting view of an impersonal life to come, that means you, as an individual, will go the way of your body.

So we are caught between the limitations of immanence and the illusions of transcendence. We can neither seize the day nor the eternal. What are we then to do?

We could start by getting clearer about what exactly pleasure is and the role it has to play in the life well lived. Pleasure has been a recurring presence in this book, but it has generally lurked in the background, only straying centre stage occasionally and briefly. Some might consider this an unjustified slight on what should be at the head of the table, served by the virtues that gather around it. If, as I contend, to know how to eat is to know how to live, then aren't the arts of living and eating ultimately about knowing how to get the most pleasure from both?

It's not as simple as that, as perennial philosophical disagreement about the nature of pleasure and its role in the good life shows. Whereas for some philosophers, such as Epicurus, 'Pleasure is the beginning and the end of the blessed life',[127] for others, like Plato, it is 'the greatest incitement to evil'.[128] Pleasure has been seen as our highest aspiration or our basest motivation.

How can it be that great minds are divided on something so basic? Because, I think, each has a part of the truth, but neither sees that they belong to the same whole. One part is provided by Jeremy Bentham, the patron saint of ethical hedonism. Bentham believed that the 'utility' of every action should be judged 'according to the tendency it appears to have to augment or diminish the happiness of the party whose interest is in question'. Of course, happiness is itself complex and not the same as pleasure. But for Bentham, 'benefit, advantage, pleasure, good, or happiness [all] in the present case comes to the same thing', and he did not think it matters where pleasure comes from, as long as it does not diminish that of others.[129] All pleasures are equal, a simple bar game such as pushpin being as good as poetry, if that's what floats your boat.[130]

The second part is provided by Bentham's godson, John Stuart Mill, who broadly agreed with his mentor about the centrality of pleasure and happiness, but who thought that the 'higher' pleasures of the intellect were superior to the 'lower' pleasures of the body.[131] Following in the tradition of Aristotle, Mill believed that our highest capacities are those that are uniquely human, while those we share with beasts are of lesser value.

The third and final piece of the jigsaw comes from the disparate, diverse and so for our purposes leaderless group of all those who believe that pleasure has at most a peripheral part to play in the good life, and may have none at all.

Although their positions as a whole are incompatible, in a very important sense all three parties get something different right, and they all get the same thing wrong. The common mistake can be found in the disagreement between Bentham and Mill over the different kinds of pleasure. This dispute rests on a distinction between higher and lower pleasures according to the kinds of things in which we take pleasure. So food, sex and other carnal pleasures are categorised as 'lower', while art, discourse and learning are 'higher'. But there is another component of pleasure that this division completely misses: it is not just *what* we take pleasure in that matters, but *how*. The young child who reads Shakespeare, without understanding what it means, is not experiencing a higher pleasure than that she gets from reading *The Very Hungry Caterpillar*. The pig eating a truffle is not exercising the same kind of appreciation as a gourmand who shaves it over pasta. What elevates or debases a pleasure has a lot to do with *how* we enjoy it, not just *what* 'it' is.

It is clearly true that some things contain more potential for higher pleasure than others. The child can in time learn to appreciate the complexities of *Hamlet*, but *The Very Hungry Caterpillar* will always remain a simple joy. You can learn to discriminate the layers of flavour and aroma in a glass of Barolo, but you'll never get more from a bottle of plonk than a big, fruity, alcoholic smack in the mouth. However, for centuries, the orthodox assumption in philosophy and in Western culture as a whole appears to have been that any experience with a strong sensuous component is by its nature irredeemably base and so only has potential for lower pleasure. If that's right, food and thinking just don't go. Plato expresses this prejudice with helpful clarity in his dialogue *Gorgias*: 'Cookery, in attending upon pleasure, never regards either the nature or reason of that pleasure to which she devotes herself, but goes straight to her end.'[132] Even if, as a matter of fact, this is almost always true, Plato doesn't consider the possibility that it need not be. Cookery does not have to be put in the service of satisfying unquestioned desires. As I have argued in this book, we can and should think about the wider significance of cooking and eating, and change the way we approach both accordingly.

So Mill was right in his basic insight that some pleasures are higher than others, and Bentham was right to deny that the hierarchy can be constructed on the basis of the kinds of things we draw pleasure from. But both were wrong to miss the key point that the *how* of pleasure is at least as important as the *what*. Perhaps the root of this mistake is the strong dualistic current in Western philosophy that keeps mind and body apart, failing to account for our psuche-somatic unity. Mill and Bentham thought of pleasures as being either bodily or intellectual, when the richest are both.

Another mistake they made was to think that pleasure is not just an important human good, it is *the* Good. But many of the things we find valuable, worthwhile or interesting are not pleasurable. Think of all the things you most value in your life. You would not desert your life partner if she became so ill that there was not much you could both take pleasure in anymore. Creative work is often, perhaps mostly, not particularly enjoyable. A pure hedonist would not choose to have children, and to call the satisfaction it gives 'pleasure' seems facile.

The mistake is not avoided if we extend the notion of pleasure to what we'd ordinarily call happiness, as Bentham suggested. True, happiness and pleasure are different. Pleasure is more connected to particular experiences and periods of time, usually quite short. Happiness is more of a background feeling, which may usually be less intense than pleasure but which lingers for longer. It's even possible, without contradiction, to insist that one is happy when in a bad mood, if one recognises the mood as a passing irritation that has nothing to do with one's underlying contentment.

But despite these differences, happiness and pleasure, as usually conceived, are fundamentally the same kind of thing: varieties of good feeling, or what psychologists call 'positive affect'. And although there are some positive psychologists who insist that positive affect is all that matters in human life, I don't think many of us find that credible. For example, Michael Haneke's film *Amour* tells the story of the declining health of an elderly woman, Anne, and her husband Georges's care for her. It's brilliantly observed, poignant and moving, but not remotely enjoyable, or even uplifting in any conventional sense. Glumly eating dinner after seeing it, I was aware that this had not been the relaxing evening off I had perhaps originally had in mind. It did not make me happy, but I was gratified that my life had been enriched, not diminished, by my choosing to see it rather than opting for a more pleasurable alternative.

We can now see what the philosophers who have denied pleasure a central role in their accounts of the good life have got right. It is a mistake to think of the pursuit of pleasure as being the primary task of life. That is not just because there is more to life than positive affect, but also because the best pleasures are generally not so much sought, but found, when we live according to the virtues. We are made happiest by activities that we undertake for reasons other than their pure hedonic potential, when we see and understand what is of value in them. That is why the moral issues around food concerning animal welfare, fair trade and the environment are not just problems to be solved so we can get on with the business of enjoying ourselves. Rather, we enjoy ourselves more fully, more humanly, when we do so in good conscience, knowing that our food's provenance is as good as its taste.

That's also why, although things like creative work and parenthood often neither give consistent pleasure nor make us happy, it is no coincidence that these things are also the sources of the deepest pleasures, when they come. The only way to make sense of this, I think, is to see the most valuable forms of pleasure as being tied up with the most valuable aspects of life, rather than to see pleasure as the only important reason why we do anything at all. Raising children brings pleasure because it is valued so much; it is not valued because it brings pleasure.

The insight is therefore that it matters how we get our pleasures. That is not a purely tactical point, that pursuing pleasure directly, for its own sake, is not usually the best way of achieving it. It is that making pleasure our primary goal draws us away from those features of experience that provide the deepest satisfactions, whether they involve positive affect or not. I don't mean to argue that there aren't some things we value largely because they give a particularly rich kind of pleasure. But it is a clue that even in those occasions, it would be a mistake to think of pleasure as simply a kind of feeling divorced from the fully psuche-somatic context from which it arises.

If we understand the real value and nature of pleasure, we will therefore abandon its direct pursuit and instead focus on what the most rewarding, satisfying way to live is, and I think we will find that involves neither grasping the moment nor hanging on for eternity. The key is to understand our psuche-somatic nature, why we are more than animals who are trapped in the moment but less than gods abiding beyond time. True, we are only ever immediately aware of now – we cannot go back in time, and we cannot stop our time from running out. But we are also creatures that exist *across* time. We have memories of the past; plans for the future; projects that take hours, days, weeks, even years; relationships that grow, develop and end. Living for the moment is not enough, because life is not a moment. And although it is in one way comprised of moments, it is not simply a series of moments, but a pattern made up of the relations across them. It's the difference between, for example, spending a year simply enjoying one experience after another, ticking off the bucket list of things to do before you die, and one when you engage in some kind of project, with a beginning, middle, end and result. Both years are made up of moments, but one is a mere series, an aggregate, whereas the other is a whole greater than the sum of its parts.

Many of the things we most value are like this. A relationship is built from days together, but it is more than a collection of days. This book is made up of around 90,000 words, but it is, I hope, more than just a collection of words.

How do we live in such a way that does justice both to our root-edness in moments of time and our existence over time? *Carpe diem* hedonism doesn't do it, because it can't accommodate the integrity over time provided by *psuchê*; striving for the eternal doesn't do it because it can't accommodate the way in which *soma* binds us to the finite and temporal. What we need instead is a fully psuche-somatic ethic that balances these two aspects of human existence. The project of constructing such an ethic is much larger than the scope of this book. Food, however, can provide a clear example of what it might look like in practice, and why it is needed.

For example, we should reject the hedonist who implores, 'Don't die with a bottle of champagne in the fridge,' and so for whom every pleasure is greedily leaped upon, and life becomes a frantic race against the clock. We should also spurn the ascetic who preaches, 'Don't put champagne in the fridge in the first place,' denying the role physical pleasure plays in our lives. Rather, we should listen to the psuche-somatic person who says, 'Don't die with *two* bottles of champagne in the fridge.' We don't need to gratify every desire immediately and so become slaves to our urges, but nor should we be so abstemious that we let the pleasures available to us pass us by. This balanced attitude embraces the role food plays in the lives of us animals without reducing us to mere slaves of our atavistic desires.

Such an approach acknowledges the proper role pleasure plays in the good life. Our higher intellects should not make us leave the pleasures of the flesh behind; rather they should enable us to enjoy them more completely. The British polymath William Kitchiner captured this idea beautifully in *The Cook's Oracle* of 1830: 'Those cynical slaves who are so silly as to suppose it unbecoming a wise man to indulge in the common comforts of life, should be answered in the words of the French philosopher. "Hey – what, do you philosophers eat dainties?" said a gay Marquess. "Do you think," replied Descartes, "that God made good things only for fools?"'[133]

We can see what it means to experience pleasure in a fully psuche-somatic way if we contrast '*Carpe diem*' with mindful appreciation. Both are injunctions to make the most of each moment, but they differ in how they understand what 'making the most' means. The hedonistic version is the pursuit of as many and as intensely pleasurable moments as possible. Mindfulness, however, is not about the pursuit of anything. In place of the fevered hunt for pleasure, it requires approaching everything we do in a frame of mind that makes us most sensitive to what it has to offer. That also means its focus is wider than pleasure, which is just one of the things we ought to attend to.

To eat as a hedonist is therefore to seek out the most delicious dishes, always looking for new experiences and to repeat the best of prior ones. To eat mindfully, in contrast, is to make sure that whatever you are eating, you are paying attention to what it is and also to what it means, being mindful of your good fortune, of what sacrifices needed to be made to bring the food to you and so on. So whereas hedonism encourages the indulgence of pleasure, mindfulness encourages a wider appreciation. That is not to say mindfulness precludes pleasure: quite the opposite. When what you are eating is delicious, being mindful makes you deeply aware of it. The difference is that whereas hedonism fosters a grasping attitude, a desire to capture the pleasure of the moment, mindfulness simply fosters an awareness of the pleasure, all the time being conscious that it is something that will pass and should not be held on to.

Another way to think about this is to consider what it means to savour something. You can savour with the attitude 'I don't want this moment ever to end' or with a simpler 'I don't want to miss anything this moment has to offer.' The former is an example of the futile desire to cling on to experiences that is typical of hedonism, the second the heightened appreciation of mindfulness.

For the Buddhists, from whom the idea of mindfulness has been appropriated, there is some merit in taking pleasure in food, but not much. 'The Buddha taught the middle way, the way beyond extremes,' Ajahn Karuniko, a monk in the Theravada tradition, told me when I met him at Cittaviveka Monastery in West Sussex. 'One extreme is indulgence; the other is extreme asceticism.' Applied to tasty food, this means 'not being afraid of pleasure but not clinging to it'. It's this clinging or grasping that causes the problems. 'When people cling to these things, when they're not there, they suffer. So if you cling to a certain sort of food, then of course when you go somewhere that food's not available, you're always wanting it.'

There is no clearer example of this than a story Jay Rayner tells of his love for Kressi, a Swiss herb-infused white wine vinegar. 'When it runs out,' he wrote, 'I feel like a bit of my life is missing.' Once, after an unsuccessful attempt to track down a bottle in London, feeling 'like an addict trying to score my next fix', he decided to fly to Geneva solely to stock up and come straight back again, only to arrive and discover it was a bank holiday and all the shops were shut.[134] When I met him and asked if even he thought this was a bit excessive, he replied, 'It's a very good vinegar, and odd as it may sound, my store cupboard really does feel slightly empty when it's no longer there.'

Rayner may be extreme, but the desire to relive food experiences of the past can create tension for anyone who enjoys eating. In *Au Revoir to All That*, Michael Steinberger says, 'For the dedicated feeder, the urge to relive the tasting pleasures of the past is constant and frequently over-whelming.' If you eat something delicious, it is only natural to want to eat it again, which is fine if it's readily available but frustrating if it's hundreds of miles away, or at a very expensive restaurant. But as Steinberger adds, 'Trying to recreate memorable moments at the table is often a recipe for heartache.'[135]

To avoid this pain, we have to master a very difficult knack. We need to be able to savour our food while at the same time not cling-ing to it. Ajahn Karuniko doubts this is possible. 'As soon as you have that thought [This is really delicious], you're clinging to it.' For him, 'Perfection of mindfulness when you're eating' is when 'You know it's pleasant, you know it's good', but once the eating is over, so is the awareness of the pleasure. I think this leads to a downgrading of the value of food that is too world-denying. Much as there is to admire in Buddhism, like all religions, I think it ultimately fails to reconcile itself to our psuche-somatic nature, always denigrating our animal aspect in some way.

It is only natural that the thought that something is delicious evokes the desire to have it again, and there is no reason why you should not want to repeat good food experiences. If you purchase some particularly good sausages, of course you'll want to buy them again, rather than inferior ones. If you discover Brie de Meaux is one of your favourite cheeses, then of course you'll keep an eye out for it. Such desires are only harmful when they are too strong. It should be possible to recognise such an excessive craving when it arises without believing one must satisfy it. There is a big difference between being guided by past experiences and compelled forward by them. 'I'll remember that restaurant next time I'm thinking of eating out' is different from 'I must go back there as soon as possi-ble.' The former is called learning from experience, the latter getting caught up in an anxious desire not to miss out. When life becomes a series of imperatives, a good meal always provoking the desire for another, then it becomes restless, without peace and ultimately unsatisfying because once is never enough. For the memory of a good meal to be truly positive, it is therefore essential that you let the experience go. Otherwise, the memory becomes not primarily a good thing you have done but another good thing you must still do again.

There are no simple practical rules for how to achieve this balance of fond memory and excessive desire. For instance, I toyed with the idea of advising that you never take home good foods you enjoy on holiday, because they never taste the same. This is especially true of liqueurs and *digestivos*, many of which seem to become pleasant by sheer force of the desire to partake of the local brew. Just enjoy them while you're there, making the experience even more special precisely because it will not be repeated. That, after all, is the right attitude to life as a whole, to see it as a kind of brief cosmic holiday before an eternity of oblivion. But that would be too strict a rule because some things you can easily pack into a suitcase, and if you can, why not? So instead of a simple rule, there can only be an attitude followed by a judgement. The attitude is, 'Make the most of it now. Don't worry about whether you'll enjoy it again'; the judgement: an answer to the question 'Am I really going to enjoy this back home, or am I just reluctant to accept that the past is done and cannot be recovered?'

In this way, it is clear that the truth perceived by those like Nando Parrado that we must make the most of every day need not imply a '*Carpe diem*' hedonism. On the contrary, making the most of every day requires that we do not devote all our time and energy in the pursuit of moments of pleasure that will pass. Appreciation is the key, and we can only fully appreciate what we enjoy if we are fully aware of the part it plays in a mortal, finite but extended life. Every day with someone you love, for example, is precious, not just because of the pleasure that day brings, but because of what it means in the context of a whole, all-too-short life.

Unlike the dogged pursuit of frivolous pleasures, a proper mindfulness thus encourages the focus on essentials that those who have tasted death often talk about. The essentials of life are the things on which we place the highest value, such as our relationships and projects. That does not mean excluding or even sidelining the pleasures of the table, however. To focus on essentials we have to be wary of running away with too lofty ideas about the importance of our work or legacy. We need the perspective to remember that for all that we might rightly try to achieve, one bit of bad news from a doctor would make us forget it in an instant.

With all that in mind, the simplicity of eating, especially with friends, comes to seem one of the most important things of all. If I had to choose between never reading or writing another book or never sharing another meal with people I love, there is no question the books would go. Sitting down to eat with my partner is one of the things that matters most to me. The table grounds me, but it doesn't reduce me to an animal with nothing on his mind apart from the next feed. It enables me to live as the psuche-somatic creature I am, capable not only of gustatory pleasure but of gratitude, a rich inner life, conviviality, aesthetic appreciation and objective judgement. We are a curious mixture of the intellectual and emotional, animals who can eat, think and be merry, and the table is the one place where we can do all three at the same time.

SODA BREAD

Bread is one of the most grounding and uplifting foodstuffs on the planet, the most basic of all foods but also the one which, when made well, is the most satisfying. Many people believe it is too much effort to bother baking at home, but if you think even the easy einkorn and spelt recipes I gave earlier are too time-consuming, then I urge you to at least try to make soda bread, an appropriately quotidian loaf for the last recipe of this book.

All you need to mix are plain flour (white, wholemeal or mixed), and for every 250 grammes, add 200 millilitres of buttermilk, 1 level teaspoon of bicarbonate of soda or 2 level teaspoons of baking powder, and 5 grammes of salt. If you can't get buttermilk – which is the healthy, low-fat but unappetising by-product of butter production – use live whole-milk yoghurt. Knead just long enough to form a dough, shape, slit the top to help the crust split when it rises and bang it in the oven at 200 degrees Celsius (400 degrees Fahrenheit, gas mark 6). The bread is ready when it has browned and makes a hollow sound if you tap its base.

What causes the dough to rise is the chemical reaction that happens when the lactic acid in the buttermilk mixes with the sodium bicarbonate, releasing carbon dioxide. Because this reaction starts immediately, soda bread dough needs to be baked as soon as it is mixed.

When it turns out well, it's delicious, especially when eaten as fresh as possible. Sometimes it hasn't risen for me. I think the problems have been over-kneading; using buttermilk too cold, straight from the fridge; and using old bicarbonate of soda. At least the odd failure helps keep us humble.

If you eat the resulting bread mindful of not just its texture and flavour but of humankind's unique ability to both bake and understand the science behind it, soda bread can be appreciated as the psuche-somatic food par excellence, a reminder of our simple, bodily needs and desires, as well as our human ingenuity.

Conclusions

As the end of writing this book came into sight, I thought about how I'd like to celebrate its completion, in that happy moment before its failings and the indifference of readers become evident. Predictably, I opted to have dinner with my partner at a favourite local restaurant. Given that 'favourite' is not fixed and does not necessarily mean 'best', I feel a little guilty naming the establishment when there are numerous other ones in Bristol that I could have chosen.* But name it I must, because the more I thought about it, the more I realised that Flinty Red provides a wonderfully concrete example of how the virtues of the table lie behind the most satisfying forms of gastronomic pleasure.

To make sure I wasn't just self-servingly projecting the virtues I value on to what is in reality just a restaurant that serves delicious food, I arranged to meet the head chef, Matt Williamson, and one of the other owners, Rachel Higgens. I simply asked them for their response to various words and phrases I threw at them: seasonal, organic, local, trade justice, animal welfare, technology, tradition, routine, conviviality. Reassuringly, each time their answers echoed the conclusions I had reached in writing this book. It seems that the pleasure I get from going to Flinty Red is not just down to Matt's impressive skills in the kitchen, but is a product of a general alignment

---

* So apologies especially to the Lido, Casamia, Bravas, the Kensington Arms, Prego, as well as others of excellent repute that I haven't even tried.

of the restaurant's values and my own. Even the format of the menu perfectly reflects my ideal of pleasure. Instead of starters and mains, most dishes can be ordered in small plates. Similarly, they have a wonderful selection of wines by the glass or carafe. Gluttony has no place here, which is sadly why the restaurant's TripAdvisor rating is not as high as it should be, dragged down by a minority whose complaint is always that the portions are too small.

The point is not that the pleasure I get when I go to a restaurant like Flinty Red is merely a side effect of the pursuit of other human goods. It is simply that even on such an occasion, when an enjoyable evening is the primary goal, there is a lot going on that has nothing to do with pleasure, but which is nonetheless essential for making the experience so rich.

Perhaps the most heartening illustration of this is that although Matt and Rachel's priorities as restaurateurs were quality and flavour, which appear to be morally neutral, time and again those ideals were best served by the most ethical practices. A maltreated animal usually makes for poor meat; a good, fair relationship with suppliers is one of the best guarantees of good supplies; the tastiest fruit and vegetables come mostly from farmers who exercise stewardship; moderation in servings facilitates the greatest pleasure; innovating within traditions you respect results in the best dishes; treating customers convivially creates the best atmosphere. Although it would be simplistic and optimistic to assume that there is never a conflict between doing what is morally right and doing what is good and pleasant for ourselves, there is a lot to the Aristotelian idea that the good life is one where self-interest and treating others well usually, if not always, go naturally together.

Although gluttony generally holds the upper hand in modern Western society, our intellectual and philosophical culture is still drawn towards the hair shirt. We need to stop thinking that the life of the mind is somehow inevitably in tension with the life of the body. That's why my own celebration involved more than a plate of my favourite pasta at home or a trip to a cheap and cheerful pizzeria, even though this book has been largely a celebration of the quotidian. That seemed far too worthy and puritanical. Since it's not every day you finish a book, it seemed appropriate to opt for a not-so-everyday meal. There are exceptional as well as everyday pleasures, and getting the right balance between the two means happily enjoying the odd indulgence.

Even extravagance sometimes has its place. The eponymous heroine of *Babette's Feast* spends all of a small fortune she inherits on a once-in-a-lifetime gourmet extravaganza for the community who took her in. It is an incredible expression both of a willingness to embrace the fleeting delights earthly existence offers and to renounce worldly wealth, with all the status and false sense of security it brings. To be too unwilling to spend money on things that are here today and gone tomorrow is to refuse to recognise that life itself is ephemeral.

How do we know when it is time for restraint and when it is time to let go? How do we decide whether we are spending too much or too little effort doing the things that give us pleasure? When, as Will Self put it, could we 'do with paying a bit less attention to what's on the end of our forks, and a bit more to what's at the end of our roads'?[136] There is no algorithm to tell us. What it takes is *phron sis*, practical wisdom, and that is why Aristotle has been the guiding philosophical light in this book. His whole approach is to look for the appropriate mean between equally erroneous extremes. He understands that to do this, we have to use judgement as well as logic and be prepared to accept that the answers we come up with are unlikely to be certain or precise. He also has an understanding of soul – *psuchê* – that is essentially tied to the body, in that soul is not a separate, immaterial substance but the distinctively human nature that emerges when the matter of our body is organised the way that it is. As Douglas Hofstadter wonderfully put it, 'The soul is greater than the hum of its parts.'[137] He saw that pleasure is an important part of human life, but that it was just one contributing factor to *eudaimonia*, a word that is often translated as 'happiness' but is better understood as 'flourishing', since it involves much more than just positive affect. A dour person who does good work that she and others value achieves *eudaimonia* at least as much as someone who lives a happy, morally decent life. Finally, Aristotle saw that it is by nurturing thoughtful, everyday habits that we become better people and live better lives. Eating is important because of, not despite, its quotidian nature. If every day of our short lives matters, then clearly we need to get the everyday right.

Aristotle's critics find this all frustratingly short on concrete advice, but that is precisely the point. The major insight of Aristotle's virtue-based approach is that there is no manual for living well that can reduce everything to a list of dos and don'ts. Yet this is precisely what people often want and expect, especially, perhaps, when it comes to food. They want to know what we should eat and what we shouldn't, what's the right and wrong way to cook a dish, where we should shop and whom we should boycott. But any list of dos and don'ts can be no more than a set of rules of thumb. That is not just because the simplicity of rules always crumbles when confronted with the complexities of real life. More significantly, it is because the *how* of life is more important than the *what*. We need to learn the right way of living, and that is about attitudes, habits, dispositions and virtues.

That is why there is no simple list of injunctions and prohibitions that could flesh out the epigraph to this book, Escoffier's line 'To know how to eat is to know how to live.' Nor is such knowledge something any one person could fully possess. Becoming more knowledgeable or wiser is not like becoming, say, a doctor of philosophy, for which you study, earn your PhD and so end up *being* a doctor. As Jonathan Rée describes Kierkegaard's idea of becoming a Christian, it is 'a matter of becoming as contrasted with being'. Living well, like being a Christian, is not 'a condition you can settle dully into' but an ongoing process of continuing to become.[138] Virtue, like self, is a verb disguised as a noun.[139]

Nonetheless, although it would be glib to reduce the virtues of the table to a list of practical, take-home bullet points, it is possible to extract some general, overarching truths about what it means to know how to eat, and so to live.

To know how to eat is first and foremost to know one's nature as a psuche-somatic being. It is to understand that eating, as with anything we do, is most satisfying when it brings together mind, body, heart and soul. We can't always do this, of course: there are times when we just have to feed and get on with it. But that should be the exception rather than the rule. We eat and live in a fully human way when we bring our minds and emotions to what we do, as well as our bodies, cognisant that we are finite beings with pasts and futures as well as presents.

To know how to eat is to know how to think about the practicalities of living well, which is the plainest way of saying we need to be able to reason about ethics. This requires knowledge of the facts, even though knowing the way things are doesn't automatically tell us the way they ought to be. It requires the kind of logical rigour that enables us to detect fallacies and contradictions, even though logic alone won't provide us with a formula for how to live. It requires accepting the role of judgement, and learning how best to use it, since there is no algorithm for the good life. And so it also requires not simply accepting the orthodoxies of the day, but checking and interrogating them.

To know how to eat is to appreciate the effects our eating choices have on others and to accept the responsibilities they entail. If our own lives have value, then so do the lives of others, who can also feel pain and pleasure, or have projects and relationships. The same faculty of reason that guides our own self-interested choices should tell us that others have interests as well and that there is nothing that makes ours more objectively important. We may have more responsibility for ourselves and family than we do for others, but that does not mean we have none at all for strangers.

Finally, to know how to eat is to be neither a pure hedonist, who seeks nothing but the next pleasure, nor an ascetic, who turns his back on his fleshy, human nature. We are right to place importance on pleasure. Life is short, and all returns to earth in the long run. To be able to savour those moments of real pleasure that life offers is to accept gracefully the gifts that the universe has blindly and unwittingly offered us. At the same time, as psuche-somatic creatures, we clearly value more than just pleasure. So our hedonism should be in a sense part-time, and also enlightened, so that pleasure does not come at the price of other things we value – such as truth, love, understanding and creativity – but as the consequence of them.

That all might sound quite simple, but what looks obvious in summary is often complex in its details. What I hope to have showed is that although it is easy enough to agree on what the core virtues are, understanding what they really entail is much more difficult. What's more, everyone's knowledge is partial and imperfect. I certainly know that I am only in pursuit rather than in command of the virtues of the table. I am sure, however, that any understanding of what the life of a psuche-somatic being should be is woefully incomplete if it neglects the large and unavoidable part eating has to play in it. The simple act of putting a piece of food in your mouth is related by a complicated network of connections to everything else in your life, and the richer that network is, the richer any satisfaction you get from that food will be.

Acknowledgements

My thanks go primarily to the people who agreed to be interviewed (listed in the 'Notes on ingredients'). There are relatively few direct quotes from these, but all the conversations helped my thinking and understanding enormously, and I could not have written this book without them. In addition to these formal interviews, I have been helped by conversations with my Italian family, Tobias Jones and Kate Lewis.

I am grateful for the loyal support of everyone at my publisher, Granta, especially Sara Holloway, Bella Lacey, Christine Lo, Brigid Macleod, Anne Meadows, Sharon Murphy, Aidan O'Neill, Kelly Pike, Angela Rose, Pru Rowlandson and Sarah Wasley, as well as to my agent, Lizzy Kremer, and the copyeditor Laura Collins.

I had the opportunity to test-drive some of the ideas and material in this book in a number of articles, namely 'Out of Sight, Out of Mind' (the *Independent*, 3 May 2010), 'Why Have We Fallen Out of Love With Organic Food?' (the *Guardian*, 4 September 2012), 'A Taste of the Divine' (*Aeon*, 17 October 2012), 'Navratri and the Lessons of Fasting for Atheists' (*Comment Is Free*, 22 October 2012), 'Joy in the Task' (*Aeon*, 9 January 2013), 'Local Versus Global Is Not the Real Issue' (the *Independent*, 25 February 2013), 'To Profit, Don't Just Concentrate on Profit' (*Guardian Sustainable Business*, 28 February 2013) and 'We Must Fight to Preserve Traditional English Foodstuffs and Techniques' (the *Guardian*, 13 March 2013).

Finally, I owe most of all to Antonia, with whom the quotidian pleasures of the table become the sweetest and richest of them all.

Notes

1 I thought of this aphorism independently and was immediately convinced it was too good not to have been said before. However, the only precedent I could find for it was attributed to the chef Auguste Escoffier without source by his biographer Kenneth James in *Escoffier: The King of Chefs* (Hambledon & London, 2002), p. 268. Furthermore, it seems Escoffier meant something a little different by it than I did. He appeared to say it in the context of two small books he had written to advise the poor on how to eat cheaply but well. Hence knowing how to eat – i.e. cook economically – meant knowing how to live, i.e. survive. What I mean by it is that you cannot know how to really, fully live if you don't know how to eat.

2 Adam Gopnik, *The Table Comes First* (Quercus, 2011), p. 7

3 David Hume, *An Enquiry Concerning Human Understanding* (1748), Section 1, §4

4 Manfred Kuehn, *Kant: A Biography* (Cambridge University Press, 2001), p. 420

5 Immanuel Kant, 'An Answer to the Question: What is Enlightenment?' (1784)

6 W. Higman, *How Food Made History* (Blackwell, 2012), p. 122

7 *Ethical Consumer*'s Ratings Information factsheet, www.ethical consumer.org/Portals/0/Downloads/categoriesA4.pdf

8 Jean Anthelme Brillat-Savarin, *The Physiology of Taste* (Vintage Classics, 2011), p. 16

9 *The Food Programme*, 'British Blue Cheese', BBC Radio Four (7 October 2012)

10 Wheat statistic from National Farmers' Union. Apple statistic from English Apples and Pears Ltd, as reported in 'Wet Weather Set to Hit UK Food Prices', BBC News Online (12 October 2012), www.bbc.co.uk/news/uk-19890250

11 Mintel press release (21 March 2012), www.mintel.com/press-centre/press-releases/841/local-produce-edging-out-organic-in-imp ortance-among-consumers

12 Caroline Saunders, Andrew Barber and Greg Taylor, 'Food Miles – Comparative Energy/Emissions Performance of New Zealand's Agriculture Industry', Agribusiness and Economics Research Unit (AERU) Research Report No. 285 (July 2006), www.lincoln.ac.nz/Documents/2328_RR285_s13389.pdf

13 World Shipping Council, www.worldshipping.org/benefits-of-liner-shipping/low-environmental-impact

14 Bristol Food Charter, www.bristol.gov.uk/sites/default/files/docu-ments/environment/environmental_health/Food%20Charter.pdf

15 Peter Singer and Jim Mason, *Eating* (Arrow, 2006), p. 141

16 'Declaration of Nyéléni', Sélingué, Mali (27 February 2007), www.nye-leni.org/spip.php?article290, reprinted on the website of Food Sovereignty Now, http://foodsovereigntynow.org.uk/foodsov/

17 John Dickie, *Delizia!* (Sceptre, 2008), p. 266

18 See Geoff Andrews, *The Slow Food Story* (Pluto Press, 2008), Chapter 8.

19 In *The Locust and the Bee* (Princeton University Press, 2013), p. 37, Geoff Mulgan argues that 'Most of the vulnerabilities of capitalism also derive from the less than solid relationship between lived value and its representations.'

20 Valsabor website, www.valsabor.com.es

21 The four global coffee-trading giants are ECOM, Louis Dreyfus, Neumann and VOLCAFE, with Olam International recently added as a major player. The five global retail brands are Kraft, Nestlé, Sara Lee, Proctor & Gamble and Tchibo. See 'Fairtrade and Coffee' Commodity briefing (May 2012), Fairtrade Foundation www.fair-trade.org.uk/includes/documents/cm_docs/2012/F/FT_Coffee_Re port_May2012.pdf.

22 See Martin Cottingham, Organic Market Report 2012, www.soil association.org/marketreport

23 Robert Blair, *Organic Production and Food Quality* (Wiley-Blackwell, 2012), p. 223 and p. 259

24 *Ibid.*, p. 259

25 'Earthtalk: What Causes Ocean "Dead Zones"?', *Scientific American* (25

September 2012), www.scientificamerican.com/article.cfm?id=ocean-dead-zones

26 Patricio Grassini and Kenneth G. Cassman, 'High-Yield Maize with Large Net Energy Yield and Small Global Warming Intensity', *Proceedings of the National Academy of Sciences of the United States of America* (2012), 109, 4 (pp. 1074–9)

27 John P. Reganold, 'The Fruits of Organic Farming', *Nature* (10 May 2012), vol. 485, p. 176

28 'Powering Up Smallholder Farmers to Make Food Fair', Fairtrade Foundation (25 February 2013), www.fairtrade.org.uk/resources/reports_and_briefing_papers.aspx

29 'Eating the Planet? How We Can Feed the World Without Trashing It', Compassion in World Farming and Friends of the Earth (2009), www.foe.co.uk/resource/reports/eating_planet_report2.pdf

30 Leo Hickman, 'Dig for Victory', interview with Monty Don, the *Guardian* (30 August 2008)

31 Michael Pollan, 'Behind the Organic-Industrial Complex', *New York Times* (13 May 2001)

32 Carlo Petrini, speech at Terra Madre 2006, as translated by John Dickie from press release in *Delizia!* (Sceptre, 2008), p. 343

33 Roger Scruton, *Green Philosophy* (Atlantic, 2012), p. 235

34 'Family Food 2011', Defra, p. 11, www.defra.gov.uk/statistics/food-farm/food/familyfood

35 Steven L. Davis, 'The Least Harm Principle May Require that Humans Consume a Diet Containing Large Herbivores, Not a Vegan Diet', *Journal of Agricultural and Environmental Ethics* (2003), 16 (4), pp. 387–94

36 Scott R. Loss, Tom Will and Peter P. Marra, 'The Impact of Free-Ranging Domestic Cats on Wildlife of the United States', *Nature Communications*, 4 (29 January 2013)

37 Jeremy Bentham, *An Introduction to the Principles of Morals and Legislation* (1789), Chapter XVII, note 2

38 Daniel Kahenman, *Thinking Fast and Slow* (Allen Lane, 2011), pp. 379–80

39 Bob Holmes, 'Veggieworld: Why Eating Greens Won't Save the Planet', *New Scientist*, issue 2769 (20 July 2010)

40 Compassion in World Farming website, www.ciwf.org.uk/farm_animals/sheep/default.aspx

41 Geoff Andrews, *The Slow Food Story* (Pluto Press, 2008), p. 173

42 Nick Gillespie, 'Poor Man's Hero', interview with Johan Norberg, *Reason* (December 2003), http://reason.com/archives/2003/12/01/poor-mans-hero/1

43 National Center for Policy Analysis, Month in Review, Trade (June 1996)

44 Lucy Martinez-Mont, 'Sweatshops Are Better than No Shops', *Wall Street Journal* (25 June 1996)

45 'Child Labour: Do's and Don'ts', Maquila Solidarity Network website, http://en.maquilasolidarity.org/node/662

46 Ethical Trading Initiative Base Code, §4.1, www.ethicaltrade.org/eti-base-code

47 Madsen Pirie, 'Misery Wrought by "Fair" Trade', Adam Smith Institute blog (6 September 2008)

48 'Good Food?', *The Economist* (7 December 2006), www.economist.com/node/8381375

49 Interview with Harriet Lamb, CEO Fairtrade International. See also Valerie Nelson and Barry Pound, 'The Last Ten Years: A Comprehensive Review of the Literature on the Impact of Fairtrade', National Resources Institute (2009), www.fairtrade.org.uk/resources/natural_resources_institute.aspx.

50 Sushil Mohan, *Fair Trade Without the Froth*, Institute of Economic Affairs, Hobart Paper 170 (2010), p. 45

51 David Hume, *Essays and Treatises on Several Subjects* (1758), vol. 1, §12511

52 Aristotle, *Politics*, Book 1, Part V

53 René Descartes, *Discourse on Method* (1637), Part 2

54 Economic Note on UK Grocery Retailing produced by Food and Drink Economics branch, Defra (May 2006), http://archive.defra.gov.uk/evidence/economics/foodfarm/reports/documents/Groceries%20paper%20May%202006.pdf

55 Robert Sommer, John Herrick and Ted R. Sommer, 'The Behavioral Ecology of Supermarkets and Farmers' Markets,' *Journal of Environmental Psychology* (March 1981), vol. 1 (1), pp. 13–19

56 'Kitchen Battle Boils Over', BBC News Online (26 October 1998), http://news.bbc.co.uk/1/hi/entertainment/201561.stm

57 Julian Barnes, *The Pedant in the Kitchen* (Atlantic, 2012), p. 14

58 Barry Schwartz and Kenneth Sharpe, *Practical Wisdom* (Riverhead Books, 2010), pp. 4 and 28

59 See John Dickie, *Delizia!* (Sceptre, 2008)

60 This tale was first told to me on a tour of Bladnoch, Scotland's second-smallest distillery. Facts were checked against the article 'Why Bourbon Barrels?', published 6 September 2012, from the website of the Islay distillery Bruichladdich, www.bruichladdich.com/library/whisky-casks-and-oak/why-bourbon-barrels.

61 My knowledge of Derrida's ideas on iterability comes from Simon Glendinning's *On Being With Others: Heidegger, Wittgenstein, Derrida* (Routledge, 1998)

62 Ferran Adrià, Heston Blumenthal, Thomas Keller and Harold McGee, 'Statement on the "New Cookery"' (2006), www.thefat-duck.co.uk/Heston-Blumenthal/Cooking-Statement

63 Ludwig Wittgenstein, *Philosophical Investigations* (1953), §607 and §88 respectively

64 San Sifton, 'Always the Same Thing', *The New York Times Blog: Diner's Journal* (5 November 2009)

65 'David Gelb's Tokyo Story', interview with David Gelb by Alexandria Symonds in interviewmagazine.com (3 September 2012)

66 *The Food Programme*, BBC Radio Four (18 February 2013)

67 Clint Witchalls, 'Medical Contradictions: So Bad It's Good for You . . .', the *Independent* (27 September 2011)

68 'Report of Committee on Nutrition', British Medical Association, Supplement to the *British Medical Journal* (25 November 1933)

69 Guideline Daily Amounts website hosted by the Food and Drink Federation, using official UK government figures, www.gdal-abel.org.uk

70 'Diet, Nutrition and the Prevention of Chronic Diseases', WHO Technical Report Series 916, p. 56, http://whqlibdoc.who.int/trs/who_trs_916.pdf

71 For a good overview of the fats issue, see 'Fats and Cholesterol: Out With the Bad, In With the Good', the Nutrition Source, Harvard School of Health, www.hsph.harvard.edu/nutritionsource/fats-full-story

72 *More or Less*, BBC Radio Four (19 August 2011)

73 R. S. Taylor, K. E. Ashton, T. Moxham et al., 'Reduced Dietary Salt

for the Prevention of Cardiovascular Disease: A Meta-Analysis of Randomized Controlled Trials (Cochrane Review)', *American Journal of Hypertension* (24 August 2011), 8, pp. 843–53

74 H. M. Orpana, J. M. Berthelot, M. S. Kaplan, D. H. Feeny, B. McFarland and N. A. Ross, 'BMI and Mortality: Results From a National Longitudinal Study of Canadian Adults,' *Obesity* (Silver Spring, January 2010), 18 (1), pp. 214–18

75 Katherine M. Flegal, Brian K. Kit, Heather Orpana and Barry I. Graubard, 'Association of All-Cause Mortality With Overweight and Obesity Using Standard Body Mass Index Categories: A Systematic Review and Meta-analysis', *The Journal of the American Medical Association* (2013), 309 (1), pp. 71–82

76 Michael Pollan, 'Unhappy Meals', *New York Times Magazine* (28 January 2007), and *In Defense of Food: An Eater's Manifesto* (Penguin, 2008)

77 David Hume, *Dialogues Concerning Natural Religion* (1779), Part 1

78 NHS Livewell website, www.nhs.uk/Livewell/Goodfood/Pages/meat.aspx

79 See John M. Doris, *Lack of Character* (Cambridge University Press, 2002) for more on the inconstancy of character

80 Angela L. Duckworth and Martin E. P. Seligman, 'Self-Discipline Outdoes IQ in Predicting Academic Performance of Adolescents', *Psychological Science* (December 2005), vol. 16, no. 12, pp. 939–44

81 See 'Rational Snacking: Young Children's Decision-Making on the Marshmallow Task is Moderated by Beliefs about Environmental Reliability', Celeste Kidda, Holly Palmeria and Richard N. Aslina, *Cognition* (January 2013), vol. 126, issue 1, pp. 109–14

82 Jean Anthelme Brillat-Savarin, *The Physiology of Taste* (Vintage Classics, 2011), Meditation 11, p. 155

83 Adam Hadhazy, 'Think Twice: How the Gut's "Second Brain" Influences Mood and Well-Being', *Scientific American* (12 February 2010)

84 Comment posted in response to Lilian Anekwe, 'Study Offers "Definitive Proof" for Bariatric Surgery Benefits' (15 April 2011), www.pulsetoday.co.uk

85 In Søren Kierkegaard, *Stages on Life's Way* (Princeton University Press, 1988)

86 Thomas of Celano, *The First Life of St. Francis* (1229), Chapter 19, §51, www.indiana.edu/~dmdhist/francis.htm

87 Versions of this appear in many reputable sources. See for example Gina Kolata, *Rethinking Thin* (Picador, 2008) p. 158.

88 T. Mann, A. J. Tomiyama, A. M Lew, E. Westling, J. Chatman and B. Samuels, 'The Search for Effective Obesity Treatments: Should Medicare Fund Diets?' *American Psychologist* (2007), 62, pp. 220–33. Tomiyama is quoted in a UCLA news release (3 April 2007).

89 See Roy F. Baumeister and John Tierney, *Willpower* (Allen Lane, 2011)

90 *Ibid.*, Chapter 2

91 Priya Sumithran, Luke A. Prendergast, Elizabeth Delbridge, Katrina Purcell, Arthur Shulkes, Adamandia Kriketos and Joseph Proietto, 'Long-Term Persistence of Hormonal Adaptations to Weight Loss', *New England Journal of Medicine*, 365 (27 October 2011), pp. 1597–604

92 Gina Kolata, *Rethinking Thin* (Picador, 2008), pp. 158–9

93 Roman Catholic Church Code of Canon Law, Chapter 2, can. 1251, www.vatican.va/archive/ENG1104/_INDEX.HTM

94 See for example 'The Puzzle of Self-Reported Weight Gain in a Month of Fasting (Ramadan) Among a Cohort of Saudi Families in Jeddah, Western Saudi Arabia', Balkees Abed Bakhotmah, *Nutrition Journal* (2011), 10 (84), www.nutritionj.com/content/10/1/84 and 'Weight Gain, Health Issues Threaten Muslim Fasters', NPR (30 July 2012), www.npr.org/2012/07/30/157594375/weight-gain-health-issues-threaten-muslim-fasters

95 Jean Anthelme Brillat-Savarin, *The Pleasures of the Table* (Penguin, 2011), p. 1. This volume contains extracts from *The Physiology of Taste*, but I prefer Anne Drayton's translation of this particular aphorism.

96 Daniel C. Dennett and Linda LaScola, 'Preachers Who Are Not Believers,' *Evolutionary Psychology* (March 2010), vol. 8, issue 1, pp. 121–50

97 Julian Baggini, *The Ego Trick* (Granta, 2011). See especially p. 123ff.

98 Daniel C. Dennett, 'Thank Goodness!', *Edge* (3 November 2006), www.edge.org/3rd_culture/dennett06/dennett06_index.html

99 Charles Lamb, 'Grace Before Meat', in *A Dissertation Upon Roast Pig and Other Essays* (Penguin, 2011), p. 14

100 'Global Food: Waste Not, Want Not', Institution of Mechanical

Engineers (January 2013), www.imeche.org/Libraries/Reports/Global_Food_Report.sflb.ashx

101 'Chorleywood: The Bread That Changed Britain', BBC News Online Magazine (7 June 2011), www.bbc.co.uk/news/magazine-13670278

102 See Kenji López-Alt, 'Do "Better" Eggs Really Taste Better?' (27 August 2010), www.seriouseats.com/2010/08/what-are-the-best-eggs-cage-free-organic-omega-3s-grocery-store-brand-the-food-lab.html; and Tamar Haspel, 'Backyard Eggs vs. Store-Bought: They Taste the Same', *Washington Post* (2 June 2010)

103 Massimo Montanari, *Cheese, Pears and History in a Proverb* (Columbia University Press, 2010), pp. 63–6

104 Thomas Nagel, *The View From Nowhere* (Oxford University Press, 1986), p. 5

105 *Restaurant* magazine (May 2012). The following year – now called Restaurant Frantzén after the departure of Lindeberg – it had risen to number twelve.

106 Henry David Thoreau, *Walden* (1854), Chapter 2

107 Aristotle, *Nichomachean Ethics*, 1118a

108 Ferran Adrià, Heston Blumenthal, Thomas Keller and Harold McGee, 'Statement on the "New Cookery"' (2006), www.thefat-duck.co.uk/Heston-Blumenthal/Cooking-Statement

109 Massimiliano Zampini and Charles Spence, 'The Role of Auditory Cues in Modulating the Perceived Crispness and Staleness of Potato Chips', *Journal of Sensory Studies* (October 2004), vol. 19, issue 5, pp. 347–63

110 Letter from Hume extracted in Professor Huxley, *David Hume: A Study of His Life and Philosophy* (Wildside Press, 2008), p. 37

111 Giorgio Locatelli, *Made in Italy* (Fourth Estate, 2008), p. 220

112 Both comments from 'The Inventory', *FT Magazine* (2 December 2011)

113 Geoff Dyer, *Yoga for People Who Can't Be Bothered to Do It* (Abacus, 2003), p. 214

114 'My Life in Food: Fergus Henderson', the *Independent* (27 April 2012)

115 *The Food Programme*, BBC Radio Four (27 May 2012)

116 'Will Droughts Hit Crisp Production in England?', BBC News Online (14 March 2012), www.bbc.co.uk/news/uk-england-17353181

117 Research by Eurest Services, reported in Ben Leach, 'British Office Workers No Longer Take Lunch Breaks', *Daily Telegraph* (15 January 2009)

118 The survey was conducted in 2005 by the vegetarian restaurant Cranks and reported by the AFP (Agence France Presse) press agency, printed in, among others, *The Times of India* (16 December 2005)

119 See 'Census: Population Estimates for the United Kingdom', ONS Statistical Bulletin (17 December 2012), www.ons.gov.uk/ons/dcp171778_292378.pdf

120 I discussed this with Radcliffe Richards in *What Philosophers Think*, edited with Jeremy Stangroom (Continuum, 2003), pp. 23–31 See also Janet Radcliffe Richards, *The Sceptical Feminist* (Penguin, 1994).

121 Pierre Bourdieu, *Distinction* (Harvard University Press, 1984), pp. 179 and 183

122 See www.parrado.com

123 'One Fish, Two Fish, Blowfish, Blue Fish', *The Simpsons*, Season 2, Episode 11, first tx 24 January 1991

124 Havi Carel, 'My Ten-Year Death Sentence', the *Independent* (19 March 2007). See also her book, *Illness* (Acumen, 2008).

125 William James, *The Principles of Psychology* (1890), vol. 1, Chapter 15, 'The Feeling of Past Time Is a Present Feeling'

126 Samuel Pepys, *The Joys of Excess* (Penguin, 2011). Quotations come from his diary entries for 23 April 1661, 6 June 1661, 4 April 1663 and 13 July 1665.

127 Epicurus, *Letter to Monoeceus*, §127

128 Plato, *Timaeus*, 69d1

129 Jeremy Bentham, *An Introduction to the Principles of Morals and Legislation* (1789), Chapter I, paras 2 and 3

130 Jeremy Bentham, *The Rationale of Reward* (1825), Book III, Chapter 1

131 See J. S. Mill, *Utilitarianism* (1863)

132 Plato, *Gorgias*, 510a

133 William Kitchiner, *The Cook's Oracle; and Housekeeper's Manual* (J. & J. Harper, 1830). Available at www.gutenberg.org/files/28681/28681-h/28681-h.htm

134 Jay Rayner, *The Man Who Ate the World* (Headline Review, 2008), p. 186

135 Michael Steinberger, *Au Revoir to All That* (Bloomsbury, 2010), p. 6
136 Will Self, *A Point of View*, BBC Radio Four (28 December 2012), transcript at www.bbc.co.uk/news/magazine-20836616
137 Douglas R. Hofstadter, 'Prelude … Ant Fugue', in Douglas R. Hofstadter and Daniel C. Dennett (eds), *The Mind's I* (Bantam Books, 1982), p. 191. He actually puts it as a question: 'Is a soul greater than the hum of its parts?'
138 Jonathan Rée, 'As If for the First Time: Becoming a Philosopher in Kierkegaard's Work as an Author', unpublished manuscript from a Forum for European Philosophy lecture given at the Institut Français in London on 24 October 2000. A shorter, edited version appears as 'Becoming a Philosopher', *Philosophy Now*, 32, June/July 2001.
139 For more on self as a verb, see my *The Ego Trick* (Granta, 2011), especially Chapter 7.

Notes on ingredients

INTERVIEWS

I am grateful to the following, whom I interviewed for this book.
Those marked with an asterisk were interviewed for a different primary purpose but are also quoted in this book.

Geoff Andrews (academic, author of *The Slow Food Story*)
Antonella (cook, Frantze, Le Rascard 1721, Champoluc)
Tom and Richard Bowles (Hartley Farm)
Estelle Brown (Incredible Edible Todmorden)
Helen Browning (chief executive, the Soil Association)
Jeff Brunstrom, Peter Rogers and Charlotte Hardman (psycholo-
    gists, University of Bristol)
Mike Bryan (chief executive, the Natural Beverage Company)
Dan Cotterill (farmer, philosophy PhD)
Dominic Coyte and Bronwen Percival (Neal's Yard Dairy)
Tim Crane and Barry Smith (oenophile philosophers)
Dom Joseph Delargy★ (abbot, Mount Saint Bernard Monastery)
John Dickie (academic, author of *Delizia!*)
Henry Dimbleby (Leon restaurants)
Dom David Foster★ (monk, Downside Abbey)
Björn Frantzén (head chef, Frantzén/Lindeberg, now Restaurant
    Frantzén)
Cat Gazzoli (chief executive officer, Slow Food UK)
Phil Haughton (founder/owner, the Better Food Company)

Fergus Henderson (chef, founder of St John Bar and Restaurant)
Charlie Hicks (greengrocer and broadcaster)
Rachel Higgens and Matt Williamson (co-owners, Flinty Red)
Nick Hindle (senior vice-president of Corporate Affairs,
　McDonald's UK)
Christopher Jamison★ (former abbot, Worth Abbey)
Ajahn Karuniko★ (monk, Cittaviveka Monastery)
Peter Kindersley (owner, Sheepdrove Organic Farm)
Harriet Lamb (chief executive officer, Fairtrade International)
Giorgio Locatelli (head chef, Locanda Locatelli)
Roger Longman (White Lake Cheeses)
Philip Lymbery (chief executive, Compassion in World Farming)
Clare and Michael Marriage (Doves Farm)
Nick Miller (Slow Food Bristol)
Nicola and Elsa Pomponio★ (restaurateurs)
Steven Poole (journalist, author of *You Aren't What You Eat*)
Jay Rayner (journalist, restaurant critic)
Jonray and Peter Sanchez-Iglesias (head chefs, Casamia)
Bhai Sahib Bhai Mohinder Singh (chairman, Guru Nanak
　Nishkam Sewak Jatha Gurdwara, Birmingham)
Becky Whay (senior lecturer in Animal Welfare and Behaviour,
　University of Bristol)

SELECTED BIBLIOGRAPHY

These are only the books that directly informed my thinking about food during the writing of this book, whether referenced in the text or not. Papers, articles and other books cited are to be found in the endnotes.

Geoff Andrews, *The Slow Food Story* (Pluto Press, 2008)
Jean Athelme Brillat-Savarin, *The Physiology of Taste* (Vintage
　Classics, 2011)

Julian Barnes, *The Pedant in the Kitchen* (Atlantic, 2012)

Robert Blair, *Organic Production and Food Quality* (Wiley-Blackwell, 2012)

John Dickie, *Delizia!* (Sceptre, 2008)

Clarissa Dickson-Wright, *A History of English Food* (Random House, 2011)

Auguste Escoffier, *Memories of My Life* (Van Nostrand Reinhold, 1997)

Peter Farb and George Armelagos, *Consuming Passions* (Houghton Mifflin, 1980)

M. F. K. Fisher, *The Art of Eating* (Wiley, 2004)

Janet Flamming, *The Taste for Civilization* (University of Illinois Press, 2009)

Fergus Henderson, *Nose to Tail Eating* (Bloomsbury, 2004)

B. W. Higman, *How Food Made History* (Wiley-Blackwell, 2012)

Kenneth James, *Escoffier: The King of Chefs* (Hambledon and London, 2002)

David M. Kaplan (ed.), *The Philosophy of Food* (University of California Press, 2012)

Søren Kierkegaard, *Stages on Life's Way* (Princeton University Press, 1988)

Gina Kolata, *Rethinking Thin* (Picador, 2008)

Charles Lamb, *A Dissertation upon Roast Pig and Other Essays* (Penguin, 2011)

Paul Levy (ed.), *The Penguin Book of Food and Drink* (Viking, 1996)

Giorgio Locatelli, *Made in Italy* (Fourth Estate, 2008)

Sushil Mohan, *Fair Trade Without the Froth* (Institute of Economic Affairs, 2010)

Massimo Montanari, *Cheese, Pears and History in a Proverb* (Columbia University Press, 2010)

Samuel Pepys, *The Joys of Excess* (Penguin, 2011)

Michael Pollan, *The Omnivore's Dilemma* (Bloomsbury, 2007)

Steven Poole, *You Aren't What You Eat* (Union Books, 2012)

Francine Prose, *Gluttony* (Oxford University Press, 2003)

Jay Rayner, *The Man Who Ate the World* (Headline Review, 2008)

David Remnick (ed.), *Secret Ingredients: The New Yorker Book of Food and Drink* (Modern Library, 2009)

Peter Singer and Jim Mason, *Eating* (Arrow, 2006)

Alexis Soyer, *The Chef at War* (Penguin, 2011)

Michael Steinberger, *Au Revoir to All That* (Bloomsbury, 2010)

Gary Taubes, *The Diet Delusion* (Vermillion, 2007)

Edward Westermarck, *The Principles of Fasting* (Pierides Press, 2010)

FILMOGRAPHY

Amour (Michael Haneke, Austria/France/Germany, 2012)

Babette's Feast (Gabriel Axel, Denmark, 1987)

Barton Fink (Joel Coen, US, 1991)

The Cook, the Thief, His Wife & Her Lover (Peter Greenaway, France/UK, 1989)

Eat, Drink, Man, Woman (Ang Lee, Taiwan, 1994)

Fast Food Nation (Richard Linklater, US/UK, 2006)

Food, Inc. (Robert Kenner, US, 2008)

Jiro Dreams of Sushi (David Gelb, US, 2011)

Pranzo di ferragosto (Gianni di Gregorio, Italy, 2008)

Index